A Jolt

The Story of the First Major Rebellion against the
British Rule in South India, 1806

SAMUEL RAJ, Ph.D.

Cover & Interior Design: Joseph Pakkianathan

Printed in the United States of America

ORDERING INFORMATION:
www.amazon.com (A Jolt—*The Story of the First Major Rebellion against the British Rule in South India -1806*)

Library of Congress Control Number: 2017914697

ISBN-13: 978-1976582486
ISBN-10: 1976582482

First Edition – August, 2020

This book is dedicated to the memory
of all who had the "I am my brother's keeper" attitude and
stood by their convictions till the end.

"Then the Lord said to Cain, 'Where is your brother?' He said, 'I do not know; am I my brother's keeper?'"
(Genesis 4:9, *Bible-Revised Standard Version*)

"Rescue those who are unjustly sentenced to death; don't stand back and let them die. Don't try to disclaim responsibility by saying you didn't know about it. For God, who knows all hearts, knows yours, and he knows you knew! And he will reward everyone according to his deeds"
(Proverbs 24:11-12, *The Living Bible*)

"Be faithful unto death, and I will give you the crown of life
(Revelation 2: 10, the last part, RSV)

CONTENTS

PREFACE

IN THE SPRING OF 2015, while visiting relatives and friends in Southern California, my nephew-in-law Luke Rynda, a retired engineer with the US Air Force told me that he read my Ph.D. dissertation on line, and that he "quite liked it". That led me to re-read the manuscript, which I wrote between 1969 and 1971, and had not looked at since my defence. I found it to be a story, a real story, and a military and political story—a narration describing the dynamics between the ruler and the ruled, the self-assured and the unconfident, people of different culture, religion and race at the dawn of nineteenth century in Southern India. I liked what I read and decided to make it available to people like Luke Rynda, who might appreciate our common humanity.

Except for editorial changes, the text remains as it was when it was submitted to my dissertation committee. I have not been an active historian since the late 1970s, and therefore I have no idea what has happened in my field during these intervening years. I've been primarily involved in working with and writing about couples and families and my own personal growth. I hope you find *A Jolt* interesting, insightful and fascinating.

November, 2016

1971 PREFACE

FEW EVENTS IN THE EARLY HISTORY of British Rule in India caused so much sensation as the mutiny at Vellore. It was the first armed attempt on the part of the Indian troops of the English East India Company to overthrow British authority. However puny the attempt might have been, it sent a surge of horror through South India, and its implication caused grave concern and apprehension both in India and England. Despite its arresting nature, the mutiny at Vellore and its aftermath has not yet received a full and objective treatment. This dissertation/book is an attempt to meet that need.

Because of the allegation that Tipu Sultan's family engineered the plot at Vellore, the first chapter is devoted to a discussion of the way in which the captive family lived and also of the character of the princes. The second chapter deals with the Coast Army. Particular attention is given to matters such as recruitment, uniform, discipline, promotion, pay and officer-troop relation to gain some insight into possible causes of grievance if there were any. Chapter three to six are basically narrative. Chapter 3 takes the narrative from the first step towards the issuance of the military orders up to the eve of the mutiny. Chapter 4 describes the mutiny in detail: as much as possible the events are portrayed by witnesses who were actually on the spot. Chapter 5 presents a comprehensive treatment of the aftermath: knowledge of which is essential for the correct understanding of the nature and character of the mutiny and what followed. Chapter 6 deals with the story of the reaction in England. The last chapter and the conclusion discuss the nature and the cause of the agitation.

A number of Indian words appear in the text of the book, which may not be familiar to the reader. Therefore, a glossary of Indian terms is given at the end of the book.

Vellore Fort

INTRODUCTION

PROMPTED BY THE INSTINCT OF SELF-PRESERVATION, the English East
India Company thrust itself to fill the power vacuum that had occurred on
the Indian sub-continent as the result of the disintegration of Moghul
Empire. Relying upon a mercenary army, composed of Indian recruits, the
Company succeeded in eliminating first its European rival, the French
Compagnie des Indes Orientales, and then its Indian rivals. By the turn of
the eighteenth century, the Company held complete sway over South India.
The last rival, Tipu Sultan of Mysore, had been slain in battle,[1] his kingdom
partitioned, and the former ruling family restored to the reduced state of
Mysore. About the same time, the rulers of the Coromandel Coast, the
Nawab of the Carnatic and the Rajah of Tanjore, were pensioned off, and
their kingdoms annexed. The other rulers, the Rajah of Travancore and
Cochin on the Malabar Coast and the Nizam of Hyderabad in the Deccan,
held on to their territories, but they had been reduced to the state of puppets
by the Subsidiary Alliance system[2]. The ones who were still left with any
degree of independence were the Marathas, but they were outside the
borders of South India. With them a bloody and inconclusive war had been
just waged.

Though the Company had emerged paramount, it was quite conscious
of the slender nature of its hold upon the Peninsula. First, there was the

French menace. Though the French were no longer a serious rival, yet from their bases in the Indian Ocean, they posed a threat to the British security, particularly in view of Napoleon's grandiose schemes. French agents, secret or otherwise, were active in the Company's territories, as well as with the Marathas.[3] Secondly, the Marathas were still a threat. It was feared that they might attack the Company's territory at any opportune moment.[4] Thirdly, there were many disgruntled elements within the Company's domain. Besides the former ruling families, numerous poligars, zamindars and other local chieftains had suffered, some very grievously, due to English incursion. These men along with their friends and supporters remained hostile to the English. Against these malevolent forces the Company counted upon a passive people and an obedient army for its security.[5]

Knowing that the people's and the army's confidence in the British would remain so long as their economic and socio-religious customs, practices and institutions were left alone, the Company followed as far as possible a policy of laissez-faire and status quo. However, for financial reasons, it did make some changes in the revenue system. Only modifications were attempted in the existing ryotwari, zamindari and mirasdari systems. Nowhere were any of them totally abolished.[6] The Company also introduced some changes in the judicial system. The judicial functions of the poligar, zamindar and amildar were abolished, and Zillah magistrates were appointed to discharge those duties. Yet the village panchayat was permitted to continue with its traditional role. Again civil laws were left alone, but criminal laws which originally favoured the Muslims, were modified to affect equity.[7] it was hoped that these changes would strengthen the attachment of the people to the Company's Government. The people's allegiance to the new regime had yet to be tested by the vicissitude of time; but before that happened, rebellion broke out in Vellore.

CHAPTER ONE
VELLORE

VELLORE LIES ABOUT NINETY MILES WEST OF MADRAS in a beautiful and fertile valley between two rugged ranges of the Eastern Ghauts. About a mile north of the city, flows the broad and sandy Pallar River. At the centre of the city lie the remains of the once famous fort of Vellore.

At the beginning of the nineteenth century, the fort still retained its medieval grandeur. The fort was nearly circular, and its wall massive. It was built of large stones and blocks of granite, which were about three to four feet thick and eighteen to twenty feet in length. Along the wall were bastions and towers at short intervals. The outer portion of the wall was crowned with "a row of handsome upright stone slabs, uniformly rounded at the top."[1]

This massive wall was surrounded by an "exceedingly broad and deep moat."[2] The moat was full of large, voracious and formidable alligators, some of whom were about eighteen feet long. It was impassable "except on a raft or by the causeways."[3] In 1805, the original causeway was replaced by a drawbridge.[4]

Beyond the valley, up on the surrounding hills there were three forts—

Sazarao, Guzarao and Mortaz Agur. They were to protect the main fort from artillery fire. So long as the hill forts were not reduced, the fort down in the valley remained impregnable.[5]

II

Immediately after the fall of Tipu Sultan, his four elder sons—Fatteh Hyder, Abdul Khalik, Mohi-ud-din and Moiz-ud-din—were moved to Vellore fort. Their presence in Seringapatam was thought to have posed a potential threat to the Myssorean settlement which was about to be instituted.[6] The four princes were married and had families of their own. The first two princes had been in charge of two divisions of the army and the other two of the palace when the Sultan fell. Abdul Khalik and Moiz-ud-din were the two princes who had been surrendered as hostages to Lord Cornwallis in 1792.[7] Besides these four princes, Tipu Sultan had eight younger sons, two married and six unmarried daughters. The Sultan also had a brother, Kerim Sahib, and numerous *mahal* women. The younger princes and other members of the family were not moved to Vellore till the summer of 1802.[8]

The treaty that concluded the last Mysore War appropriated an annual sum of not less than Rs.700,000 for the maintenance of Tipu Sultan's family. The treaty also stated that the Company's Government was at liberty to reduce the stipulated sum in case of any member's decease or to suspend the allowance, in part or whole, "in the event of any hostile attempt on the part of the said family, or of any member of it, against the authority of the contracting parties, or against the peace of their respective dominions, or the territory of the Rajah of Mysore."[9]

The Sultan's family was given comforts "on a manificent scale, suited to the rank in which they were born."[10] The elder princes were housed in the renovated apartments of the old Nawabs of the Carnatic. Each prince was given his own private apartment but the public apartment was shared by

14

them all. Their residence was called a "palace." Others were housed in the newly-built quarters.[11]

The elder princes were given an annual allowance of Rs.50,000 each, and no restriction was imposed upon the manner in which they spent their money. They were also exempted from duties on all consumer goods "as honorary, rather than pecuniary, marks of favour."[12] Further, they were permitted to have, besides their women and servants, muriadmians or gentleman companions. However, some restrictions were placed upon their number lest they would become so numerous "to endanger the public tranquility, or form a point of union for the adherents of the late Sultaun."[13] The next three princes—Muhammad Yussain, Subhan Sahib and Muhammad Shak'r Ulah—too were given the same treatment after their arrival in Vellore, but their annual allowance was fixed at Rs.25,000 each. However, their marriages were solemnized with special grants from the Government. A plan to build three two-storey apartments at the cost of nearly Rs.58,000 for them was under consideration when the mutiny broke out.[14]

The other five princes—Jam-ud-din, Suneer-ud-din, Muneer-ud-din Gholam Muhammad and Gholam Ahmed—were promised similar treatment when they reached the age of majority, which was fixed at 15. Until then they lived in common apartments, and they were given monthly allowances. Jam-ud-din and Suneer-ud-din's allowances amounted to Rs.450 each; Muneer-ud-din, Ghulam Muhammad and Gholam Ahmed's to Rs.350 each. In 1805, the first two princes' allowances were raised to Rs.700, and the last three princes' to Rs.500.[15]

Tipu Sultan's two married daughters, Bibi Begum and Asmut Ulnissa Begum, were allowed to remain near Seringapatam, and they were given no allowances.[16] The six unmarried daughters—Ummeer Ulnissa Begum, Fatina Begum, Budi Ulnissa Begum, Umdah Begum, Nur Ulnissa Begum and

Kulima Begum—were taken to Vellore, and their monthly allowances were fixed at Rs.150 each. Ummeer, Patina, Budi and Umdah were married during the year 1805. A grant of Rs.10,500 was given for the ceremonies of each wedding. After the marriage, each husband was also provided a monthly allowance of Rs.200.[17] The marriages of Nur and Kulima were scheduled to take place in 1806, but unfortunately due to the mutiny the Government abrogated them. It refused to permit the consummation of Nur's wedding which had begun on July 3, 1806, and ordered the annulment of Kulima's engagement.[18]

The Sultan's brother, Kerim Sahib's annual allowance was fixed at Rs.12,000.[19] He lived in a separate apartment, near the princes' residence. Kerim Sahib was slightly deranged, and the Sultan had kept him in confinement.[20] In October, 1804, he was joined by his wife, his sister (Hyder Ali's daughter and wife of the Nawab of Savanore in the Maratha country) and her two sons (Hussain Khan and Jaffer Ali Khan), who had until then lived in Seringapatam. In recommending their removal to Vellore, Arthur Wellesley declared that their stay in Seringapatam "might do mischief and certainly can do no good."[21] Prior to the mutiny, a grant of Rs.3,500 was authorized to solemnize Kerim Sahib's daughter's marriage.[22]

The *mahal* women were given modest treatment.[23] High ranking women were given each a separate room and a small amount of pocket money; others might have been housed in pairs and were provided only with necessities. The women had come from different parts of India, and they furnished their rooms according to the fashion of their home districts.[24] They had the habit of making petitions for special indulgences whenever a dignitary's wife visited them.[25] Some of the old eunuchs of Hyder Ali were still attached to the *mahals.*[26]

While granting indulgent treatment, the Government kept strict surveillance over the princes, their families and their adherents. To ensure the security of the princes, sentinels were posted at the main entrances of their respective apartments and around their enclosures. No one was permitted "to pass over the walls of the enclosure or out from the house in any other part than through the proper gate or door."[27] The main gate was always closed at 10.00 p.m. except under extra-ordinary circumstances and with the permission of the officer-in-charge of the princes.[28] But the sentinel remained at the post day and night. The Indian troops furnished the necessary guards, and the guards were forbidden to converse with the princes but were expected to pay them every military compliment.[29]

At the time of relief, the officer of guard did not receive charge of the princes as he would do in the case of the regular prisoners. This deficiency in security was remedied by an *hirkarh* system. Four *hirkarhs* or trusty servants were attached to each prince, and one of them at least remained with the prince day and night except when he retired to the women's apartment. The *hirkarhs* also had some other assignments. They identified the prince's servants and adherents to the guards, who might not be familiar with them, and reported to the officer-in-charge all the occurrences in the household. Originally these *hirkarhs* were placed at the princes' arrival in Vellore upon the pretext that their servants were strangers and that they needed assistants.[30] Apart from these *hirkarhs,* who were really spies, some of the princes' servants were on the Government's secret pay roll.[31]

A *hirkarh* establishment was also stationed at the entrance of the fort. A register of the princes' servants and adherents was provided to facilitate their identification. All strangers were stopped at the gate and their arrival was reported to the officer-in-charge. Only upon his permission was the visitor allowed to go into the fort.[32]

The princes' servants and adherents were admitted by tickets. The ticket had the bearer's name, and that of his patron, and the seal and signature of the officer-in-charge of the princes. With that ticket the bearer was permitted to pass and repass the gate as often as he liked so long as the gate was open. However, the bearer was permitted to visit only the prince whose name was found on the ticket.[33]

The princes were at liberty to visit one another if they so desired. When a prince left his apartment to visit another, the *hirkarh* reported it immediately to the officer, and three or four guards escorted him.[34] The princes were also allowed to ride out of the fort. But this necessitated a more complicated arrangement. When a prince wanted to ride out, he informed the officer, who subsequently prepared an escort to accompany him. The officer himself led the escort, which consisted of a detail of British cavalry and such other guards as he thought expedient to add. Further, the officer regulated the precise number of attendants who composed the *sowaris* and arranged the order of procession in such a manner as to place the leading horses "within the most unequivocal control of a portion of the cavalry guards."[35] The 19th dragoons were stationed at Vellore for the purpose of providing the necessary escort. But as the princes did not avail "themselves of that liberty" for some years, in 1805, the dragoons were removed and the privilege of riding out was tacitly withdrawn. If the princes rode out "for the performance of ceremonies or for any other reason," the commanding officer in Arcot furnished the guards.[36]

Precaution was also taken to prevent foul-play through covered *doolies* or carriages.[37] No covered *dooly* was permitted to leave from any prince's apartment without prior notice. Before a *dooly* left, the officer-in-charge was notified. Subsequently, he or his chief assistant came and took charge of the prince from whose apartment the *dooly* was to leave. Thus, even the possibility of practicing deception through covered *doolies* was eliminated.[38]

The princes were forbidden to correspond with any person of significance. All their incoming and outgoing mails were opened, and copies of the same were transmitted to the governor in Fort St. George.[39]

III

Once in every ten days, the officer-in-charge of the princes submitted reports to the Government. These were filed in duplicate, one for Fort St. George and another for Fort St. William. They described briefly the disposition of the princess, their servants and adherents, and also of the Muslims in Vellore and neighbourhood and narrated the arrivals and departures of notable personalities and conspicuous characters.[40]

These reports make interesting reading. They portray the activities in and around Vellore. "Moiz-ud-deen almost every night has players and singers in the women's apartment where they generally remain until 3 or 4 o' clock in the morning," reads part of a report.[41] "One of the women of the late Sultaun's Mahal died on the 17th at night . . . Futteh Hyder is pleased at this . . . as she possessed some property, money and jewels etc. upon all of which Futteh Hyder will now seize," states another.[42] "Sultan Mohy-ud-deen has sent back to his uncle Moyen-ud-deen the person who came from him some time ago."[43] The reports also reflect the reaction of the princes when additional measures were taken curtailing their freedom. "Since the receipt of the Governor's last instructions, I have placed two additional *hircaras* or spies over Futteh Hyder. He has necessarily become informed. . . He mentioned it to the Native Doctor and observed that there surely ought to be no cause for suspicion in regard to him, for he had quitted his army in the field and had come . . . to . . . the English," runs another. ". . . I asked him [Moiz-ud-din] for a copy of the letter for the purpose of transmitting to the Governor. He seemed very much averse to giving me a copy of it, not from any consideration (he said) of the contents of the letter, but merely on account that it was addressed to a female, as the letter simply contained expressions of duty and of affectionate regard and was of no importance . . . ," adds the same report.[44] A good many reports end, "Nothing extraordinary. The Princes are in good health."[45]

The *pettah* or village too was carefully kept under surveillance. It had about 20,000 inhabitants.[46] Out of this number, there were about eighteen hundred registered and twelve hundred unregistered servants, *muri-admians* and relatives of the princes. *Hirkarhs* were posted day and night at the entrances of the pettah. They checked on persons of "suspicious appearances" and intercepted letters of doubtful nature. The Government also banned all forms of arms from the *pettah.*[47]

The princes were born of different mothers and differed much in their habits and dispositions. The eldest son Fatteh Hyder was born about 1771 or 1772. He had the largest number of women. According to Thomas Marriott, the officer who had known the princes for many years, Hyder had such "incestuous connexion [which was] abhorred even amongst the most profligate and abandoned Mussalmans." He was also extraordinarily rude and mean to his mother and women. Being the first born, Hyder entertained political aspirations even after his removal to Vellore. He was a keen observer of contemporary politics. After the Treaty of Amiens, when the French returned to take their settlements, Hyder had an agent, Mahomed Malick, in Pondicherry. With the passage of time, he came to profess attachment to the English and hostility towards the French. His prime claim to succeed his father made him an object of envy among the brothers.[48]

The second son, Abdul Khalik, was born about 1779 or 1780. Khalik was extremely jealous of Fatteh Hyder. The day after the fall of Seringapatam while Fatteh Hyder was still holding his forces against the English, Khalik threw himself at their mercy in the hope of obtaining their father's throne. Despite his disappointment at that, he continued to profess attachment to the English, but his hostility to Hyder became deeper. In Vellore, he endeavoured "to calumniatye . . . accuse and criminate . . . Futta Hyder of treacherous designs against the British Government." Once he sent out a letter to Dhundiah, who was then at war with the English, with

Hyder's forged signature and seal, and immediately informed Lieutenant-Colonel Doveton, the officer-then-in-charge of the princes, that Hyder's seditious letter was on the road. Unfortunately for Khalik, its bearer Sheikh Par, when seized by and confronted with the authorities disclosed the true origin of the letter.[49] Failing to eliminate Hyder through accusation, Khalik tried to poison him. Marriott states that Abdul Khalik put on "a cloak to cover the deformity of the most malicious and rancorous heart," and in him "human nature" reached its "greatest depravities." He was a sodomite in sexual life and inhuman in the treatment of his women, bordering on sadism. Khalik was an extreme miser too. He spent a great deal of time with an old Brahmin accountant settling his pecuniary concerns and disputing bazaar prices.[50]

The third son, Mohi-ud-din, was born in 1782. Unlike his two elder brothers, he was a likeable person. Marriott describes him as "amiable, gentle, mild and generous." His disposition was non-aggressive and his conduct "irreproachable." He would "give up every point, and submit to any condition" to avoid dispute. Mohi-ud-din was said to have been "really satisfied with the dispensations of Providence and . . . really contented with his condition." Marriott adds, "I could never see the least attempt at duplicity, prevarications and decity."[51] Mohi-ud-din was an avid reader, and he was much interested in history and biography. He was alleged to have had no political aspirations.[52] This was strange as he was the only legitimate son of Tipu Sultan, and was revered as "sultan" in the family.[53] For a year prior to the mutiny, Mohi-ud-din was believed to have drawn closer to his younger brother Moiz-ud-din.[54]

The fourth son, Moiz-ud-din, was born about 1784. Marriott describes him as "good natured, lively affable and generous," but adds that his temper was "fury and sometimes passionate, but as easily calmed as enflamed." "In all his actions," Moiz-ud-din exhibited callous "carelessness and indifference." Marriott prefers to call it "want of reflection." He had also no "man of respectability" among his *muri-admians.*

Moiz-ud-din was a great lover of horses. He enjoyed greatly watching, riding, feeding and reading about them. He was much interested in music too. He had a grand collection of vinas. He insisted that his companions learn to play them. Further, he deeply enjoyed controversial discussion between Shiahs and Sunnis, the two major sects of Islam. Personally, like his grandfather Hyder Ali,[55] Moiz-ud-din was "much of a deist." He laughed at Fatteh Hyder's conversion from Sunnis to Shiahs. He often said, "Everyman should go to heaven his own way, but the faith of Islam is most desirable from the prospect it holds out of so much sensual bliss in the next world." Moiz-ud-din also talked "on all subjects," but "the naivete of his questions" betrayed that he had "not made them his study." He expected Thomas Marriott, whose visit was ever eagerly awaited, to furnish him information about current politics.

Moiz-ud-din was a great spendthrift. He was "always deep in debt and always endeavouring to borrow." According to Marriott, "His vices are all venal in short. He is a true Moorman—believing in totality he will live today and let the morrow take thought for himself." Whenever he had opportunity, he bought either horses or dancing girls. "For five minutes after [visits], Marriott states, "he will ask permission to buy a dancing girl, or anything else." Moiz-ud-din also took great delight in vexing Abdul Khalik on account of his stinginess. For some time prior to the mutiny, Moiz-ud-din was on voluntary stoppage of Rs.1,000 a month to reduce his debt.[56]

The next three sons, Muhammad Yussain, Subhan Sahib and Muhammad Shak'r Ulah, were born in 1785, 1786 and 1789 respectively.[57] Yussain was said to have had "a religious turn of mind." Subhan was extremely quick tempered, though he was "ready to hearken to advice."

22

Shak'r Ulah was "the handsomest of Tippu's sons." He was extremely intelligent, and he delighted in opposing Moiz-ud-din. Shak'r Ulah wrote to him "severe and sarcastic letters" whenever he found opportunities. These three princes deprecated the discrimination shown in their allowances. They formed "a league" against their elder brothers and opposed them at every turn. Marriott stated "the character of these three young men would be very different had they not four elder brothers."[58]

The last five sons, Jam-ud-din, Suneer-ud-din, Muneer-ud-din, Gholam Muhammad and Gholam Ahmed, were born between the years 1794 and 1797. Unlike all other princes, Jam-ud-din, Muneer-ud-din and their older brother Muhammad Yussain were born of the same mother.[59] The last five princes were too young to exhibit any distinctive traits. They were all said to be "very fine boys."[60]

IV

The officer-in-charge of the princes and their household at the time of the mutiny was Thomas Marriott.[61] He was known to Tipu Sultan's family perhaps from about the early 1790's. Marriott was entrusted by Lord Cornwallis with the honour of taking back the two hostage sons to their father.[62] In 1799, he escorted the four elder princes to Vellore,[63] and then he returned to Seringapatam and took charge of that part of the family which remained there.[64] Upon its arrival in Vellore, he became the assistant paymaster of stipends (officer-in-charge of the princes) and town major of Vellore. In January, 1805, Lord Bentinck appointed him the sole custodian of the Mysore family. His younger brother Charles was later appointed to assist him.[65]

The Marriott brothers seemed to have received rapid promotions in the service. Thomas became a major in April, 1804.[66] Not long afterwards, Charles became a captain. With great delight, their father Randolph Marriott wrote to his old friend Warren Hastings on May 8, 1806:

We have now exceeding good [news] . . . from our young men.
The Major 'Thos' is quite settled at Vellore, and Mrs. Hastings'
friend Charles 'now a Capt' is appointed his deputy 'each with
handsome salary exclusive of their pay'.[67]

Few weeks later Randolph again informed his friend, "I have the
further pleasure to inform you that my son Thos has got at Lt. Col'cy, and
that he hopes soon Chr will be a Major . . ."[68] He adds again, "Tom was
appointed a Lt. Colo . . . when he had been 15 years in the country and some
of the officers of 22 and 23 years standing are yet only captains."[69] The
Marriott brothers also appeared to have had excellent rapport with the
Governor. "Lord and Lady Wm Bentinck have been staying two or three
days with them, at Vellore," reports Randolph.[70]

Thomas Marriott was very popular with the princes and their families.
He conversed very fluently in their own language. He was also well
acquainted with their manners and customs.[71] Lord and Lady Bentinck,
while visiting Vellore, found the princes and their women extremely pleased
with Thomas Marriott.[72] Lord George Valentia tells that the Mysoreans had
"adopted" Marriot into their family and called him "brother".[73] The princes
reposed a great deal of confidence in him. Consequently, Marriott was able
to have "personal conversation with the mothers and females of their
families, without the personal presence of the princes themselves." In fact,
whenever Marriott went to speak to any of the women, the princes retired
on their own accord.[74]

Thomas Marriott believed that the princes had reconciled themselves to
the reality of their situation. They had seen their father's kingdom divided,
South India reduced, the Nizam and the Peshwa made puppets and the
Maratha confederacy shattered. They had also observed the fate of their
cousin, Fatteh Ali, Kerim Sahib's son, who escaped to the Marathas at the fall

of Seringapatam. Fatteh Ali was not made a rallying point by their adherents; rather he had become "almost destitute of the common necessities of life." Marriott thought that the princes could hope only in the French, and in that connection, he felt that they had deep interest in the Anglo-French war.[75]

Moreover, Marriott believed that the princes' adherents had no interest in changing the lot of their patrons. He said:

> I feel confident that there is scarcely a murdi-admian or servant about the place but in reality, thinks it more for his own individual interest, that his master should remain in his present condition, than that he should endeavor to better it, by any hazardous or precarious attempt. Indeed, few of them would wish to change their present lazy indolent but secure, and profitable way of life for the more hardy and precarious one of the field. While nature predominates, there is little reason to disbelieve that self-interest will actuate the generality (sic) of mankind.

Nonetheless, Marriott admitted that the *murdi-admians* filled their respective prince's ears "with gross flatteries, foolish or slanderous stories, false ideas of his present condition and vain hopes of his future grandure."[76] Marriott, further, added that the enmity among the princes was so intense that they could not unite to rise against the English.[77]

At the time of Thomas Marriott's appointment as the paymaster of stipends, a triple authority was instituted in Vellore. Until then the commanding officer of the Vellore garrison was also in charge of the princes and the *pettah*. In April, 1805, Lieutenant-Colonel John Fancourt of His Majesty's 34th Regiment was appointed to the command of the garrison,[78] and the *pettah* was placed immediately under R. C. Ross, an assistant to the collector of North Arcot.[79] Fancourt had earlier served in San Dominico. He was said to have been "a good hearted man,"[80] who "lived religiously."[81]

Nonetheless, Fancourt was blunt and tactless. He was also impulsive and quick-tempered. Lord William Bentinck stated that his "want of temper and judgement" was "extraordinary" and "too notorious to be questioned."[82]

V

Soon after the division of power and responsibility, Fancourt, Marriott and Ross began bickering. Fancourt accused Ross's assistants of being contemptuous "of the commandant's authority."[83] Ross complained that Fancourt was meddling with the civil and criminal disputes in *pettah*.[84] Marriott charged that Fancourt was obstructing his work.[85] Marriott also pleaded his inability to "watch over" the adherents of the princes without his control of police in the *pettah*.[86]

The Governor Lord William Bentinck bore patiently the charges and counter-charges which crowded his desk for a year.[87] At last his patience became exhausted. On May 6, 1806, the very day when the first symptom of mutiny was exhibited, Bentinck recommended to the Board John Fancourt's removal from Vellore at the next favourable opportunity to "a command where the same intermixture of authorities" did not exist.[88] The Commander-in-Chief Sir John Francis Cradock deeply resented the Governor's suggestion.[89] He castigated Bentinck's recommendation as having been introduced "with great solemnity and interesting preamble." He proposed a court-martial to try Fancourt and asked the Governor to prepare his charges.[90] Cradock's rebuff infuriated Bentinck. He condemned Cradock's proposal as "incompatable with the nature of the question before the Board"; reiterated that Fancourt was "entirely unqualified for the station" he was in, and proposed "his immediate removal from that station."[91] The other two Board members, William Petrie and James Strange, regretted the disagreement between the Governor and the Commander-in-Chief, but added that they did not find "sufficient ground for removing" Fancourt from Vellore.[92] Unfortunately for Fancourt, Bentinck did not use the veto but yielded to the decision of the majority. The blessing that almost came in disguise slipped away from Fancourt.

The garrison that John Fancourt commanded consisted of six companies of the first battalion of the first regiment and the whole of the second battalion of the fourth regiment of the Indian army and four companies of His Majesty's 69th Regiment. The regiments were commanded by Lieutenant-Colonel Nathaniel Forbes, Lieutenant-Colonel John Darley, and Major J. K. Cootes respectively. The rank and file of the 69th were housed in the British barracks inside the fort. Some of their officers resided in the *pettah*, while others lived in the fort. The Indian troops resided in the *pettah*, and only when they had early morning drill did they sleep in the fort. Like the officers of the 69th Regiment, some of the British officers of the Indian troops resided in the *pettah*. Besides these, 1,200 Indian and 40 British invalids and a host of officers' servants also lived in the *pettah*.[93]

The two Indian battalions at Vellore for some reason did not get along well. That is attributed to some "old enmity" which existed between them. They seldom co-operated with one another. They even refused to celebrate their feasts and festivals together.[94]

VI

On February 12, 1806, an untoward incident took place in Vellore which in some ways prefigured the tragedy which was to occur in a few months. While shooting at some pariah, stray dogs, Lieutenant Louis Baby of His Majesty's 69th Regiment shot the four-year-old child of Sheikh Madar, a sepoy of the first battalion of the first regiment. On the following night the child died of double wounds near "the joints of the thigh bones."

According to the cyc-witnesses, Baby had cleared off everyone from the direction of his targets. But the child was found about 135 yards away from where Baby stood, and the dog which he aimed at was to have been about 25 yards from him in a different direction. Further, Baby did not notice the child even after it had been shot. Not until the child was taken to Dr. Wynnes' place for dressing, did Baby know that it had been wounded "by the fire . . . directed at the dogs." The Government appointed a committee to examine the cause of the mishap, but it could not explain satisfactorily how the shot aimed at the dog hit the child which was in a different direction.[95] This tragedy in its apparently inexplicable cause and effect foreshadowed the ensuing disaffection in the Coast Army.

Vellore Fort - East Moat

CHAPER TWO
THE COAST ARMY

THE YEAR 1806 WAS THE DIAMOND JUBILEE of the Coast Army.[1] In that year, its Indian establishment consisted of twenty-three regiments of infantry, eight regiments of cavalry, one battalion of Fencibles, two companies of foot artillery, one company of horse artillery, forty-two companies of gun lascars and two battalions of pioneers. The infantry regiments were paired off into battalions, which in turn were divided into one grenadiers[2] and eight battalion companies. The numerical strength of each battalion was about nine hundred sepoys and eighty sepoy boys.[3] Though the two wings of the regiment were intended to be kept together, they seldom were. Each cavalry regiment was divided into six troops, and their total strength was 402 troopers. The Fencibles numbered about a thousand, and they were under the direct command of the governor. The size of the foot and horse artillery corps was very small: their combined strength was no more than 250 men. The gun lascars and the pioneers were auxiliary corps: the former manned the guns, and the latter supported the troops on manoeuvres.[4] The establishment had 55,050 men fit for duty.[5]

In peace time, the Indian troops along with the British were stationed in detachments of varying sizes in different places across South India. As the territory over which they were stationed was so vast and the communication was slow, it was necessary to establish headquarters in the Southern, the Central and the Northern divisions of the area. Roughly the River Coleroon demarcated the South from the Central division and the Krishna the Central from the Northern. Divisional headquarters were Trichinopoly in the South, Madras in the Central and Vizagapatam in the North. At the time of the Vellore mutiny, Colonel Alexander Campbell was the commandant of the South and Major-General Dugald Campbell in the North. The Centre was under the Commander-in-Chief's direct supervision till July 1806, when Major-General Fuller became the commandant.[6] The divisional headquarters was the liason between the Adjutant-General's office at Fort St. George and the direct garrisons in the divisions.

II

The Coast Army consisted of two different classes of volunteers. First, there were those who for various personal reasons such as financial need, a desire for adventure or a desire to make a career in the army enlisted voluntarily at the recruiting centres in the different divisions. The number of these volunteers was very small. It was not enough even to fill the vacancies which normally occurred in the army during peace time. Recruitment was indeed a serious problem. The Commander-in-Chief Sir John Francis Cradock frankly admitted in 1806 that it was carried out with "great difficulty."[7] Nonetheless, recruits had to be found; and therefore, from time to time, the commanding officers of the garrisons sent Indian commissioned officers into the countryside and hamlets to try to encourage villagers and vagabonds alike to enlist. To ensure that these officers pursued their business diligently they were paid a reward for each recruit they enlisted. The men who joined the army as a result of this procedure formed the second class of "volunteers." Whether the recruits belonged to the former or latter class, the dominant reason why most of them joined the army was financial. John Munro, the Quartermaster-General, observed that only those who were "unable to procure subsistence by any other mode of life" found "a refuge" in "our service."[8] All recruits spent the first four months after enlistment in basic training. Only then they were allowed to enter the ranks of a battalion.[9]

Besides the adult recruits, some boys were enlisted into the army through what was called "the sepoy-boy establishment," which was reserved for the sons and close relatives of the men who were in the army or who had died in the service. These boys were enlisted in one or two ways. Some were enlisted when they attained the age of eleven. They received a monthly wage of Rs.3.50. They also received basic training appropriate to their age, and when they were 15 or 16 years old, if they were physically fit, they were transferred to the regular ranks of the army. Other boys were enlisted when their fathers died. These boys continued to receive their fathers' pay until they reached the age of puberty, when they were placed on the regular establishment of the army. If for some reason, they chose not to remain in the army, their pay was terminated.[10]

Before a recruit was given his uniform, he took the oath of "fidelity and attachment." He swore that

I, A.B. sepoy, do swear to serve the Honorable Company faithfully and truly against all their enemies, while I continue to receive their pay, and eat their salt. I do swear to obey all the orders I may receive from my Commanders and Officers, never to forsake my post, abandon my Colours, or turn my back to my enemies, and that I will in all things behave myself like a good and faithful sepoy, in perfect obedience at all times to the rules and customs of war. I do also faithfully promise and swear that whenever I have an inclination to quit the service, I will give a month's notice of it before to my Commanding Officer, and when I have received my discharge, I will return my arms, accoutrements and ammunition in the same good condition I may have received them from the Honorable Company.[11]

After the recruit took the oath, his name, description, age, caste, village and district were entered in the regimental register and then his uniform and accoutrements were issued.[12]

III

The uniform which was given to the sepoy was quite different from his ordinary dress. As uniform the sepoy wore a red jacket (over a white undershirt), a pair of white drawers and a blue turban. The red jacket was cut in the front and buttoned down from top to waist and sloped sharply to the hips. Its collar, facing and cuffs were of the same colour. The drawers extended to just above the knee, and were bordered with navy blue. At the top, they were fastened around the waist by a blue sash. The turban was quite unique and in no respect was it similar to the head dress worn by South Indians. The turban was made of an iron and wooden frame, which was neatly and artistically covered by a blue woolen cloth. The turban, when worn, inclined slightly to the side, and it was ornamented with a rose, a brass button, a band lining. Some corps' turban had also a tuft or leather cockade or both. Indeed, the turban had no affinity to the turban of South India, except the name it bore.[13]

The above described turban was instituted on May 1, 1797, and from that day it was worn by all battalions except one—the second of the thirteenth regiment (formerly the 36th) which continued to wear its original head dress. Its turban was truly very different from the others. Like the others, it too was blue, but when worn the turban inclined a little from the front to the rear. The turban was encircled by a plaited calico band, the ends of which were gathered up behind, and from them two cotton tassels were suspended. It had a leather cockade at the left side with a tuft of hair. The sepoys and their officers did not cut their hair, which plaited and turned up behind under the turban. The grenadier company was marked out by yellow band and tassels with white tuft and the others with white band and tassels with red tuft.[14]

From the regular sepoy's uniform, the grenadier's and the Indian officer's differed slightly. They had a few minor trimmings and additions to designate their respective stations. The commissioned officers appeared to have worn a pair of long trousers and boots. Non-commissioned officers and privates did not have footwear except sandals. But in some corps socks and boots were being introduced, though unofficially.[15]

Unlike the infantry, the pioneers and gun lascars wore blue jackets. In other aspects their uniform was very similar to that of the infantry. Not much is known about the uniform of the other three corps. Nevertheless, it is clear that the cavalry, the foot and the horse artilleries had red turbans, and their Indian officers wore "white pantaloons and hussar boots."[16]

To maintain regularity, it was usual, at least among the infantry corps, to set apart "the most expert and well dressed" person in a company as "pattern man" and everybody was expected to copy him. No deviation was tolerated. A naigue was held responsible to see that everyone adhered strictly to the established practice.[17]

With regard to the face—moustache, beard, sect mark and ear ring— no uniformity was practiced in the army. Beards were verbally prohibited in many corps, and in some by standing orders. Moustaches were universally tolerated. Neither their shape nor their size appeared to have been regulated. In some corps even small beards might have been permitted. However, no corps tolerated long beards.

Among the corps where shaving was regulated, beards were shaved off twice a week—on Wednesday and Saturday or the day before troops furnished guards. At times some men did appear on parade unshaven, and they were cautioned. At least in one corps the practice was to order the unshaven "to be shaven with a blunt razor without soap or water to the greatest amusement of their comrades who always looked on and laugh'd at them."[18]

The sect marks and ear rings were quite common among the troops. Only in one corps was the practice totally prohibited by standing regulations; among several it was neither "usual" nor "customary." In many corps however, a small mark on the forehead and a little ring in the ear were overlooked—a happy compromise between traditional practice and the urge for innovation. Nonetheless, no large mark or ring was permitted. The commanding officers were more inclined to discourage these "peculiar practices" of the Indians than to encourage them.[19]

IV

Patterned after that of the European armies, the discipline was strict, rigid and severe. The troops found the morning drills and garrison duties quite unpalatable and irksome. They often compared their iron discipline and regimented lives to their counterparts in the armies of the Indian rulers, who had less drill and duty and more leisure. The severe discipline and exacting duties, it was believed, made recruitment difficult.[20]

For the same reason, some of the Indian soldiers deserted; however, by far the largest number deserted when the battalions were ordered to move to another division or when they were ordered into action. The authorities tried to stop desertion by imposing the death penalty on all convicted offenders, but this deterrent was not very successful. In order to encourage the apprehension of deserters, the authorities offered rewards ranging from Rs.10.50 to 17.50 for each deserted captured. The information recorded in the regimental registered prove very helpful in tracking down the deserter. The deserter's description was widely circulated, and the local civil authorities were ordered to assist the military search parties. Usually, the deserter was caught and then the law took its course.[21]

As a rule, no soldier was subjected to punishment except by a sentence of court-martial. There were two categories of court-martial: the regimental and the general. The regimental court-martial dealt with all minor offences of privates and non-commissioned officers. The members of this court were taken from all ranks, but its president was a subadar. Any senior officer was empowered to order a regimental court-martial. The general court-martial dealt with the offences of commissioned officers as well as capital crimes. Its chairman and members were exclusively Indian commissioned officers. The commanding officer alone would order a general court-martial. A capital sentence passed by this court had to have the approval of the governor-in-council for its execution.[22]

However, when immediate punishment was required either as an exemplary or restraining measure the senior officer present on the spot acted according to his discretion. Soon after the occasion, at the first opportunity, he sent a report to his superior, giving an account of the incident and explaining the measure he had adopted together with his reasons for it. The senior officer's discretionary powers, however, were not without restriction. No officer, whoever he might have been, could inflict corporal punishment upon a soldier. He also could not reduce or dismiss commissioned officers. These were prerogatives of the general court-martial and the governor-in-council.[23]

V

The highest rank to which an Indian could be promoted was subadar. Recruits were normally enlisted sepoys. From that rank, the sepoy was promoted to naique, to havildar, to jamadar and to subadar. Since there existed a strong prejudice among the high caste troops against the promotion of members of a lower caste, the latter were discriminated against in favour of higher caste candidates. Lower caste men were promoted "in cases of very extraordinary merit only."[24] For non-commissioned ranks—naique and havildar, a (British) captain recommended the candidate and the commanding officer of the battalion confirmed the recommendation; but for the commissioned ranks—jemadar and subadar, the commanding officer of the battalion made the recommendation and governor-in-council issued the commission.[25]

No Indian, however brilliant he might have been, could rise above the rank of subadar. Prior to 1785, Indians were promoted to commandant, a rank higher than subadar. S. G. Hill suggests that the rebellion of Yusuf Khan, who was commandant and also one of ablest Indian military leaders during the mid-eighteenth century, was a factor that led to the abolition of the rank of commandant.[26] Also, in 1785, Muctum, who was an acting commandant of the ninth battalion, was executed for inciting a mutiny among his corps.[27] In abolishing the rank, the Government declared:

> There are but few instances where they have been of much service, but frequent ones where they have done mischief . . . When they are clever men, their influence over the Native officers and sepoys becomes dangerous, and when they are not so, they can be no use.[28]

Even prior to 1785, the Indian commandant had only the trappings of a battalion officer, and in no way was he placed on equality with his British counterpart. He was made dependent and subject to all British commissioned officers. S. C. Hill observed rightly:

> It is clear . . . that at no period in the history of the Indian army was the native officer ever placed upon the same footing as the European . . . [29]
> Whatever the honour paid by brave men to bravery and skill, independent of race or colour, the fact remains that neither in

honours, nor rewards, neither in rank nor salary, were the native or Indian officers ever placed on an equality with the European.[30]

The Government might have abolished the ranks of jamadar and subadar as well. But in retaining them, it hoped to ascertain the pulse of the rank and file—a task no English could possibly do. The "special duty" of the jamadar and subadar was "to make themselves acquainted with the private views, attachments and connections of the men of their companies," and to report them regularly to their commanding officers. If they were ever found to manifest "either neglect or indifference to this essential part of their duty," they would at once be dismissed.[31]

VI

The Indian soldier's pay was higher than the daily labourer's. In 1806, a private in the infantry received Rs.7.00 a month whereas a labourer received about Rs.4.00 a month.[32] The pay scale of the army was as follows:[33]

Ranks	Calvary and Horse Artillery	Foot Artillery	Gun Lascards	Pioneers	Infantry
	Rs	Rs	Rs	Rs	Rs
Private	10.50	7.83	7.83	7.83	7.00
Naique	17.70	8.50	8.50	8.50	8.50
Havildar	21.00	10.50	10.50	10.50	10.50
Jemadar	31.50	24.50-42.50	24.50-42.00	24.50-42.00	24.50
Subadar	91.00-129.00	--	--	--	42.00-72.00

Besides the regular wage, the troop received allowances when they took the field. On such occasions all corps, except cavalry and horse artillery, were treated alike and were given the same allowance. The subadar received Rs. 21.00, the jamadar Rs.10.50, and all the non-commissioned rank and file Rs. 3.50 each day.[34]

The remuneration of privates and non-commissioned officers was very low indeed. The wage scale that was in operation prior to the Vellore mutiny was established in July 1800. At that time, the increase was given in consequence of repeated appeals by the troops to the Government. While granting the increase, the Government admitted "that the rate of pay at present allowed to the Native infantry does not bear a just proportion to the expense of maintaining themselves and their families, nor to the duties attached to the profession of arms."[35] Yet the increase was illusory as the following table shows:[36]

Ranks	Old Scale (Rupees) Prior to 1800	Revised Scale (Rupees) After July 1800
Sepoy	6.00	7.00
Naique	8.47	8.75
Havildar	10.50	10.50
Jemadar	24.50	24.50
Subadar	45.50 (no maximum)	42.00-72.00

It is true that after July 1800 troops no longer had money deducted from their wages to pay for their clothing. Admitted that was beneficial, but the gain was not much. The sepoy gained Rs.0.42 a month, the naique Rs. 0.58, the havildar Rs. 0.87, the jamadar Rs. 1.75 and the subadar Rs.3.50.[37]

The increase, however, were not large enough to make any appreciable benefit to the sepoy and non-commissioned officers. The troops rightly complained of their "depressed situation and low allowances."[38] The justice of their complaint receives further support when one realizes that even in 1806, the Company's troops, on the whole, and particularly the lower ranks, were paid much less than Tipu Sultan's troops during the 1790's. The following table demonstrates: [39]

Ranks	Coast Army in 1806	Tipu's in the 1790's
	Rs	Rs
Sepoy	7.00	9.00
Naik	8.50	10.00
Havildar	10.50	12.00
Jemadar	24.50	14.00
Subadar	42.00-72.00	50.00

One must also remember that after the liquidation of Tipu Sultan's army, a number of his soldiers joined the Coast Army. Obviously, those men had to take a cut in their pay, which must have irked them. It was true that the Bengal troops were paid exactly the same amount as the Coast Army.[40] But the cost of living was lower in Bengal. There a rupee would buy about 30 to 40 seers of rice, whereas on the Coast the same rupee purchased only about 13 to 20 seers of rice.[41] Furthermore, the English private whom the Indian sepoy met day after day received almost twice as much as he did.[42] No wonder, the Indian troops complained about their pay. On the other hand, they were paid promptly, and to the Company's credit, it did not in the 1800's make a practice of keeping the wages of its troops in arrears.[43]

Usually, at the end of his military career, the private as well as non-commissioned officer found himself without any savings. But the pension which the Company provided saved him from beggary. He was pensioned off at half pay whenever he was deemed unfit either for active service or when he was on the invalid establishment. However, if he was discharged on account of the loss of a limb or by wounds received while in the service, he was pensioned off at full pay. All Indian officers were treated similarly.[44]

If the Indian soldier or officer of the infantry, gun lascars, pioneers and foot artillery was considered unfit for active service but fit for garrison duties, he was not pensioned off, but transferred to the invalid establishment. The personnel in the cavalry and horse artillery were always pensioned off. The invalid establishment was not an attractive form of service. Upon his becoming invalid, the private's pay was reduced to Rs.5.00, and the officer's to half of what he was getting, unless he was invalid as a result of wounds received in action. Despite this loss in remuneration, the invalid was obliged to remain in the Presidency Town, attend parades, perform garrison duties and observe all forms of military discipline. In fact, the invalids performed all the duties of regular sepoys except marching "upon field service." Obviously, this indulgence was "more than counterbalanced by the reduction of their pay, and that state of inferiority and degradation" to which they were subjected.[45]

While in the service, the troops also received medical attention. To every regiment, at least in theory, one surgeon, two assistant surgeons and two Indian doctors were attached. Whenever a considerable detachment was made, one of the assistant surgeons or the Indian doctors accompanied it. No garrison was without a medical man. Some garrisons like Vellore also had a good-sized hospital, which catered to the needs of neighbouring villages and towns as well. In the early part of the nineteenth century, these medical centres were the popularizing agents of the recently-introduced vaccination, which was alleged to have caused much sensation among Indians.[46]

VII

In terms of the population, Muslims were heavily represented in the army. The cavalry and horse artillery were almost completely dominated by them. A small portion of high caste Hindus were admitted into these corps. At times when shortage of recruits occurred, some lower caste men were admitted. In other branches, Muslims constituted about one-third and Hindus about two-thirds. There were also some Jews and Indian Christians in the army. Unlike the Bengal army, most of the Hindu sepoys came from lower castes.[47]

Most of the Indian officers in the army were Muslims. Muslims were generally regarded as better soldiers. H. H. Dodwell estimates that "not quite two-thirds" and "something over one-third" must have been Muslims and Hindus respectively. Almost all the Hindu officers were of higher castes.[48]

The soldiers came from all parts of South India. The largest number came from the Tamil country. Andhra furnished the largest second group, Mysore the third and Travancore and Cochin the least. After the overthrow of Tipu Sultan and reduction of the Southern poligars, a number of their former sepoys joined the Coast Army. A few sepoys had also come from outside of South India.[49]

The Indian troops were commanded by British officers. The 1796 Regulations allotted 45 field and 15 staff British officers to a regiment. Colonels were appointed to command regiments and lieutenant-colonels to battalions. Every regiment was assigned 1 colonel, 2 lieutenant-colonels, 2 majors, 7 captains, 1 captain-lieutenant, 22 lieutenants and 10 ensigns as field officers, and 2 adjutants, 1 paymaster, 1 surgeon, 2 assistant surgeons, 2 sergeant-majors and 2 quartermaster-sergeants as staff officers. This high allocation of British officers remained only in theory and it was not realized in practice.[50]

The reason for the shortage of officers was the unpopularity of their office (besides the difficulty in securing adequate number of officers from England due to the European war). The Company's military ranks no longer carried the degree of popularity they once did. Due to the increasing grip of the Government during the latter part of the eighteenth century, the officers' opportunity to make quick money and to wield influence and power gradually declined. Finally, the 1796 Regulations transferred the real power and authority from the commanding officers to the adjutant-general and quartermaster-general's offices and left the former without any effective power over their corps. They were made more "cyphers" and they no longer had any power of patronage or reward.[51] The Regulations also abolished the bazar and table allowances,[52] which drastically cut down the commanding officers' financial resources and the sepoy allowance,[53] which was enjoyed by subalterns, and left all officers only with their pay and regular allowances. The Regulations went a step further. Hitherto company commanders had been responsible for issuing pay to Indian troops, and they had not been required to furnish any records certifying the authenticity of such payments. A major or captain who was in charge of a battalion made "a fortune for himself over a few years by defrauding his men or by keeping his battalion under-strength."[54] This dishonest practice, according to Arthur Wellesley, was extremely widespread. But the new regulations required that "after every issue of pay, acquittance rolls signed by every individual of each company showing that he had received his full demand" were to be delivered to the commanding officers of the regiment; and a paymaster was appointed to examine the accuracy of the pay rolls. Thus, the opportunity of making a fortune through deceitful means was also curtailed.[55] In addition, in 1796, the British wing of the army was separated from the Indian wing. As a result, the British officers of the Indian branch were denied the opportunity of commanding British troops. This was deeply resented by the officers. They felt that the regulations made them feel "inferior" and "contemptible."[56] Because of these reasons, many able officers sought and obtained appointments either in the staff or civil department.[57]

VIII

The British officers in the Coast Army were of two types: the Company's and the King's. The Company's officers had originally come to India as young cadets by the patronage of a proprietor, a director or someone else who had influence with the Court of Directors. From that position of cadetship, they had risen through the ranks on the basis of seniority. As they had spent all their adult life in India, they were quite familiar with Indian customs, manners, attitude and values. The King's officers came to India as full grown men, having had their training in Europe, America or West Indies. Naturally, they were "utter strangers" to India, and "their opinions and habits" had been formed solely upon "European ideas and usages." The King's officers enjoyed better treatment than the Company's officers. The King's officers were promoted sooner, and given higher commands and more favourable furlough privileges. Possibly, it was because the governor and the commander-in-chief were King's appointees.[58]

The younger officers, whether the Company's or the King's were in general ill trained. Upon their arrival, because of the scarcity of officers, they were quickly promoted to the rank of lieutenant without passing through the ranks. This unfortunate promotion, John F. Cradock stated, made them ill-disciplined, presumptuous and self-conceited. He also noted that the officers were lamentably ignorant of the "country languages."[59]

The relationship between British officers and their troops was in general formal and somewhat cool. As expected, the King's officers kept a distance between themselves and their "inferiors." The Company's officers, particularly the younger men, followed a similar path. Whether they were King's or Company's officers, their attitude towards Indian officers was largely exclusive. John Cradock admitted that Indian officers were strangers to the British officers' "confidence or even friendly conversation."[60] Edward Parry and Charles Grant, Chairman and Deputy Chairman of the Court of Directors, observed that the British officers went so far as not to allow Indian officers "to sit down in their presence."[61] The British officers were also abusive of their men. On parade grounds at times officers used wrong words of command, and then they threw the blame upon the troops and reviled them.[62] In demonstrating these haughty demeanors, no doubt, the officers merely reflected "the general hardening of European attitudes towards Indians," which was taking place about this time.[63]

The Indian troops were no less exclusive than their officers. The barrier of caste, which excluded one caste member from another also excluded the troops from their officers. However, occasionally some officers were invited to attend Indian festivals; and the guests were honourably treated. But in all the courtesies which the troops extended to their guests, the rules of "pollution" were kept scrupulously. No sepoy except the pariah who considered himself as being "the same as the master's caste"[64] would ever deign to associate himself freely with his officer. In fact, the prejudice was so strong that a high caste sepoy would "rather die of hunger than eat anything in common" with his officer. This bigotry however did not have any material effect on their military relationships.[65]

IX

The early history of the Coast Army reveals that the Indian troops once having entered the Company's service remained attached to it. Some of them had been brought up in it as their fathers before them. Their fortune had been closely tied to the Company's. They had fought the Company's wars and shared its trials and sorrows. Its victory was their glory and its defeat their disaster. Though not always satisfied, they were still grateful for the benefits of the Company's service. To a large extent "a sense of loyalty to their salt" was ingrained in them. "Biting the hand that fed" was extremely rare. Their patience could be often "taxed even up to a breaking point without much adverse repercussions."[66] They remained with the Government through thick and thin so long as confidence was reposed in them. Their attitude during the Company's darkest hour in the Second Mysore War (1780-84) was a classical example. Despite the outstanding arrears, distressing conditions of their families and Mysorean overtures with brilliant offers, they stuck to the Company's cause.[67] The troops had even risen above their cherished prejudices when tactful appeals were made to their attachment. During the Anglo-French wars in the 1780's and the

1790's some corps had volunteered for overseas expedition.[68]

This does not mean that the troops never faltered from the habit of obedience. At times when they believed that they were wantonly exploited and their prejudices insolently slighted they became obstinate and even violent. The very troops which patiently endured the horror of the Second Mysore War mutinied in Trichinopoly and Arnee when they felt that their goodwill was being unduly exploited. In Trichinopoly, they held the fort to ransom until their arrears were cleared.[69] In Arnee, they tortured their officers.[70] In Vizagapatam, another group of sepoys shot at the officers for their unwelcome measures.[71]

The Vizagapatam incident was very significant as it was the first organized attack upon the officers in the Coast Army. The sepoys stationed in the Northern Circars expressed considerable aversion when ordered to sail to Madras, as crossing seas was prejudicial to their caste. But the officers insisted that they must. On October 1, 1780, eight companies boarded at Muslipatam without disobedience but rather reluctantly. Two days later another four companies were paraded at Vizagapatam to embark on the *Sartine*, but suddenly they began to shoot at their British officers and every Englishman they found. Three officers were killed on the spot, a few wounded, and the others fled to safety. Then the mutineers plundered the cantonment and escaped to Hyderabad.

The cause of this tragedy was the officers' indifference to the sepoy prejudice and their determination to carry the orders through. In these two aspects, the prelude to the Vizagapatam incident foreshadowed the prelude to the Vellore mutiny.

Vellore Fort - West Moat

Vellore Fort - West Moat from a different angle view

CHAPTER THREE
THE OBNOXIOUS ORDERS

THE SEED OF THAT TRAGIC EVENT which was soon to occur in Vellore was sown almost immediately after Sir John Francis Cradock's arrival in India. In the Indian soil of that time, it took only a few days for the seed to germinate, grow, blossom and bear the bitter fruit.

John F. Cradock was appointed as the Commander-in-Chief of the Coast Army in October, 1804. After a long voyage around the Cape, he landed at Fort St. George in February, 1805. The new Commander-in-Chief had already served in Ireland, and from his experience there he considered himself an expert in dealing with "subject" people. Rigid discipline alone he felt was the surest means to maintain "the authority of a few over the multitude."[1]

At his arrival, John F. Cradock found the governing principles of the Coast Army much pleasing to him. They were, in his words, "to maintain the complete ascendency of authority over the troops," and "to abolish to the greatest practicable extent the observance of local usages." The Indians, it was assumed, were "deficient" in "the energies & qualities of mind," and, it was hoped that "a rigid discipline" would compensate this supposed deficiency. Furthermore, the trend in the Coast Army, Cradock felt, was "to disregard on duty all distinctions, and observances of cast, and to assimilate the conduct & appearance of the sepoys under arms to that of European troops." However, in all these Cradock believed that "the real religious ordinance of the sepoys" was respected.[2]

A quick observation indicated to the new Commander-in-Chief that while the Indian troops had been somewhat approximated to the British in discipline, dress and appearance, there was no uniformity in the army. Rules and regulations varied from regiment to regiment, and at times from battalion to battalion. The previously-issued code of regulations had become almost obsolete. The variety and diversity which was so conspicuous in the army distressed Cradock's soul. And he decided to institute a new set of reforms.

Early in March, 1805, about three weeks after his arrival, John Cradock submitted to the Madras Council a recommendation for compiling a new code of regulations for the efficient maintenance of the army. In the minute, Cradock stated that he was contemplating only "to reduce into one view the several orders in force and which are already sanctioned by [the] Government." However, he added that there would be slight alteration or variation for the purpose of discipline and economy, and such new matter will be distinguished in the manuscript that will be submitted for the final approbation of Government." To compile the proposed code, Cradock recommended Major Frederick Pierce, the Deputy Adjutant-General, whom he described as "perfectly qualified from his experience and talents."[3]

The Council found the Commander-in-Chief's recommendation entirely satisfactory, and it gave unanimous approval. Subsequently, Cradock informed Pierce of his new assignment and promised him additional "remuneration for the trouble."[4] In his direction to Pierce, Cradock stated "that the regulations to be framed should, as far as might be practicable, be assimilated to the customs and usages of His Majesty's service."[5] Cradock also instructed Pierce to bring to the attention of the

Government those regulations which were new and therefore would require governmental sanction.[6]

Once the task was assigned, Major Pierce proceeded to do a thorough job with the "ambition" to receive the Commander-in-Chief's approval. In compiling the new code, Pierce gleaned liberally from the previous code and standing orders of many battalions. He altered and innovated them as he judged best. After several months of tedious work, the task was completed. The finished product was a volume of twenty-seven sections, with many paragraphs or articles, running to nearly a hundred and fifty pages. Those regulations which had already received governmental sanction were first enumerated, then those that were new and therefore required Government's confirmation were listed. Unfortunately, amongst the former was a regulation that had never been before sanctioned by the Government. That was the fatal tenth paragraph of the eleventh section. It reads:

> It is ordered by the Regulations, that a native soldier shall not mark his face to denote his cast, or wear ear-rings, when dressed in his uniform; and it is further directed that at all parades, and upon all duties, every soldier of the battalion shall be clean shaved on the chin. It is directed also, that uniformity shall, as far as it is practicable, be preserved, in regard to the quantity and shape of the hair on the upper lip.[7]

Major Pierce was quite aware that the Government had never before sanctioned the above regulation. However, with a persuasion that this order was "a regulation of the well conducted part of service," he inserted it amongst the orders which had already received Government's confirmation. Pierce also thought that such details were solely within the Commander-in-Chief's jurisdiction and therefore needed no governmental approval.[8]

No sooner was the Code compiled, it was submitted to the Commander-in-Chief for his scrutiny. Cradock summoned his lieutenants,[9] and with them spent several successive days examining the Code paragraph by paragraph. As Cradock was reading the compilation to others, the tenth paragraph of the eleventh section arrested his attention. He asked his lieutenants, "Whether it would interfere with the prejudices of the natives?" To which Frederick Pierce and the Adjutant-General Patrick Agnew answered "that it would not, and that was not the custom in well-regulated corps for native soldiers to appear in the manner forbidden by that paragraph."[10] Immediately, Cradock remembered that "in reviewing a considerable number of native battalions he had never perceived the marks of cast, or the ear-ring which the orders prohibited."[11] Thus flattering themselves that this order was "not only unobjectionable but the invariable course of every regiment," the military authorities left that paragraph as it was, and there it remained.[12]

On January 21, 1806, the proposed code was transmitted to the Government for confirmation.[13] In the minute which accompanied the code, Cradock stated:

> The whole is comprised in twenty-seven sections alphabetically arranged; and the additional Orders to which I request the attention of the Board, as requiring the sanction of Government, are as follows: [14]

The additional orders were then enumerated.

The proposed code remained with the Board for over six weeks. As instructed the Government checked the additional orders and gave its approval. Unfortunately, the Commander-in-Chief, who drew the attention of his lieutenants to the tenth paragraph of the eleventh section did not even mention its existence to his colleagues. Consequently, the Board sanctioned the code without any knowledge of an explosive regulation within its pages.[1]

II

While the proposed code was under preparation, a new pattern of
turban too was approved for the Indian troops. Sometime in the early part of
1805, Major Paul Bose, commanding officer of the second battalion of the
fourteenth regiment, recommended to Adjutant-General Patrick Agnew a
new pattern of turban for his battalion. He criticized the present turban as
being very loose on the head. Agnew examined Bose's pattern, and found it
extremely pleasing. Therefore, he suggested to Cradock that the same should
be adopted for the whole army. Consequently, Cradock ordered Bose to
prepare three similar patterns of turbans for his consideration. Accordingly,
Bose prepared and sent them with three sepoys from Wallajabhad, where he
was stationed at that time. The three sepoys wearing three different turbans
presented themselves for the Commander-in-Chief's inspection. Cradock
compared them with the old turban and concluded that these were
inexpensive, better fitting, and superior in military appearance. Among the
three Cradock opted for the one which was subsequently adopted for the
army. The three sepoys, a Muslim, a Rajput and a Telugu, wore the turbans
without "the smallest dislike or objection . . . They declared themselves
much pleased with them." The chosen pattern was left in the Adjutant-
General's office a long time for the inspection of interested persons.[16]

The proposed turban was not very different from the old one in
material. Like the old, it was made of blue woolen cloth covering an iron
frame and ornamented with a brass button. However, the new one had a
few more additional ornaments—a leathern cockade, a cotton tuft made like
a feather and a tape or bond.[17] It inclined "from front to rear instead of from
side to side" as the old one.[18] Unfortunately, its shape resembled "the leather
caps lately introduced into His Majesty's European regiments."[19]

On November 14, 1805, it was announced to the troops that the
Commander-in-Chief was determined to issue a new pattern of turban. But

the turbans were not actually made for some more months.[20]

On March 11, 1806, the Code of Regulations, long in preparation, was published to the army. It stated:

> The Right Honorable the Governor in Council is pleased to annul, and to declare to be abrogated every regulation which has heretofore been in force, and that militates against the spirit, and evident meaning of any code now established; to which his Lordship requires a most pointed obedience from every individual subject to the Government of Fort St. George.[21]

The tenth paragraph of the eleventh section of the new Code of Regulation caused consternation among some British officers. Lieutenant-Colonel James McKerras, commanding officer of the second battalion of the twenty-third regiment, suspended the communication of the whole paragraph to his corps. He told his Adjutant, Lieutenant John M. Coombs, "not to mention the order to the sepoys, observing he would rather lose his commission than enforce, as he conceived it would be productive of great dissatisfaction."[22] Several other officers too either deferred or suspended communicating the order to their corps.[23]

During the months of April, May and June, the long-expected model turbans arrived in different garrisons. The troops were ordered to return their old ones and make up the new.[24]

These orders, which had the effect of approximating the Indian troops' dress and appearance to the British, soon caused suspicion among Indians. To the Indians who associated at least a part of their religion with external features, the order to remove their distinguishing marks perhaps seemed an encroachment upon their religious practices. And when that order was accompanied or followed by others introducing British dress, they began to attribute sinister motives to the Government's action. Furthermore, the Indians of that day had a living memory of coercive proselytism.[25] As those orders were issued soon after the emergence of the British as the unrivalled power in India, they appeared to signal that the new conquerors were not going to deviate from the footsteps of former invaders. Once suspicion arose, people began to share their fears. With every wagging tongue the rumour of forced proselytism spread like a forest fire.

Vellore was not without its share of wagging tongues. The Indian troops' families and the princes' servants and adherents not unnaturally expressed suspicion, concern and apprehension. In the light of the shaving, trimming, no-sect mark and no-ear ring orders, the earlier alterations and innovations in dress appeared to have sinister motive. Scrutinizing eyes readily observed that the sepoy had already the turn screw on his breast and stock around his neck. The turn screw appeared like the Christian cross, and the stock seemed to have been made of the objectionable leather. Suspicious persons insinuated that the sepoy needed only the hat to make him complete "Farginhee."[26] Though no one in Vellore at this time had seen the proposed turban, it is possible that some were acquainted with its shape from those who had seen it elsewhere. Eventually, lone voices called the sepoys to resist the new turban. The cup was fast filling up, and another drop, it would spill over. The new turban was that drop.

III

Among the Indian troops, the earliest objection to the new turban was manifested in the first week of April.[27] Jemdar Muhammad Cawn and a few other Indian officers of the first battalion of the first regiment swore at the Durgah "that they would never consent to wear the new turban; that their dress had been lately subjected to great innovations by the introduction first of waistcoats, next of stocks, and now of hats, which, if they were to agree to wear they would lose cast."[28] The long-expected turban arrived in Vellore late in April. After their arrival, probably early in May, Imam Khan, a sepoy of the first battalion of the first regiment, told Jemmal-ud-din, Moiz-ud-din's foster-brother, with whom he was on intimate terms, "that the 2nd [battalion of the] 4th [regiment] were ordered to wear topees. That the topees were also ordered for them, but that the sepoys were resolved never to wear them, but to resist and declaring that they would rather die than wear them."[29] From that time onwards the Indian officers and sepoys who visited Jemmal-ud-din's home, which was in the *pettah*, discussed the new turban.[30]

Late in April the British officials in Vellore learned for the first time that some objection had been raised against the turban. Sheikh Nutter and Esop Cawn, two sepoys of the first battalion of the first regiment, informed Lieutenant-Colonel Nathaniel Forbes, their commanding officer, that a Muslim school teacher had refused to read prayers on the funeral of a sepoy's relative. The school teacher was alleged to have stated that he would not have anything to do with those who were "connected with such villainous unbelievers who wore topees." Forbes took the matter to Lieutenant-Colonel Thomas Marriott, who was then acting for the absent collector. Both officials decided to make him "a severe example." Accordingly, the school teacher was beaten severely and sent away from the *pettah*. Sadly, the school teacher's attitude was dismissed as insolent and isolated[31]

The Indian troops' first open objection to the new turban came when the grenadiers of the second battalion of the fourth regiment was ordered to surrender the old turban and make up the new. In the morning of May 6, Captain James Moore, under instruction from his Commanding Officer Lieutenant-Colonel John Darley, directed Sheikh Imam, kot havildar of the grenadiers, to order the "off-duty" men of his company to report to the store for making up the new turban. In response, Sheikh Imam stated that the grenadiers "wished to speak to him." Therefore, Moore directed Imam to march the "off-duty" men to his quarters[32].

About nine o' clock the grenadiers arrived at Captain Moore's place. On their way they agreed among themselves "for the first time" to resist the new turban unanimously. As Captain Moore inquired the cause of their objection, they responded "nearly at the same time," "putting their hands up to their turbans," that "they wished to wear their *present* turban." Because, they continued, if they wore the new turban "their families would not live with them . . or . . prepare their rice for them." And they concluded saying that "if they served the Company they must wear their present turbans." At this time, the grenadiers had not yet seen the new turban. Moore did his best to persuade the men that the turban was in no way offensive to the caste. But the grenadiers remained unyielding. Perceiving that the "dislike was general," Moore ordered them back to their barracks and sent a note to Darley stating that grenadiers were repelled by the new turban and proposing that they might perhaps change their mind if they saw it. Sheikh Imam took the note to Darley, and brought back a new turban to show it to the men in the barracks. Sheikh Imam claimed that he warned the grenadiers not to object. That "if they objected they would be surely punished and . . . eventually be obliged to wear it." One of the grenadiers, Ranga, came forward and said, "[Even] if his throat should be cut he would not wear the new turban." At this time a group of sepoys from the first battalion of the first regiment crowded in and encouraged the grenadiers to stand firm[33] The grenadiers said to one another that if one or two resisted they would be hung or shot; but if they all remained united and opposed, the Company could not "cut off all their heads." Despite Sheikh Imam's admonition, the grenadiers remained obstinate. Sheikh Imam returned to Moore and Darley and reported that the men did not want to wear the new turban.

The grenadiers' obstinacy stirred the Commanding Officer's indignation. Darley felt that the situation demanded immediate action.

Thinking that he himself should handle the men, he came to the barracks, with More and Lieutenant Benjamin Baker, the Adjutant.

At first Darley paraded the grenadiers in the barracks. But soon finding that it was "an awkward place," he ordered them to proceed to Captain Moore's quarters. It was about eleven o' clock, and the sun was hot. The men were halted in the shade of some trees near Moore's quarters. Under the trees, the grenadiers encouraged one another to remain resolute and not to betray their comrades.

The apparent solidarity broke down as the grenadiers were summoned into the house one after another to confront the British officers. Unfortunately for the sepoys, Darley first selected Sheikh Imam, the Kot Havildar, and Ram Nick, the Havildar Writer, and ensured a favourable precedent. He asked them whether they had any objection to the new turban. They replied, "They had no particular objection." Then Darley ordered them to take off their turbans and tie their handkerchiefs around their heads. They obliged immediately.

The other two havildars were then summoned. The same question was put to them. But their reply astonished Darley. They stated that the new headdress was not a turban but a hat. And "if they wore [it], their cast would not supply them with water neither would they marry their daughters." Dismissing their explanation as nonsense, Darley asked the havildars whether they knew that the new turban was issued by the authority of the Commander-in-Chief and the consequence of disobedience to such an order. They said, "Yes." Darley further inquired whether not the Articles of War had been explained to them. They replied, "Yes, notwithstanding they could not wear the new turban without bringing disgrace upon themselves!" At this response, Darley was enraged, and he snatched their sashes[34] and put them under guards.

Darley then tackled the four naiques. He called them in one by one, and asked whether they had any objection to the new turban. Each replied like the last two havildars. Darley's reaction was swift. He removed their knots and placed them under guards.

The obstinacy of the last six non-commissioned officers led Darley to suspect the commissioned officers of the company. Therefore, he sent for Sheikh Imam,[35] the Subadar, and Chan Singh, the Jemadar, who were on garrison duty. The former arrived first and then the latter. As they arrived, Darley asked them why their men were discontented and who the instigators were. They both expressed surprise at the men's behaviour and disclaimed all knowledge of their grievance. Consequently, Darley ordered them to remove their turbans and tie handkerchiefs around their head as an example to their company. That "they instantly did."

Darley now gave a second opportunity to the six delinquent non-commissioned officers. Darley brought them before their Indian superiors, who had been an "example", and explained "the impropriety of their conduct, desiring them to follow the examples of their officers." Feeling betrayed and humiliated, the junior officers declared, "since our superiors are inclined to take the turban so will we!" Darley then returned their sashes and knots to them.

With confidence that the sepoys would automatically follow the example of their officers, Darley called them in one by one. They were asked whether or not they were satisfied with the new turbans. Out of the thirty-nine sepoys, twenty-one declared they were not, and the remainder said they were. The brave Ranga apparently lost his nerve and he was in the latter group. In the presence of Darley, Moore and Baker, the Indian commissioned officers remonstrated with the twenty-one obstinate sepoys but in vain. Consequently, Darley put them under guards and reported the matter to Lieutenant-Colonel John Fancourt, the commanding officer of the garrison.

During the afternoon, Mir Ghalam Ali, Indian adjutant of the battalion, went and told the recalcitrant grenadiers that if they consented to wear the new turban as others had done he would get them released. But if they remained obstinate, their conduct would be reported to the headquarters, and "some of them would be blown away from a gun or hanged." Despite Ghalam Ali's pleadings, the sepoys remained stubborn.

Understandably the fate of the twenty-one grenadiers was the main topic of conversation and concern among the Indian troops in the garrison during that afternoon. The grenadiers who consented to wear the turban were spoken of contemptuously and accused of betraying their fellow sepoys. About five o' clock in the evening when the companies came for roll call "there was an *universal* abuse against the company [grenadiers]." They were urged to go and intercede "with the Colonel to have their men released." Consequently, Ranga, perhaps feeling remorse for his cowardice in the morning, took the lead; and about twenty others followed him. They went to their Commanding Officer's residence to plead for their imprisoned colleagues. As they approached the gate, Darley, seeing them through the window, came out and asked them what the business was. Ranga stepped forward and replied that they wanted the sepoys "to be released;" otherwise "they also wished to be confined with them!" The grenadiers' unexpected protest provoked Darley to fury. He hit Ranga with the bamboo he had in his hand. But it broke! Then outrageously, Darley drew his sword and pushed Ranga with it, shouting at the protesters to get out of his place. But the sword also snapped! However, they dashed back to the barracks as fast as they could.

Almost immediately after the grenadiers' departure, Darley was told that the sepoys had "fallen in" for roll-call without their belts or side arms.

The grenadier, the first, the second, and a part of the third battalion companies, whose Indian commissioned officers were absent, had their belts on; but the other companies, whose Indian commissioned officers were present, did not[36]. Darley came and asked the battalion, company by company, what "the reason for such unmilitary conduct" was? The response was identical. They said that they were objecting to the new turban and the imprisonment of their colleagues. Darley became bitter and disgusted. He suspected intrigue. He immediately ordered the Indian officers to surrender their swords. Then Darley commanded everyone to remain in the barracks, and went to consult John Fancourt. In reporting the event later on, he stated, "Convinced at that time that it was necessary to adopt strong measures, and knowing that the inferior ranks are seldom guilty of disobedience of orders unless supported by their officers, I immediately divested the whole of the Native commissioned officers of their swords."

After some time, Darley returned with Fancourt. Fancourt paraded the battalion and asked the men the cause of their misbehaviour. They stated that the new headdress was "a hat and not a turban," and that if they consented to wear it, "they could not get water from their cast nor their cast would marry their daughters."[37] Fancourt noticed that the Indian commissioned officers were without their swords and inquired the reason. Being told that Darley had "divested them of their swords," Fancourt ordered them to be returned immediately, adding that he "saw no reason for depriving them of their swords." Later under Fancourt's instruction, Lieutenant Baker ordered the sepoys to put on their belts. This order was obeyed immediately. Fancourt then warned the men that their behaviour was "highly improper," and dismissed them.[38]

Immediately after the dismissal, Darley summoned the Indian officers and told them that he was going to execute the Commander-in-Chief's orders on the following day, and warned that if their men should again object to the new turban, "he would hold them responsible." He cautioned the Indian officers that they had "better go back to the barracks and talk to their men."

IV

That very night Fancourt dispatched an express letter to the Commander-in-Chief, without Darley's knowledge. In the letter, he stated that the second battalion of the fourth regiment was in a "mutinous state," refusing to wear the new turban, and asked for instruction.[39]

The following day was marred by no irregularity until the evening. At morning roll-call, Darley repeated his determination "to execute the Commander-in-Chief's instruction." He then ordered the men to take off their turbans and leave them at their feet. That was instantly done. Subsequently, the battalion was marched off into the barracks. Later, Darley ordered some men from each company to carry the old turban to the store. These orders too were obeyed "without the least murmur."

At evening roll-call a strange incident occurred. As the battalion turned "right-about" for dismissal, there arose "a general and repeated cry of *dhoot.*"[40] It began "at the centre and extended towards the flanks." The cry drove Darley to fury. He immediately re-ordered the battalion to "fall-in," and asked the Indian officers to point out the men who made the noise. But all the officers declared that it was a general cry and they could not distinguish the guilty. In frustration, Darley dismissed the men and marched them off into the barracks. At that time, they "behaved in perfect order."

Again, Darley summoned the Indian officers as he did the previous evening, and expressed his grave concern over their men's "unmilitary conduct." He asked them to go to the barracks and ascertain the names of the guilty and report to him in the morning. Consequently, the next morning, the Indian officers waited on Darley but again pleaded their inability to comply with his demands.

On May 7, Darley submitted to Fancourt an account of the events that transpired the previous day. This account suggested to Fancourt the prudence of suspending the new turban for some time. Therefore, he sent another express to Cradock expressing his intention to suspend the execution of the turban order. He also enclosed a copy of Darley's report for the Commander-in-Chief's information.

Fancourt's first express reached the Adjutant-General's office in the afternoon of May 7. Adjutant-General Agnew took the letter immediately to the Commander-in-Chief who at that hot hour of the day had retired to the Brodie Castile in the pleasant suburb of Madras. Cradock's reaction to Fancourt's letter was not unpredictable. He resolved to enforce obedience at all cost. In response the Fancourt's inquiry, the Commander-in-Chief wrote:

> While the Commander-in-Chief regrets the cause which requires such measures, he feels it to be his duty to check, by the most decided resolution, the symptoms of insubordination which you have reported in the 2nd battalion 4th regiment of native infantry.
>
> His Excellency has therefore ordered to Vellore a detachment of H. M.'s 19th dragoons, who will receive and escort to the Presidency for trial, before a General Court-martial now sitting, the 19 (sic) men confined by Lieutenant-Colonel Darley, against whom he will prefer charges, and prepare to support the same by the requisite evidence.
>
> You will also direct the non-commissioned officers of the grenadier company (the two, who did not object in the first instance to deliver their turbans, excepted) to be reduced to the ranks; the Commander-in-Chief deeming a man who hesitates a moment to obey an order unfit to bear the character of a non-commissioned officer.
>
> You will further, through Lieutenant-Colonel Darley, direct the native commissioned officers of the 2nd battalion 4th regiment N.

I., immediately to make up and wear the turban of the prescribed pattern.

Disobedience, or hesitation, on their part will be instantly followed by their dismission (sic) from the service in public orders on your report. Lieutenant-Colonel Kennedy has orders, should you require it, to march the 19th dragoons to Vellore to assist in enforcing obedience.

It is the intention of the Commander-in-Chief immediately to relieve the 2nd battalion 5th regiment, but though he thinks proper to remove them from Vellore, he will not admit hesitation even in their obedience to the orders he has given.[41]

After dictating such a resolute letter, Cradock instructed Agnew "first to wait on Lord William Bentinck and communicate the circumstances to His Lordship," and then to transmit the dispatch. Consequently, Agnew waited on the Governor. According to Agnew, "The honorable Governor concurred in opinion with the Commander-in-Chief." Agnew then edited the final draft and dispatched it late in the evening.[42]

Fancourt's second express arrived at the Adjutant-General's office on May 8. Fancourt's proposal to suspend the order had no impact upon Cradock. In fact, it made him only more obstinate in his resolve to enforce obedience. "His Excellency sees no cause to relax from the orders he has already given, which you will accordingly enforce" was the response.[43] Furthermore, Cradock condemned the second battalion of the fourth regiment as being "at present unworthy to participate in any promotion" and ordered the places of those reduced non-commissioned officers to be "supplied from other corps." In the same letter, Cradock stated that the second battalion of the twenty-third regiment had been directed to relieve the second battalion of the fourth regiment from Vellore.[44]

V

On the following day, May 9, Cradock officially informed the

Government about the objection raised against the new turban and the measures he had adopted to ensure obedience. Cradock stated in his minute:

> Having previously ascertained that the intended change of turban did not at all clash with any religious prejudices of the Natives, I took immediate measures to enforce obedience, and to punish those most prominently guilty. . .

After citing the details of the measures he had ordered Cradock added,

> deeming Vellore an improper station for a corps that at any time forgets the duty of strict obedience, I have directed a battalion from Wallajabhad to relieve the 2nd battalion of the 4th regiment with the least possible delay.[45]

Though Cradock stated confidently that there was nothing offensive to the Indian prejudice in the new turban, he felt that the agitations of May 6 and 7, required at least some investigation. Therefore, he came to Vellore on May 14 and ordered a court of inquiry to investigate the cause of the late disturbance. The court was to begin its session as soon as Lieutenant-Colonel James McKerras, the commanding officer of the second battalion of the twenty-third regiment, who was to be its chairman, arrived in Vellore. Lieutenant-Colonels Forbes and Marriott were nominated as members. Cradock also ordered the detainment of the second battalion of the fourth regiment in Vellore until the court completed its proceedings. Moreover, he asked John Fancourt to transmit the complete proceedings and report of the court of inquiry to Nundydrug where he was then proceeding in order to escape from the heat of Madras and to recuperate his health.[46]

The day after Lieutenant-Colonel McKerras' arrival, the court of inquiry began its sitting.[47] The court first examined the British officers and then the Indian officers and grenadiers. In their depositions, the Indian officers declared categorically that the new turban was free from anything offensive to their prejudice. One of the Indian officers, Hurrupah, Havildar Major, went so far as to say:

> There is no objection at all to the turban; nor will the wearing of it, to the best of my opinion, degrade a man of the highest cast, nor will it affect the prejudice of cast.

Another, Mir Ghalam Ali, stated with equal force, "I think that any cast man might wear it without suffering degradation and that there is nothing about it to prejudice the cast of any one." Despite these distinctive and positive assertions, the general evidence indicated that these were not the true reflections of the troops' feelings. The court of inquiry was quite conscious of the ambivalent attitude of the Indian soldiery. In the report, it observed, "the Court, finds itself considerably embarrassed, not only from the delicacy of the subject but also from the labyrinths of contradictory evidence in which the subject is involved." However, the court concluded the sepoys' prejudice to the turban was the chief cause of their "mutinous" conduct. It added:

> The Court locates, rather imputes, the cause which led to their first act of insubordination, to have originated in the jealous and lively prejudices of the Natives, in any matter respecting dress (which in this country is so intimately connected in the cast and religion) acting upon the weak minds of illiterate and uninformed men.

The attempt "to crush all symptoms of irregularity and enforce obedience to the General Orders at this first instance of insubordination," the court continued, "led to the subsequent ones." However, the court regretted that the evidences were not adequate enough to substantiate the second observation.[48]

After the conclusion of the proceedings, the court, at Lieutenant-Colonel Fancourt's request, met and gave its private opinion. It stated simply "that there is nothing in the new turban which can really affect the prejudices of cast."[49] Late in May, the proceedings, the report and the private opinion of the court were transmitted to Nundydrug for the Commander-in-Chief's information.[50]

To Cradock the court's findings did not provide any new information. He wrote to Agnew, "You will perceive I imagine by the perusal [of the court's proceedings, report and opinion] that nothing of a very prominent nature beyond what had already reached our knowledge appears [to have occurred]." Cradock dismissed the evidence against the new turban as "fancied objection" "from the silly minds of the sepoys" and the unfavourable statement as "false testimony so widely prevails," but he accepted the ones in favour of the turban as genuine and trustworthy. He did not realize that some might be sincerely more prejudiced than others. In fact, Cradock was blinded by his suspicion of intrigues and instigation, which he regarded as the real cause of insubordination. Therefore, he asked Agnew to lay all the papers before James Leith, the Judge Advocate, to carry "the guilt of the late mutinous conduct to the real authors." Cradock suggested that the Indian commissioned officers of the battalion should be watched with "double vigilance." Cradock also directed the court's findings to be transmitted to the Government.[51]

The twenty-one sepoys[52] who were imprisoned by Darley in Vellore were later escorted to Madras, and in the middle of June they were put on trial before a general court-martial for "contempt of authority and disobedience of orders." Sheikh Abdul Ryman, a Muslim, and Anantaram, a Hindu, who were considered foremost in the resistance, were tried first, the court found them guilty and sentenced them "to receive nine hundred lashes each, with a cat of nine tails, on their bare backs at such time, and place, as His Excellency the Commander-in-Chief may be pleased to direct, and furthermore to be discharged from the Honorable Company's service as turbulent and unworthy subjects."[53] The Commander-in-Chief confirmed the sentence and decreed that it should be "put into execution in that public and impressive manner, which their mutinous and hardened conduct so forcibly requires."[54] The other nineteen were tried subsequently and found guilty. But they were pardoned "in consequence of their acknowledgement of error, deep contrition, and solemn promises of future good conduct."[55]

The six non-commissioned officers, who first hesitated to obey the order, were also punished. They were reduced from their ranks and the vacancies were filled from other corps.[56] The guilty battalion itself left the theatre of disobedience for Madras on May 25. No further symptom of discontent was noticeable. Darley reported that the battalion was "now wearing the turban lately ordered . . . is . . . in as perfect and complete state of subordination and good discipline as is any other corps in the Madras Establishment."[57] Outwardly, Cradock's repressive measures appeared successful.

VI

But the ostensible acquiescence was a delusion. According to one account about May 10, there were about two hundred sepoys of the second battalion of the fourth regiment ready to attack the cavalry which escorted the twenty-one prisoners and another four to five hundred sepoys to mutiny in the garrison.[58] Lieutenant Thomas Macleane reported that he himself heard some sepoys say "that they would sooner die than wear them [the new turban]."[59] It did not take too long before the fever became contagious. Voices within the first battalion of the first regiment, which was already averse to the turban and a silent witness to the impunity with which the remonstration of the second battalion of the fourth regiment was treated, suggested that "the first of the first" should take the lead and set an example.[60] The simmering flame was undoubtedly fanned by other Indians who lived in the *pettah*, including the princes' servants and adherents.

It was suggested by imaginative minds that the Government's unflinching attitude was a sure indication of the sinister motive behind the late innovations. The innovations, it was hinted, were only the prelude to coercive proselytism of the sepoys first and then their countrymen. Undoubtedly, from whomever such wild but not unreasonable views originated, they were shared and expressed by many of the princes' servants and friends. According to eye-witnesses, the princes' people warned the sentries whom they met day after day:

> The Feringhees have conquered the country. Now when they shall have made you Christians by putting on those hats, they will put a stop to all our religious ceremonies both Musselman and Hindoos. You must all eat together. Nobody will give you wives or even water out of their hand.

And they also implored:

> Do not wear that hat. If you do, we shall become Feringhees. If you sepoys consent to wear that hat, what will become of us? The whole country will be ruined; bazar people, ryots, and all of us will be obliged to wear it.

To such warnings and pleadings, at times, the sentries responded sarcastically, "Well, we will put on those hats and perhaps make you put them on too!"[61]

During this period, it is more than probable that the Indian officers and sepoys who resorted to Jemmal-ud-din's place began to express apprehension. They even began to talk of mutiny in vague terms. One of the sepoys or the princes' adherents or servants might have suggested the idea. The sepoys and many people in Vellore knew that discontent was prevailing in many other garrisons. In their "evening-chats," they might have even expressed hope for a general uprising. However, in the month of May, no substantial plan for a mutiny was formulated.[62]

On May 16, the second battalion of the twenty-third regiment came to Vellore from Wallajabhad. The new battalion was the youngest in the Madras Establishment, and it had just come from Madura. It was raised around Shankarancoil in Tinnevelly district, and was composed chiefly of Hindus, who had been formerly in the service of the Southern poligars. There were only about 180 Muslims in that battalion.[63]

Soon after its arrival, while the second battalion of the fourth regiment was still in Vellore, the new battalion was ordered to make up "the turban of new muster." The order was obeyed without any ostensible objection. It is alleged that the two older battalions abused and taunted the new as it prepared the new turban.[64] Yet, their mutual "coolness" prevented them from launching an active opposition to the turban. While they were still unable to submerge their hostility for a common cause, the second battalion of the fourth regiment left Vellore for the Presidency.[65]

VII

In many other garrisons too, the late orders created a great deal of discontent. A considerable alarm was expressed in Madras, Wallajabhad, Hyderabad, Nundydrug, Bangalore, Trichinopoly, Palamcottah, and several other places. But in Wallajabhad alone the troops became mutinous enough to draw the attention of the Government.

On June 9, Major Paul Bose, designer of the new turban and commanding officer of the second battalion of the fourteenth regiment, ordered his grenadier company to make up the new turban. As the company was making and fitting the turbans "without the slightest objection," a crowd began to gather not far from where the grenadiers were, and then uttered "a torrent of the vilest abuse" against them for consenting to wear "those hats." Bose became irritated and ordered the crowd to be chased and dispersed. But to his annoyance, the crowd soon regathered and began hurling abuses. The grenadiers appeared for a time indifferent to the crowd, but suddenly one of them refused in a most positive manner "to put on his turban." Immediately, Bose seized him and ordered a drum head court martial to decide on his conduct. At that moment, to Bose's bewilderment, six or seven others threw off their turbans in a turbulent manner. At that sight the crowd which was just being chased off dashed back and cheered the "delinquents." Bose feared that the situation might overwhelm him. But fortunately for him, the greater part of the company remained obedient, and with British officers' support, Bose reduced "the refractory . . . to reason and subordination."[66]

During this embarrassing moment, Venkata Naik[67], subadar of the grenadiers, remained utterly indifferent to what was transpiring. He exhibited no interest in his colleagues' struggle to maintain discipline until he was shouted at by a British officer. Obviously, Venkata Naik's attitude infuriated Bose. He wrote to Lieutenant-Colonel George Harcourt, commanding officer of the garrison,

> the subadar of the grenadier company stood in the midst of them his arms folded calmly witnessing (I had almost said enjoying) a scene of the most flagrant disrespect and insubordination without betraying a least desire to check it.[68]

Bose insinuated Venkata Naik to be the "secret cause" of the disobedience.

To Harcourt the episode of June 9th signaled that mischief was in the offing. Therefore, he decided to take preventive measures. He dispatched Venkata Naik under "close arrest" to Madras and wrote to the Adjutant-General recommending his dismissal by a special order as the nature of the "crime" was too delicate for a court-martial trial. Harcourt also appealed for a detachment of His Majesty's 59th Regiment to serve as deterrent in Wallajabhad.[69]

On June 13, Harcourt sent another plea to the Adjutant-General to expedite the arrival of His Majesty's 59th Regiment. He complained that the repugnance to the turban was mounting and the sepoys might mutiny unless overawed by British troops. He proceeded to state that the grenadiers who wore the turban had been "repeatedly insulted and abused" and the sepoys were holding secret consultations to resist the turban. Hurcourt further added that the sepoys were being encouraged by a rumour that the second battalion of the fourth regiment had succeeded in resisting the new turban even after its arrival in the Presidency.[70]

George Harcourt's recommendation was approved by the Government. On June 21, 1806, Subadar Venkata Naik was dismissed from the Company's service by a special order for "having neglected to exert himself as it was his duty to have done in support of the discipline." On the same day, three companies of His Majesty's 59th Regiment marched from Poonamalleee, near Madras, to Wallajabhad "as a measure of necessary precaution."[71] However, nothing occurred in Wallajabhad.

VIII

In the early days of June, the discontent in Vellore took a concrete form. Some men of the first battalion of the first regiment initiated the conspiracy to murder all the British officers and soldiers in Vellore, and then they cautiously invited others to join them.[72]

The most significant event, in all probability, that led to the formation of conspiracy was the halt of the second battalion of the first regiment at Vellore on its march from Seringapatam to Wallajabhad. While the visiting battalion was in Vellore, sometime late in May[73], a meeting took place between some officers and sepoys of both wings of the first regiment, at a tomb called Aminpeer, in which the turban was discussed. The second battalion told the first battalion:

> That the 2nd Battalion 1st Regiment would look to the 1st of the 1st
> for an example, and that if the 1st of 1st wore it, the corps would
> become enemies to each other; but if the 1st of the 1st refused it,
> and any disturbance took place, the 2nd of the 1st would come up
> and support them.[74]

At this meeting no plan was formulated, but a strong inducement was given to the first battalion to take the lead.[75]

The conspiracy must have been formed shortly after the departure of the second battalion.[76] Probably Jemadar Sheikh Dewan was the initiator.[77] Perhaps, Imam Khan, Muhammad Jaffer, Sied Modin, Sheikh Nutter, Rymaun, Sheikh Seconder and Sheikh Cassim were Sheikh Dewan's co-authors.[78] Jemmal-ud-din must have been informed as soon as the conspiracy was formulated.

Once the plan was initiated, the conspirators began to enlarge their circle. Reliable men were sought and informed. The circle, in fact, kept expanding till the very night of the massacre.

The earliest ones to join the conspirators from the second battalion of the twenty-third regiment were Subadars Sheikh Adam and Sheikh Homed.[79] Besides the common antipathy to the "topie," Adjutant Coombs' "severe treatment" seemed to have induced them to defect.[80] Between the two, Sheikh Adam was a man of great leadership. No sooner was he informed of the plot than he became the leader of the conspirators.

Participants entered into the conspiracy with a solemn and impressive oath-taking ceremony, which was held either in the mosque, or Sepoy Rymaun's or Subadar Adam's residence. The ceremony began with a prayer and then the oath was administered in small groups. The Muslims drank milk, touched their respective sword and an open Koran and repeated the prescribed oath. The Hindus swore according to the custom of their respective sects. The oath consisted of three articles: "Inviolable secrecy," extermination of all "Feringhees," and the establishment of a Muslim kingdom under Moiz-ud-din.[81]

The number of the persons who took the oath was indeed small. Only about one-fourth of the Indian sepoys and officers were sworn into the conspiracy. A little larger number, perhaps another one-third were in secret consultation. But the majority of the soldiers, probably anywhere between half and three fourths, knew that "something was in agitation."[82]

The first battalion of the first regiment was greatly committed to and better informed of the conspiracy than the second battalion of the twenty-third regiment. About three hundred men in the first regiment took the oath whereas only three commissioned officers and one non-commissioned officer[83] in the twenty-third regiment did. In the first regiment, with the exception of three commissioned officers and five havildars,[84] all subadars, jemadars, and havildars and almost all grenadiers were in secret consultation; whereas in the twenty-third regiment only three commissioned officers (besides the ones who had taken the oath) and two sepoys[85] were in secret consultation. However, with the exception of two commissioned officers,[86] all other officers "well knew of the disaffection of the corps, and that some plans were in agitation."[87]

IX

Muslims and Hindus entered into the conspiracy with equal willingness. The exact ratio between the two religious groups cannot be ascertained. The conspirators with equal care debarred some Muslims and some Hindus, whose fidelity they had cause to suspect, from their secrets. The initiators were largely Muslims, but the Hindus joined them almost immediately.

Some of Moiz-ud-din's adherents participated in the conspiracy. The number is unascertainable. Jemmal-ud-din took the oath, perhaps on June

18, with a few Muslim and a Hindu officer[88]. A few more might have taken the oath. Certainly a greater number were in secret consultation. About twenty sepoys held a meeting with Moiz-ud-din's servants in his horse stable.[89] Many adherents of other princes too knew that the sepoys were restless and also that "something was in agitation." Prince Shak'r Ulah's mother pleaded with Marriott about the middle of June "not to enforce the wearing of the new turban."[90]

Among the princes, Moiz-ud-din alone was fully acquainted with the plot. According to Jemmal-ud-din, Moiz-ud-din was informed of the conspiracy in the afternoon of June 23. He told Moiz-ud-din,

> The sepoys were resolved to mutiny . . . consultation of the subject had been carried on for about two months . . . Principal people had taken an oath on the subject and I also had taken the oath.

The conspirators, Jemmal-ud-din continued, wanted Moiz-ud-din and Mohi-ud-din to "come out and join" them after they had accomplished their business "to set up a Musselman Government." Moiz-ud-din's reaction was distinctively characteristic of him. He responded, "No, no, this is a trick to bring me into disgrace as was formerly attempted with Fattah Hyder." Jemmal-ud-din assured him that it was not a "trick" at all, but the sepoys were definitely proceeding with their plan. Moiz-ud-din, however warned Jemmal-ud-din "to take care."[91]

It would be unnatural if Moiz-ud-din did not find the offer too tempting. A person who suffered notoriously from "want of reflection" would hardly dissociate himself from a popular clamour whatever risk it might entail. Perhaps impetuous Moiz-ud-din dreamed of freedom and even elevation. Moiz-ud-din told Mirz Sied Churudmud Ali, an adherent of Tipu Sultan's family, towards the end of June, "Keep up your spirits: I shall be out in a few days."[92] He later told Jemmal-ud-din to tell the sepoys to choose

73

him or Mohi-ud-din and not both.[93] Moiz-ud-din also, according to Marriott, desired to be allowed to have *Murdandh* on the night of July 8 and 9. [94] Besides, Moiz-ud-din asked Marriott to permit him to purchase a horse, if not, at least to try it.[95] There is no other evidence to suggest that Moiz-ud-din took the matter seriously.[96]

Though Moiz-ud-din was informed of the intended mutiny only on June 23, Jemmal-ud-din encouraged the conspirators in his patron's name almost from the time he was first acquainted with it. Jemmal-ud-din asked the sepoys to take and keep the fort only for eight days; meanwhile, he assured them that ten thousand men would arrive from Gurrumcondah Poligar, whom he described as "a powerful man and great friend of the Princes." Letters were also written for the Vancatygherry and Callastry Poligars, soliciting their assistance, which would definitely come. Jemmal-ud-din further stated that many *sirdars* in the service of the Rajah of Mysore were still loyal to Tipu Sultan's family and they would certainly throw off their allegiance and join the insurgents' ranks the moment they were acquainted with uprising. Jemmal-ud-din promised an increase in the sepoy's pay. He suggested that the sepoy should have Rs. 17.50 instead of Rs. 7.00 a month. He further stated that the families of all those who might fall in the uprising would be provided for.[97]

Jemmal-ud-din's encouragement was matched by the sepoys' wildly-optimistic imagination. The sepoys said that they were sure to receive assistance from their comrades in various other garrisons. One stated, "The cavalry at Connatore would join them." Another observed, "The cavalry at Arcot would welcome their initiative." The second wing of the first regiment in Wallajabhad had already given its assurance. The moment they commenced the insurrection they thought that they would receive assistance from the four companies of their own battalion stationed in Chittur. They even talked of a triumphant march to Madras. Apparently their tongues wagged too much for them to plan anything substantially. They neither made contact with other garrisons, save for one or two stray letters between insignificant persons, nor adopted any joint plans. They hoped to receive assistance from other troops because they said, "they were all their countrymen." The only substantial steps the sepoys ever took was to ask some pensioners and gun lascars in the *pettah* to man the guns for them. Yet the sepoys exhorted themselves to be optimistic and buoyant.[98]

Despite the note of buoyancy, at least some Indian soldiers had a sense of reality, perhaps many of them had at saner moments. Esoph Cawn, a sepoy, confessed, "When I entered into the scheme, I had my death in view, and thought of nothing."[99] Muhammad Jaffer, an initiator and active member of the conspiracy, implored his friend Mustapha Beg, who later became a traitor, to take care of his wife and two children.[100] There were others who asked their friends or relations "to take care of the children, and each offering to sacrifice his own life for the other."[101]

X

The conspirators had a very dramatic escape on June 17. On the 16th midnight, Mustapha Beg, a Muslim sepoy, came to Lieutenant-Colonel Forbes' residence, which was in the *pettah* and insisted that he must speak to his commanding officer. As he was persistent, the guard went in and called Forbes. When Forbes came down from upstairs, Mustapha Beg desired that "he might be heard apart." That being granted, the sepoy, "under great agitation," said, "Sir, the Mussulmen of the battalion have all united to attack the European barracks and kill all the Europeans on account of the *topee*. I, Sir, am ready to wear it, but the Mussulmen have united against it." "From the agitation and the unconnected manner" in which Mustapha Beg spoke, Forbes thought that "his understanding was disordered!" However, to allay suspicion, Forbes sent Mustapha Beg aside, and called the naique, who was on guard, and asked whether there was any "disaffection in the 1st battalion." Instantly the naique called out, ". . . the sepoy was a mad man . . . no attention should be shown to what he said . . . the battalion were all old soldiers and well affected!" Overhearing the naigue's remarks, Mustapha Beg rejoined, "Many people would unite in impressing . . . the Colonel that he was mad!" Forbes then asked other guards. They all unanimously declared, "The sepoy was deranged!" Being anxious to return to bed and at the same time desiring to know the truth, Forbes ordered the naique to take Mustapha Beg to Jemadar Rangapah, "a confidential and trusty officer," with the message that he should inquire into Mustapha Beg's account and report to him in the morning.

First thing in the morning, Rangapah waited on Forbes with the report that there was "no evidence to support" Mustapha Beg's assertion. He observed that the very person whom Mustapha Beg furnished as witness pleaded ignorance of the allegation. While Rangapah was still with Forbes, Sheikh Ali, the Indian Adjutant, arrived. Forbes narrated the "midnight" episode and asked him whether there was any evidence of disaffection in the battalion. Ali denied any such insinuation and accused Mustapha Beg of being a "very bad man," habituated to "irregular and extravagant conduct."[102] Ali stated further "that the battalion were all perfectly satisfied with the turban and vying who should first get it ready to wear." The Adjutant went so far as to say that "if anything like what Mustapha Beg had stated took place, he would be blown from a gun."

Forbes remained still unsatisfied. He therefore directed Rangapah to verify the account with Jemadar Sheikh Cassim and Havildar Dowd Cawn, two officers whose names Mustapha Beg had stammered in the night. To Rangapah's inquiry, Sheikh Cassim "disclaimed all knowledge of the circumstance, with the Koran placed on his head, as the most sacred form of oath." Dowd Cawn admitted a part of Mustapha Beg's account but asserted that the informer had unfortunately misunderstood the conversation.[103] Consequently, Rangapah reported "that the whole story was without foundation."

That evening Forbes invited all the Indian officers of the battalion to his residence and held a conference with them. He related Mustapha Beg's account and asked whether there was any aversion to the turban. If so, he continued, it was only necessary to represent through the proper channel and their grievance would be redressed. The Indian officers responded,

> They were all much pleased with it [turban] . . . No one man had the smallest objection to it. On the contrary . . . they were all exerting themselves to get the best topees and tufts.

That being the case, they stated that Mustapha Beg had done a "great injustice" to the stalwart battalion! They demanded that Mustapha Beg must be made "a severe example" and blown away "from a gun." Forbes became convinced of their sincerity and dismissed the Indian officers after expressing his confidence in them.

Forbes reprimanded Mustapha Beg for his improper conduct and put him in irons. Forbes was completely deceived. The only voice that dared to save the British lives was despised, condemned and punished.[104]

XI

Besides Mustapha Beg's alarm, there was another warning. But it was so vague, indistinct, and faint that none heeded it. From about June 20, almost daily, Ruston Ali Shah, a fakir from Cuddapah walked through the streets of Vellore, paused at different places and cried out in Hindustani and Telugu, "One sepoy has joined with many. . . yet in seven days, all the coffers will be killed. . . Rivers of blood will flow; heaps of dead will be carried away. . . Mussalman flag will be hoisted. . ." Some called the prophet "fool"; others said, "Mind what he says!" The trumpet gave uncertain sound;

none understood what the warning was about.[105]

The date of the insurrection was revised several times. At first, it was to have taken place even before the new battalion was "admitted into the plot."[106] But it was postponed in the hope of gaining its consent and cooperation. It was then to have occurred the night after the new battalion was informed. But as the leading conspirators, Subadar Sheikh Adam and Jemadar Sheikh Cassim, were on guard, the insurrection was deferred. It was further delayed to enable the troops to receive their pay. Again it was put off till Monday, July 14.[107]

Towards the end of June, the Commander-in-Chief, who was still recuperating in the coolness of Nundydrug hills, received a letter from Lieutenant-Colonel James Brunton in Seringapatam informing him that his coercive measures, instead of reducing the opposition, had produced a "common cry that the next attempt will be to make the sepoys Christians." Cradock became greatly anxious. He immediately wrote to the Government in Madras that he had "the strongest reasons to suppose that almost universal objection" arose against the turban; yet, he stated that he would "persevere to the full extent" if he were given "the sanction of Government."[108] He also enclosed Brunton's letter for the Government's information.

The Government in Madras too was lamentably ignorant of the sepoys' mounting feelings. Making an interpretation favourable to the "turban order" the Governor himself ordered the same pattern for his own Fencibles.[109] Bentinck found no symptom of discontent anywhere in the army after it had been crushed in Vellore and Wallajabhad. He was obsessed with the notion that all was well. The Commander-in-Chief's dispatch did not awake him from complacency. Lieutenant-Colonel Brunton's warning was dismissed as an exaggeration from one who "had been for a long time in a deplorable state of health."[110]

However, on July 4, Bentinck presented the Commander-in-Chief's letter to the Council. As a result, the Council decided to issue a general order to allay the sepoys' "unfounded apprehension," but to uphold the turban order.[111]

At the Council session, William Petrie wanted to take the turban issue "as a question of high and delicate political importance than as one partially relating to the details of discipline," but he did not express it as such.[112] The expressed consensus was that there was no real cause for objection but only a "clamour arising from an unfounded prejudice,"[113] and any concession to such a clamour from "an act which received the confirmation of public authority" would result in serious injury.[114]

The proposed general order declared that the Government evinced "a sacred regard for the religious principles of the Native troops, as well as of all other inhabitants of this country," but that

> in the present case, it appears after the strictest enquiry, and according to the testimony of Natives of the highest cast that the opposition which has been experienced, in the late change of turbans, is destitute of any foundation in either the law or usage of the Mahomedan or Hindoo religions.

That being the case, the order continued, "His Lordship in Council repeats his determination to . . . suppress all marks of insubordination and groundless discontent . . ."[115] The proposed general order was immediately dispatched to Cradock with the observation that if he concurred "in its adoption," he should circulate it "in such mode" as he saw it.[116]

That very day while conversing with Adjutant-General Agnew, after observing that the Commander-in-Chief appeared to be apprehensive of the sepoys' discontent, Bentinck stated:

. . . If any concession is made, I expect the worst consequences. If the matter is allowed to take its course, I am convinced that nothing . . . will ever move the troops even to momentary discontent. It derives consequence from discussion, but in itself, the subject has none . . . [117]

Bentinck did not imagine at all that a silenced sepoy might be a sleeping volcano which might erupt unexpectedly. He confessed years later:

The wildest dreamer in politics could hardly have imagined that the question lay between the revocation and the mutiny . . . to have acted at that time on the possibility of its occurrence, would, to say the least, have been thought unreasonable and preposterous.[118]

Cradock was much elated by the Government's response. He was now given a free hand for full coercion. He felt a peculiar gratification at the proposed order, but suspended its publication as he thought that the reports he had earlier received were "exaggerated."[119] While the Commander-in-Chief's acknowledgement was on the road, the unsuspected exploded in Vellore.

XII

In the afternoon of July 9, the second battalion of the twenty-third regiment was informed that it was to have a parade early in the following morning.[120] On such occasions the sepoys slept within the fort in order to be on the parade ground early. As the occasion seemed conducive for the meditated act, it was suggested that they should mutiny that very night. However, no decision was immediately taken. That evening Jemadar Sheikh Hussain, being drunk, articulated the plot in the barracks. Some fearing that it might reach their officers' ears warned their colleagues against delay. Consequently, about eight o' clock in the evening, a consultation took place in the barracks; and it was decided to begin the scheme at 2.00 a.m.[121]

The message was shortly passed on to alert all who were involved. Jemmal-ud-din waited on Moiz-ud-din with the gleeful news.[122] The prince responded, "I cannot believe this, are you sure, are you sure, are you sure, is it positively to take place this night?" Jemmal-ud-din assured him and asked, "we only require you and Mohudden to come and join us." Moiz-ud-din replied:

> Very well. If it does take place what can I or Mohudden do? There are 12 of us, all sons of Tippoo Sultaun. You are the fighting people and have the means in your own hands. You take which of us you like . . . When you call upon we will follow you. Indeed, on such an occasion were you to call a horse-keeper, he would follow you! [123]

Nothing dramatic occurred at Vellore in that evening[124]. It was just another evening when the cool breeze returned after a hot day. At Mohi-ud-din's apartment the festivities of the evening, part of the wedding ceremony began on July 3, came to an end before 9:30. Many ladies remained at Mohi-ud-din's place for the night; many men in the tents pitched outside, Mohi-ud-din himself "in his stable."[125] The gates of the palace and the fort were closed as usual at 10 p.m. All the British families retired to bed totally unaware of what that night held for them. As the late evening wore away, the stillness of the night settled over Vellore.

That night the garrison guards were furnished by His Majesty's 69th Regiment and the first battalion of the first regiment of the Indian branch of the army. The former furnished guards at the gateway, main guard, general magazine, and the British barracks. The latter furnished guards at the palace, arsenal, Ambur gate, spirit store, and regimental magazine. The guards at the main gate were furnished by both regiments. Fifty-eight British and 264 Indian officers and sepoys were on duty that night.[126] Including the guards, there were 100 British officers and staff, 330 British privates, 227 Indian officers and staff, and 1,341 Indian privates in that garrison on that night.[127]

About midnight Captain J. J. Miller, who was scheduled to go "the round," being indisposed, asked Subadar Sied Hussain to go for him. But Sied Hussain too was indisposed. Consequently, Jemadar Sheikh Cassim, a chief conspirator, was invited to go. Not unnaturally he willingly obliged. Cassim took a havildar, two sepoys and a drummer (to carry the lantern) as escort and began "the round." No sooner had he gone around the palace than he dismissed the escort, returned and slipped into bed.[128] Apparently, all was calm before the hurricane.

The Sepoys

CHAPTER FOUR
THE MUTINY

AT TWO CLOCK THE NIGHT RELIEF was instituted as usual. But unlike
other nights only a few returned to bed, while many lingered around and
began to prime and load their muskets. Many who were lately posted also
began to get their muskets ready for action.

At Fetteh Hyder's apartment, Ramu and Ramjuny, a Hindu and a
Muslim, were posted. No sooner had the officer of the guard vanished into
the dark than Ramjuny turned to his fellow sentry and said, "Before the
daybreak, all the coffers in the garrison shall be dispatched." With the
accent of curiosity, Ramu asked what he meant. Rajuny insolently observed,
"All the Hindoos and Pariahs have agreed to wear the *topee*, but the
Moormen are determined not to wear it." Then he contemptuously sneered,
"What! You Hinduoos have . . . no whiskers left. Will any of your cast give
you water if you wear the *topee?*"

To Ramjuny's insulting remarks and inciting queries, Ramu responded
plainly and simply: "I was formerly in the French service, and now . . . I am
in the English service. I must wear what they desire me else what will
become of my wife and children. If I did not like it, I might get my
discharge." Ramjuny then placing his hand on his chest, retorted, "This is
the breast that has been nourished by the Sultaun, not by the Company's
salt." While these sentries were conversing, the moon arose, and with it a

greater part of the garrison.[1]

About 2.15 a rumour passed through the barracks alerting the sepoys. "Get up," it was whispered, "the time to exterminate the coffers has come." The first regiment was first alerted, and then the twenty-third. Not all sepoys responded briskly. Several, who had no knowledge of the intended insurrection, thought only of the early morning parade, and asked the disturbers, "What business do we have to get up at such an early hour? . . . it is not yet four o' clock!" They received no explanation. The disturbers merely poked them with their swords and ordered them to get up, dress up, and fall in at once. Many responded immediately, while some others continued to remain in bed.[2]

While the sepoys were getting ready, some briskly and others reluctantly, some with the full knowledge of the intended insurrection, and others only with vague idea of what was ahead, a jamadar with a few sepoys went and asked Arnachellum, guard of the battalion store, for ball cartridges. Arnachellum refused to open the store without either the Commanding Officer's or the Adjutant's permission. As Arnachellum remained obstinate, the rebels pushed him aside, broke open the store and brought loads of ball cartridges to the barracks.

Meanwhile Subadar Sheikh Adam paraded the sepoys and solemnly explained to them the nature of their undertaking. The sepoys were then supplied with ball cartridges, which had been just brought in, and were organized into groups. Before they parted, Sheikh Adam told them that if they behaved well and completed satisfactorily "the intended business" they would be given five pagodas each in the morning.

II

As the moon rose above the eastern rampart, the sepoy groups took to their respective positions. One large party marched to the British barracks and another to the main guard. They were to commence their attack

84

simultaneously. Several smaller groups went to attack the British guards at their posts. Several others took their positions to obstruct the British officers from joining the soldiers in the barracks. The time was 2:30.[3]

The British guards were wholly unaware of the preparation in the sepoys' barracks. The fifteen-minute preparation was carried out so silently and calmly that even the early morning stillness remained undisturbed. To the guards, the first indication of the impending disaster was the footstep of the destroyer.

Hearing a "trampling of feet" near the barracks, Serjeant Cosgrave[4] called the sentry at the guard house to express "his astonishment that the patrol should pass that way." Just as he finished speaking, a volley of missiles hit the guards. Some were killed instantly and some others wounded. As the stunned survivors got under arms, a host of sepoys attacked them. Soon the rebels surrounded the barracks and through windows and every other opening, they showered destructive missiles upon the sleeping inmates.[5] Later, the mutineers brought a six-pounder with grape to bear upon the unfortunate fellows.[6]

The attack in the dark naturally snared the sleeping soldiers. The very first assault killed many, wounded many more, and threw all the survivors into utter bewilderment, panic and confusion. The wounded and surviving jumped out of bed and tried to shelter themselves as much as possible from the murderous missiles which were flying in. They hid themselves under beds, behind shelves, chests of drawers and anything they found.[7]

The attack on the barracks was almost immediately followed by another on the main guard.[8] Hearing the discharge of musketry, a British sentry called Corporal Piercy saying that "a shot or two was fired somewhere about the 69th barracks." The sentry had not completed speaking when the sepoy guards rushed at their unsuspecting colleagues and began killing them. Almost instantly they were joined by a sepoy party. Out of the twenty-three guards, Piercy and three others alone, by pretending to be dead, escaped the slaughter.[9]

Once the silence of night was broken by musketry fire, a great tumult ensued. Firing soon became throughout the fort. The rebels raised the hellish cries of "Ding, ding, Vallekarra,"[10] and "Marrow, marro Banchute."[11] The noise of the firing and the shouts of the insurgents filled the air.[12]

The uprising caught all the British families and officers unexpectedly. Awakened by the discharge of musketry, they immediately wanted to know the nature of the excitement. Some men went out of their homes and others called out from their windows. But hardly any received answer. However, the insurgents' horrid shouts and their firing indicated in unmistakable terms the diabolical nature of the uprising. Alarm and consternation seized all the British homes.

The initial reaction at John Fancourt's home perhaps might be considered illustrative of the feelings in many other homes as they sensed the menace which had surreptitiously trapped them. In a moving account, Amelia, John Fancourt's wife, narrates:

> . . . we were both awaken'd at the same instant with a loud firing. We both got out of bed, and Col. Fancourt went to the window of his writing room, which he opened and call'd aloud and repeatedly to know the cause of the disturbance to which he received no reply . . . Col Fancourt then went downstairs, and about five minutes after [he] returned to his writing room and requested me to bring him a light instantly. I did so and placed it on the table. He then sat down to write and I shut the open window from which he had spoken to the sepoys fearing some shots might be directed at him. As he sat . . . I looked at my husband saw him pale as ashes. I said, 'Good God, what is the matter, my dear St. John.' To which he replied, 'Go into your room, Amelia.' I did so for I saw his mind so agitated, I did not think it

right to repeat my question at that moment. I heard him two minutes after leave the writing room, and go out of the house . . . I bolted all the doors in my room and brought my children into it. I fell on my knees and fervently pray'd that Col Fancourt's endeavours to restore peace to the garrison might be crown'd with success and his life spared thro' the mercy of God . . . [13]

The reaction of the younger and single officers perhaps was somewhat different from that of the families. Many dashed to their neighbouring apartments and began to consult and take measures for self-defence. One of the young officers, Lieutenant John Ewing, the moment he heard the firing, went out, disarmed the guards who were over apartment, and secured their arms and ammunition.[14] Not long afterwards, Captain Maclachlan, Lieutenants Michell, Baby, Jenur and Serjeant Brady came to Ewing's apartment. Later, they were joined by Surgeon John Jones, Assistant Surgeon John Dean and Lieutenant Theodore Cutcliffe, who was already wounded. This group eventually became the nucleus to launch the offensive. Lieutenants John M. Coombs and Gunnings fled to Marriott brothers' apartment. At Serjeant James Walter's quarters, five other serjeants sought refuge. The latter unfortunately did not find the shelter too secure.[15]

III

The uprising even surprised some sepoys and Indian officers. Their exact number cannot be ascertained, but obviously it was much less than one-fourth of the men in the garrison. The unapprised ones were told that "it was a general business," planned "with good consent," and that they "must join and accomplish it fully." All who hesitated to participate in the scheme were abused and taunted. At times they were even manhandled. Many followed "the multitude to do evil" without qualm. Several pretended to be one with the mob to escape its wrath but either ran away to the coconut garden, which was near the magazine, or deserted the fort through the sally-port at the first opportunity. A few alone stuck to their oath to the Government and completely dissociated themselves with the rebellion. Some indomitable characters withstood the mob's fury and even protected some fugitives. But no one actively opposed the insurrection until the arrival of relief.[16]

Lieutenant-Colonels John Fancourt and James McKerras were the first ones to fall among the officers. When Fancourt came out of his home, he was warned by some friendly sepoys not to proceed. But he dismissed the warning with a "never mind," and dashed off to the main guard calling the sepoys to fall in. Fancourt had not gone far from home when Abdul Cawder shot him, and he fell mortally wounded.[17]. McKerras was shot near the post office without the slightest warning. Like Fancourt, McKerras, awakened by the musketry fire, came out to ascertain the nature of the uprising. While proceeding towards the main guard, where numerous sepoys were, McKerras, seeing near the post office Sheikh Dumus, a sentry, asked him in Hindustani, "What is it all about?" Dumus stoutly replied, "Nothing at all, Sir." Then as McKerras turned right, without any suspicion, Dumus shot him. McKerras then sat on the steps of the post office exclaiming, "Lord, Lord." The villain immediately rushed upon and killed the Colonel with the bayonet. According to an eye-witness, James Frost, "After Colonel McKerras was expired, the sepoy struck his corpse, with the butt end of the firelock and kicked and spat upon it, exclaiming, 'It was you that ordered us to wear this *topee*.'"[18]

IV

Between 3:00 a.m. and day break, the mutineers attacked the officers' quarters. The first apartment to incur the full measure of the sepoys' wrath was Lieutenant Coombs. Among all the British officers, the sepoys hated Coombs the most because of his ruthlessness. About forty to fifty sepoys of the twenty-third regiment rushed to his apartment and through every window they poured volley after volley of fire. Then, they set fire to the building to ensure the extermination of all who might be inside. But unluckily for the mutineers, their chief target Coombs, escaped along the verandah in the dark and then into Lieutenant-Colonel Marriott's apartment.[19]

While that party was burning Lieutenant Coombs' apartment, a smaller party of first regiment sepoys, led by Shwash Khan, attacked the apartment where Captin J. J. Miller and Lieutenants C. R. Smart and W. Tichbourne lived. Shwash Khan is alleged to have been Smart's foster-brother[20]. Fortunately for the officers, just prior to the arrival of Shwash Khan's party, they quitted their apartment in the hope of reaching the British barracks. Consequently, the mutineers did not find the intended victims. So they fired a few shorts into different rooms and plundered the house and went on their way.[21]

About the time Shwash Khan's party was plundering the young officers' quarters, another scene, more graphic, took place at Conductor Samuel Gill's home, where William Mann, deputy commissary of stores, Mrs. David Potter, a merchant's wife, and her children had taken shelter. Mrs. Potter relates:

> About 3 o'clock a number of sepoys came and called to the conductor by the appellation of serjeant that Colonel Fancourt wanted the keys of the stores to take out ammunition as the Princes were fighting with the sepoys. I approached the sepoys and asked them what it was they wanted. They told me to call the serjeant, but seeing Mr. Mann they said, ask him for the keys. And they told Mr. Mann and the sergeant to come along with them for Colonel Fancourt wanted them. On which Mr. Mann said if Colonel Fancourt sends another orderly I will come. They then said to me, 'Go away, go away.' I asked for what. Then they immediately shot the conductor. On this I turned around to make my escape with

my family, but my children being in the way I fell over them. And Mr. Mann fell also in the act of jumping over us, by which means he escaped a shot that was fired at him. The sepoys incensed at Mr. Mann's escape, then took aim at me. I took shelter behind a pillar, and the shot went through the knee of my child, whom I . . . [was holding] by the hand . . . [22]

William Mann, who fortunately escaped here, was not too lucky. He was killed elsewhere in a short time.[23]

Not long after this scene transpired, another group of mutineers attacked Lieutenant Ewing's apartment which then sheltered nine officers. Here the insurgents for the first time met stubborn resistance. An exchange of fire ensued, and then the mutineers withdrew. Luckily for the officers, none of them was hurt. After an hour, the party sallied to the adjoining apartment as that was considered better suited for defence. When the officers quitted Ewing's house, Serjeant Brady went out "to procure information of what was going on."[24]

About 4:00 a.m. a party of mutineers came into Surgeon William Pritchard's compound with the shouts of "Ding, ding Valekarrah." As they came to the door, William Pritchard escaped through the upstairs window and hid himself "on a terrace at some distance from the house."[25] He had left behind his wife to settle the account with the insurgents. In a letter to a friend in Scotland, she describes what transpired then:

. . . he [her husband] had not left me a minute when 15 or 20 sepoys rushed upstairs, some with burning brands and all with fixed bayonets. On entering the room [that] I was in, they fired two or three shots, and pointed their bayonets at [me] while my poor women and dear children were clinging to me, the former entreating them to have mercy on me and the latter screaming with terror. Finding there was not an officer or European man in the house, they turned their attention from murder to plunder.

Everything in the upper rooms was presently demolished. My cot, drawer, glasses etc. broke to pieces. My cloths and every article of value packed up, ransacking every box and place for money and repeatedly coming to me to ask where it was deposited. During this perilous time, I was sitting on a window. . . When the ferocious monster (sic) had loaded themselves with spoil, they left the house . . . [26]

While looting was in progress at Pritchard's home, another party went to Fancourt's. For some reason, perhaps because it was dark, the rebels refrained from plunder but not from murder. Here Lieutenant Thomas O'Reilly, an officer of the main guard, was done to death. Amelia Fancourt, eye-witness to the scene, describes the circumstances:

. . . As I stood at the lower end of the hall which was quite open to the verandh, a figure approached me. It was so dark I. . . was dreadfully frightened expecting to be murdered. . . I had however the courage to ask who was there? The answer I received was 'Madam, I am an officer.' I then said, 'But who are you?' To which the gentleman replied, 'I am an officer of the Main Guard.' I enquired what was the matter. He said it was a mutiny, that every European had already been murdered. I made no reply but walked away to the room where my babes and female servants were. The officer went out of the opposite door of the hall where we had spoken together and never got downstairs alive, for he was butch'd most cruelly in Fancourt's dressing room . . . [27]

About 5:00 a.m. a minor assault was launched against Lieutenant-Colonel Marriott's house, where Charles Marriott, Coombs and Gunnings also had taken protection. The mutineers at first fired through the windows. One shot hit Charles Marriott "just above the hip." Then the attackers broke in and took possession of the ground-floor. The fugitives retreated upstairs and sealed off the entrance against the insurgents. The mutineers then laid a siege which lasted until sometime after 7:30 a.m.[28]

In the early hours of insurrection, a stranger courted death out of curiosity. That was Major Charles Armstrong of the first battalion of the sixteenth regiment, who was travelling to Madras in the hope of embarking for England. As he neared the fort, he heard the tumult. Seeing some men on the rampart, Armstrong alighted from his palanquin and asked them what the disturbance was. The response was a volley of fire, which laid him to ground. Later some adherents of the princes came and dispatched him with sticks and plundered all his goods.[29]

V

After the organized attack in the initial stage of insurrection, the mutineers gradually lost all discipline and order. They began to disperse for plunder and loot rather than press on towards complete victory. The British barracks were yet to be thoroughly assaulted and the remaining soldiers put to death. Numerous officers were still to be searched out and dispatched. But the lure of loot was so tempting that the mutineers neglected the essential task for plunder raids. Before day broke the trained sepoys had become largely hordes of looters and vandals.

The insurgents also exhibited a tragic want of imagination. They took no measure to defend the fort and external attack which would inevitably come sooner or later. The drawbridge was not removed. The two outer gates were left open. A gun was installed against the main gate, but no serious consideration was given to manning it. No step was also taken to secure the strategic hill forts. Worse still, the mutineers left the officers who lived in the pettah wholly unmolested.[30] It was one of them, Major J. K. Cootes of His Majesty's 69th Regiment, who signaled to the neighbouring garrison sixteen miles away in Arcot for immediate relief.[31]

The dark hours of insurrection brought release to the sepoy prophet of doom, Mustapha Beg. The very thing he forewarned and for which he was so ironically thrown into the cell now facilitated his release. Taking advantage of the commotion and darkness, some of Mustapha Beg's friends broke open the cell and set him free. Mustapha Beg absconded immediately, as he feared "revenge from the sepoys."[32]

However, when he felt safe, on July 28th, Mustapha Beg came out of his hiding. The Government gave him a sum of Rs. 7,000.00 in cash, a pension equal to that of a subadar of infantry for life, a gold medal in the name of the Governor-in-Council and a badge of honour and distinction. These honours were published to the army in a general order.[33]

VI

Throughout the dark hours of the morning, the palace had no part in the insurrection. The gates remained closed, and there was no movement to or from the palace. But a lamp was lit in Moiz-ud-din's apartment not long after the commencement of the insurrection.[33] Some Mysoreans also came from the *pettah* in the early hours of insurrection and joined the mutineers. A rope was suspended from the ramparts, near Captain Willison's home and not far from the gateway, facilitated their entrance into the fort.[34]

When the day-light broke, bands of insurgents went to the palace and invited the four elder princes to come out and join them. The princes' reaction ranged from extreme indifference to calculated approbation. Fatteh Hyder reacted with total indifference. The mutineers called at his door, waited awhile and sensing no audible response, cursed him and walked away.[35] Abdul Khalik was more civil and polite. Then he "went in immediately and shut the door."[36] Sultan Mohi-ud-din was rather more cordial. He spoke to the invitees, and they tarried at his door for a while.[37] Moiz-ud-din went further. His reaction if not warm, at least bordered on approval.

Moiz-ud-din responded to the insurgents' invitation despite his *hirkarh*'s objection. According to Gurupah, the *Hirkarh*:

About six o'clock a crowd of sepoys came in and desired one of Mouz u deen's [Moiz-ud-din's] servants to call his master. On which I said he is a prisoner, it is not proper to bring him out, let him stay where he is . . . the sepoys . . . said if I opposed them I should be put to death. Then the Prince, Mouz u deen, came out and stood at the gate. I then told Prince Mouz u deen if he came out he would be considered guilty by the Company . . . it was therefore better for him to go within, but he remained where he was along with the sepoys, paying no attention to what I said . . . [38]

The mutineers told Moiz-ud-din that they had killed almost all the Englishmen and taken possession of the fort, and now it was time to celebrate victory. They asked for his flag, and after some time an old flag of Tipu Sultan was brought out. Then about thirty mutineers and Mysoreans went to the flagstaff; and having offered a Muslim prayer, they hoisted the flag with shouts of *din*.[39]

After the flag had been hoisted, many insurgents congregated at the palace yard. Tents were pitched, chairs and benches placed for their comfort. Water was given to quench their thirst.[40] Then pilau, rice, curries, sweetmeat, sherbet and butter milk were served. Betel and pauk were also distributed. The rebels, after hours of killing, looting and plundering, now sat down to eat, drink and relax.[41]

Special arrangement was made for the Hindus. Murti sepoy says:

". . . a great many sepoys came into the palace to get water as they were tired, and out of Sultan Modeen's house were brought new pots full of water for them and some Pariahs and Moormen drank out of them. A havildar of the 23rd battalion told Sheikh Adam the Gentoos would not drink out of those pots and that he must get puckaulas for the Gentoos. A puckaully was accordingly brought out for them . . ."

At this time the insurgents endeavoured to get Moiz-ud-din out. They ordered his horse-keeper to saddle his master's horse[42], and asked the prince to mount on and assume the leadership. But this was expecting too much too soon from the impetuous Moiz-ud-din. He served them with food and drink, but he was not prepared to risk coming out. Moiz-ud-din is alleged to have stated that he would not come out until the hill forts were taken and Lieutenant-Colonel Thomas Marriott's body was brought to him. He is also reported to have ordered Sied Hussain, the son of the famous general Sied Guffar, to go and capture the hill forts.[43]

While the great body of mutineers were feasting and relaxing at the palace yard, the carnage did not completely cease. It was kept up by bands of roving insurgents. The broad day-light, which had just come, undoubtedly facilitated their hunt.

VI

About 6:00 a.m. Captain Miller, Lieutenants Smart and Tichbourne, who had escaped from their apartment in the night, were murdered by Shwash Khan's party when it returned the second time. These three officers unfortunately did not succeed in their attempt to reach the barracks. One of them, Miller, was wounded in the attempt, but others managed to bring him home. After returning home, they sat in their living room, and anxiously awaited for the events to take their course. After a long time, they suddenly spotted the approach of some insurgents. Immediately, they went and hid themselves in a bath, and their servants bolted the doors. But the insurgents broke open the door and searched every nook and corner of the house. After a few minutes elapsed, Lieutenant Smart, hearing Shwash Khan's voice, and perhaps with the confidence of his protection, but most foolishly, showed "himself at the window," calling "Oh! This is a man of my company." Instantly, Shwash Khan shot him "through the head," shouting to others to do the same. Immediately, the sepoys rushed into the bath and dispatched all three. The sepoys then gathered all the papers in the apartment, piled them over the slain bodies and after having set fire to them, walked away from the house.[44]

Many other officers too were butchered in different places about daybreak. Captain David Willison was dragged out of his home and murdered. Dutchman Bee, the Captain's maid-servant, gives a brief but comprehensive description of the murder:

> . . . about 30 sepoys came to his house, abused him for wearing a cap and making them wear topees. They dragged him out by the belt, threw him down and shot him, continuing to abuse him and asking if he considered them a parcel of chucklers to make them wear hats.[45]

Serjeant Frost was murdered while hiding under a bed. A party of mutineers and princes' adherents broke open the door, searched the house, found him under a bed and shot him. According to the Serjeant's wife, "they were also going to kill her but she showed a child and begged for mercy which they gave, but plundered her of everything."[46] Serjeant James Walter, along with five other serjeants, was murdered in his quarters. Unfortunately, the details of the slaughter were not found anywhere. James Walter's wife, Charlotte's account is very brief and not very revealing. According to her, "a party of sepoys with a number of the prince's attendants charged down on their quarters and killed her husband with five other garrison staff serjeants." She further adds that some sepoys were going to kill her and other women, but the prince's people intervened and saved their lives, as they wanted to make them their wives. The insurgents then plundered the house and the ornaments which the women had on them—gold rings and necklaces—and walked away.[47]

Lieutenants John Ely, Philip Winchip and George Jolly were cut down about the same time near the sepoy barracks. Ely was first shot and

wounded; and then in his and his wife's presence, their eldest daughter—
they had two more—was butchered as a revenge for the death of the sepoy's
child in February.[48] Ely was then taken to the barracks. Mrs. David Potter,
who was near the gate, narrates which transpired then.

> I saw some sepoys bring Lieutenant Ely from the ramparts, who
> was wounded, and had a handkerchief tied around his body. He
> was making salaams to the sepoys for mercy, at which time a
> Moorman. . . belonged to the palace . . . made a blow at him,
> which the door prevented taking effect. And afterwards he
> pursued him as he retreated into the guard room and cut him
> down.[49]

Another eye-witness, James Frost, describes Lieutenants Winchip and
Jolly's murders:

> I saw Lieutenants Winchip and Jolly brought into the barracks.
> They were ordered to sit down. They entreated to be liberated,
> giving up all the same time their watches and all their valuables to
> the sepoys, and the sepoys told them to go to their quarters. And
> they rose up accordingly; at which time four or five Moormen
> belonging to the palace exclaimed as the coffers are come into the
> barracks, suffer them not to go out again alive. On this, one of
> them, but whether Lieutenant Winchip or Jolly I know not, was cut
> down by one of the Moormen. Seeing which the sepoys pursued
> the other that was going off, and shot him. On this they gave the
> shout, "Deen, Deen"[50]

Mrs Pritchard, another eye-witness, adds:

> After he (Winchip) had fallen, one of the sepoys put his hatt (sic)
> upon the point of his fire-lock and bayonet, and after flourishing it
> about some time, threw it down and trod upon it about [with]
> seeming exultation.[51]

Lieutenant Popham and Paymaster J. S. Smith too were killed sometime before or during these hours. But no evidence relating to the circumstances of their death survives.[52]

A soldier of the H. M. 69th Regiment gives the following account:

Mr. Williams, one of our assistant surgeons, who being awakened about two o' clock at night by six sepoys breaking open his door and firing into the quarters, got up and it being dark fortunately knocked one of the men down and jumping over the body made his escape and getting into a cook room, he completely blacked his face, neck and hands, and by that means walked for sometime quietly along the fort. But alas as he was going a little farther to gain the ramparts and join our men . . . but his small cloths should give way and showed he was not quite as black as he wished to appear. No sooner was this discovery made . . . he had half a dozen musquets fired at him, but he escaped and concealed himself in a sentry box where he had time to consider which evil was to be preferred trying to join our men on the ramparts and be shot on his way by the sepoys or as he is an excellent swimmer jump into the ditch that surrounds the fort and be swallowed by an alligator of which it is full. . .Williams was going to prefer the latter when an alligator popped its head up and seemed ready to receive him. So he thought he had better remain where he was. After some time, a party of our men coming near him, he put out his head and said, 'It is I, it is I," quite forgetting he looked like a Black fellow. The soldiers exclaimed, "We will soon, 'It is I,' you,' and began firing at him, but he again fortunately came off uninjured.

The sick in the hospital too fell victim to the prevailing carnage. About forty sick were taken out in their very hospital cloths and dispatched. Many of the Indian sick too joined their colleagues in the murderous work.[53]

The mutineers also did not spare any Indians who opposed their scheme. Two *hirkarhs* were found shot dead and one wounded.[54] At least two sepoys were shot, although not seriously.[55] The insurgents wanted to kill Sheikh Ali too, Indian adjutant of the first battalion of the first regiment, presumably due to his lack of sympathy with them.[56] They also wanted to kill John Jones, the manufacturer of cockades for the turbans, as well as his Indian workmen.[57]

VII

The grim hours of loot and carnage were not unmixed with humanity and compassion. Several instances of kindness and sympathy shown to the unfortunate ones could be cited. At the very beginning of insurrection, Numbiyapen sepoy and Muhammad Jacob lance naique went and warned Captains Greensill and Marret of their danger and asked them to flee from the quarters.[58] Permaul naique tried to protect several British fugitives, though he succeeded in saving only two, James Alexander and Francis Henshaw. According to the survivors, "they feel themselves indebted to him for their lives. . . No man could have done more."[59] Sam Rao rescued John Read from the jaws of death.[60] It was due to two sepoys' kindness that Lieutenant-Colonel Fancourt's life was prolonged till the evening. Twice Murti brought him water to drink; Ramu rescued the wounded from another assailant's hand.[61] A sepoy took Amelia Fancourt and her children to a place of refuge—a fowl house—and "the same sepoy" brought her "little boy half a loaf of bread to satisfy his hunger."[62] Mulllyander havildar and Ballagru sepoy took Mrs. Pritchard and her child from a "cook room" to their barracks, gave them blankets for their comfort and attended tenderly to all their needs.[63] There were some civilians too who protected British lives. The parsee merchant of the fort granted asylum to four fugitives. He "disguised them in a parsee dress and concealed them in his house."[64] John Jones too was saved by some Indians.[65] Perhaps, if one could know the whole story, one could cite many more acts of love and mercy.

In fact, broadly speaking, even the mutineers' disposition was marked with restraint and fellow feeling. During the many hours of their sway not a woman was molested or a child ill-treated, except one who was shot as a "revenge."[66] The mutineers were not even interested in killing all the officers. A party of mutineers met Lieutenant-Colonel Thomas Marriott in an open ground but left him unmolested.[67] The mutineers were prepared to let go Lieutenants Ely, Winchip and Jolly. But it was only the princes' people intervention that cost them their lives.[68] The mutineers' treatment of young James Frost illustrates again that they were not bent on destroying all the Englishmen.

In an interesting account, James Frost describes the manner in which the sepoys dealt with him:

> A sepoy of the 23rd battalion taking me for Lieutenant Combes, called out to some others, 'Here is Lieutenant Combes, come and dispatch him.' On that I cried out, 'I was not Lieutenant Combes, but the post office writer.' The sepoy then told me to come out saying, 'I suffer you to escape because you are country born. Was you an European I would stab you this moment.' . . . They took me with them to the barracks, telling me to obey their orders. There Hanamuntoo lance naigue of the 1st grenadiers . . . accoutered me with a jack and drawers like a sepoy, making me stand sentry.[69]

VIII

Even at the height of their success, the sepoys were quite conscious of the transitory nature of their triumph. Consequently, desertion became rampant. Many having loaded themselves with plunder escaped through the sally-port. Some went to the pettah and shared their loot with their friends: several were spotted dividing their spoil up on the surrounding hills. Some feeble and futile efforts were made to bring the deserters in. Some were seen standing on the ramparts and "abusing the sepoys in the pettah for not coming into the fort." But hardly any one responded.[70]

Those who remained behind in the fort were no better than the deserters. No trace of discipline and order existed among them. In addition, they kept smoking hookah and drinking arrack. Some even got drunk.[71]

The desertion and total break-down of discipline caused concern among the leaders of the insurrection. Sheikh Adam and Sheikh Cassim implored Moiz-ud-din to come out, assume the leadership and rally the disordered sepoys. But, alas it was too late.[72]

The people in the pettah had no faith in the permanence of the sepoys' triumph. They said that the troops' victory would evaporate as the sun got hotter. Peechan, a barber, tells that when the people of the pettah saw Tip Sultan's flag hoisted on the flagstaff, they said, "it would not remain long."[73]

The British officers, who lived in the pettah, did not fully realize the nature of insurrection till the daybreak. After sunrise, Forbes and some others made a few futile attempts to enter the fort. But they found it impossible to unlock the two inner gates. Consequently, they retired to Sazarao, the strategic hill fort, and secured it. Here they were joined by some "loyal" sepoys.[74]

About daybreak, Sergeant Brady returned to his brother-officers with "the lamentable account of the murder of every European on the different guards; of the Mysore flag being hoisted; . . . many men in the European barracks killed and wounded . . . and the whole fort . . . to be in possession of the insurgents."[75] Sometime later, one of them Lieutenant Mitchell quitted his shelter with the intention either of reaching the barracks or Captain Barrow's apartment. A little later a party of insurgents, perhaps in a plundering raid, attacked the rear of the house in which these officers were, and broke the door. The officers returned fire and tried to keep the attackers at bay, but the assailants were more than a match. Therefore, they immediately retreated to the barracks through the front-door. In the barracks, they found the survivors "in the greatest confusion, every man sheltering himself in the best way he was able from the shot which were frequently fired from the guns." Here they also found Lieutenant Michell. A quick calculation revealed that there were about two hundred able-bodied men, and they were all equipped with at least some ball-cartridges. It was immediately decided that Captain Maclachlan should assume the command, and the men should sally out through the window opposite to the parcherry and gain the adjoining ramparts. That was done promptly. They sallied out in small groups and took post in the nearest bastion. Once all the men were collected, they advanced to dislodge the insurgents who happened to be in the northeast cavalier. It was gradually done but at a high price. Several were killed and wounded. Captain Maclachlan was among the latter. He was shot through the thigh and incapacitated. At the northeast cavalier, the party was joined by Captain Barrow, who managed to escape from his apartment, and he then took the command. Leaving a detachment at the cavalier, they proceeded along the rampart to take possession of the gateway.

Once the gateway was taken, some soldiers went down "to ascertain if the gate was open." It was found that the two inner gates were locked and a six-pounder was placed opposite to the gate "for its defence." But there was no ammunition with it. At this time, the mutineers in the palace yard maintained an "extremely heavy fire." Near the gateway hung the rope by which many had entered the fort a few hours earlier. The same now furnished an opportunity for these well-nigh worn out men to escape. The opportunity was too tempting. However, only a few decided to escape, though others advised against it. Lieutenant Ewing and thirty others having descended by the rope, went and joined Lieutenant-Colonel Forbes in the hill fort. The greater majority while regretting the departure of their comrades, resolved to hold the gateway as well as to advance and take possession of the grand magazine, which was at the other end of the ramparts. Consequently, leaving behind a detachment to prevent the six-pounder from falling into the mutineers' hand, the main body proceeded with Captain Barrow to the southeast cavalier. While advancing, Barrow was shot "through both his legs," and several others were killed and wounded. Leaving the wounded at the southeast cavalier, others, now under Surgeon Jones' command, proceeded to reach their destination.

At the flagstaff, which was on the way, a soldier attempted to pull down the Sultan's flag, but he was shot down "from the pettah." At this time, the insurgents both from the palace and the pettah kept up "a very heavy fire" and the men were "falling fast." However, a considerable number succeeded in reaching the grand magazine, and as the soldiers burst open the door, to their "general disappointment," they found "nothing but loose powder." Many of the soldiers became utterly desperate, and they "wished to proceed towards, and attack the sepoy barracks." But Surgeon Jones "instantly opposed" the idea and ordered them to retreat immediately to the gateway. Then men promptly returned with the anxious hope of seeing the relief at any time. While returning Serjeant MacManus and Philip Bottom volunteered, went and pulled down the Sultan's flag.[76]

Soon after their return, Serjeant Brady, gazing down the Arcot road, saw a solitary horseman galloping towards Vellore. Farther away in the distance he saw a cloud of dust rising above the trees denoting the approach of cavalry.[77] Recognizing the leading horseman to be Lieutenant-Colonel Robert Rollo Gillespie, with whom he had served in St. Domingo, Brady exclaimed, "If Colonel Gillespie be alive, he is now at the head of the nineteenth dragoon, and God Almighty has sent him from the West Indies to save our lives in the east."[78]

IX

Robert Rollo Gillespie,[79] commandant of the Arcot garrison, received J. K. Cootes' message at 6:00 a.m. as he mounted his horse with the intention of riding over to John Fancourt's home for breakfast. Gillespie and Fancourt were old friends, who had served together in St. Domingo under General George Simcoe. Gillespie was supposed to have gone to Fancourt's home in the evening of the 9th to spend a few days with his friend. While he was mounting his horse for that purpose, some letters arrived from the Government which required his immediate attention. Therefore, he sent an apology and promised to come for breakfast.[80]

As soon as Gillespie received the message, he returned to the cantonment and ordered a squadron of His Majesty's 19th dragoons and a strong detachment of the 7th regiment of Indian cavalry under arms. He then left orders for Lieutenant-Colonel Joseph Kennedy "to advance with the whole of remaining forces in cantonment" except a detachment of Indian cavalry and a troop of 19th dragoons, which were to remain at Arcot to support the rear and keep open if necessary the communication with the cantonment. Having made these necessary arrangements, Gillespie, with the troops under arms galloped to Vellore.[81]

Perhaps about 8:15 a.m. Gillespie arrived at Vellore.[82] Upon his arrival Gillespie was relieved to find the drawbridge left down and the two outer gates still open. The third gate was opened to him by some soldiers let down by their comrades from the gateway.[83] Gillespie tried to force through and break open the fourth and final gate. But his efforts were thwarted by the insurgents who had by now fully realized the gravity of their situation. The insurgents' fire was so fierce that Gillespie was forced to withdraw and await the arrival of the guns.[84]

About an hour later, Lieutenant-Colonel Kennedy arrived with his party and guns. Immediately, Gillespie ordered the artillery serjeant, who had the direction of guns, "to blow the gate open." But he did not know "how to go to work." Therefore, John Blackistan of the Engineers Corps "ventured to give an opinion." At once, Gillespie put the guns under Blakistan's orders.

Blakistan states:

> . . . I immediately directed the serjeant to load without shot, intending to run the muzzle of the gun close up to the gate, and make use of it as a petard; but, finding that it was already loaded, and with shot, I told him to discharge the piece, and that he might as well lay it for the bolt, pointing with my sword to where I thought it was. He did so, and the gate flew open.[85]

No sooner was the gate burst open than Gillespie ascended to the rampart by a rope, perhaps the same one by which Lieutenant Ewing and others descended and made their escape to the hill.[86] On reaching the rampart, Gillespie made a general observation of the horror-stricken fort. "After scaling the wall," he states:

> I remained for several minutes over the gateway, and in the house over the gateway, as well as at the corner or the paymaster's house in order to make every observation on the transactions passing within the walls of the fortress. I had Serjeant Brady of the 69th Regiment with me, who explained where the enemy were, and the different positions which they occupied. During this time, I saw no officers, whatever in any part of the fort. I from thence proceeded along the walls to the cavalier to the northeastward. I there made a further observation, and looked out for officers, but could find none, but three wounded officers of the 69th . . . [87]

As soon as he located the positions of the rebels, Gillespie organized the remainder of His Majesty's 69th Regiment, who were still in the gateway, for the descent. Leading the men, Gillespie charged down into the fort. At that time, the insurgents "kept up an incessant fire" at them, and "many . . . were destroyed by it." At that moment the cavalry too charged in, troop after troop and squadron after squadron.[88] The insurgents, in a brief moment, were simply overwhelmed by the sheer number of assailants. No effective

105

resistance was either attempted or possible. Only in the old British barracks was anything like resistance offered. Even here it did not last more than a few minutes. Within ten to fifteen minutes, the entire fort was in Gillespie's hand. The insurgents threw their muskets and fled, but the vengeance swiftly overtook them. Most of the sepoys who were taken, whether guilty or innocent, were butchered. Hell was now truly let loose. Building after building was searched and the victims were taken out and slaughtered. Even the palace was not exempted. "Upwards of a hundred sepoys, who had sought refuge in the palace," says Blakistan, "were brought out, and, by Gillespie's order, placed under a wall, and fired at the canister-shot from the guns till they were dispatched."[89] Retribution pursued even those who fled through the sally-port. They were intercepted and cut down outside the fort.[90] "Revenge! Revenge! was the cry and many a sword drank deep," continued Blackistan. The retribution was brief but total, complete and untinctured with mercy. Many years later, recollecting the devastating carnage, Blakistan confessed:

> ... For my own part, I must say, that nothing like pity entered my breast during that day... Even this appalling sight [dispatching more than a hundred sepoys with canister-shot] I could look upon, I may almost say, with composure ... yet, at this distance of time, I find it difficult to approve the deed, or to account for the feeling under which I then viewed it.[91]

Gillespie would have butchered the princes too but for Marriott's intervention. Gillespie's biographer relates:

> ... he would have consented to the demands of the enraged soldiers, who were bent upon entering the palace. But the entreaties of some persons who had the care of the princes prevailed.[92]

Once the fort was retaken, and the rebels were silenced, the awful intelligence was transmitted to the smug authorities in Madras. Marriott sent an express about eleven o' clock.[93] A few minutes later, Gillespie sent another.[94] That evening George Harcourt, the commandant in Wallajabhad, who had been earlier informed by Joseph Kennedy, also sent an express to the Adjutant-General.[95]

Throughout the afternoon the victors gathered and assessed the loss of that tragic day. The findings were indeed painful and the loss was truly lamentable. It was found that fifteen British commissioned officers had been killed, and three wounded; eighty-three non-commissioned rank and file butchered and ninety-four wounded (subsequently fifteen died of wounds); one child killed and another wounded.[96] About 650 sepoys and Indian officers were slaughtered and seventy-five taken captive.[97] Later on, almost six hundred sepoys were picked up, and about another five hundred returned on their own accord.[98] More than Rs.197,360 worth of cash and property had also been looted.[99] Indeed, the loss of that tragic day both in life and property was truly great, but the greater loss to the army and government was still to come.

Indian and British Soldiers

CHAPTER FIVE

AFTERMATH: PANIC

THE VELLORE MUTINY INITIATED A PERIOD OF PANIC never before known in the history of the Coast Army. As the news flashed from garrison to garrison, an obsessive fear gripped the British officers. They felt as if they were sitting on a live volcano. One eruption had occurred; they did not know how soon others would follow.

In Vellore the reaction of the Indians was quite natural. At the approach of cavalry, many fled the *pettah*. The slaughter that followed produced great grief among the sepoy families. Even the people of neighbouring villages felt that execution had been "too severe."[1]

Not unnaturally, that very afternoon rumours spread among Indians that at that very moment "fighting was going forward in most garrisons in India." On the following day, it was rumoured that "a general rising" was to take place on the night of July 12th or 13th. However, nothing transpired though the atmosphere remained electrified. The British officers somewhat endeavoured to nullify the rumours and restore normality. On the 12th, Gillespie issued a proclamation inviting the innocent to return and resume their peaceful occupation and promising them "every lenity and protection."[2]

The impact upon the British officers was astounding. They could hardly believe that the sepoys whom they long regarded harmless and docile had

109

proved so violent. It was impossible, they thought, that the very men who deferred so much to their officers would murder them in the dead of night without the slightest warning unless they had been incited. Who were the instigators? Who else could that be but their inveterate enemies, the sons of Tipu Sultan? The role of Moiz-ud-din and several Mysoreans appeared to confirm that Tip Sultan's family was the real architect of the massacre.

With that assumption, Gillespie proceeded to act. At first he wanted to remove the princes to Madras, but later he changed his mind and doubled the guards over them. He also ordered a military court under Lieutenant-Colonel Joseph Kennedy "to trace the whole business to its origin."[3] The evidences deposed before the court appeared to confirm Gillespie's assumption. ". . . it appears," Gillespie wrote to Colonel George Harcourt, on July 12, "in such strong colours, as almost to amount to positive proof . . . that the whole was carried on at the instigation of Mozu-ud-dun (the third son of Tippoo) for the express purpose of enabling him to make his escape to Mysore, where it seems he expected to be joined by a numerous train of followers."[4] George Harcourt simply accepted Gillespie's conclusion. On the following day, after his arrival in Vellore, Harcourt wrote to Bentinck, "I am satisfied that their [the princes'] guilt will daily be more apparent, and that the further proceedings of the committee . . . will justify me if I am not already supported by those proceedings."[5]

II

The Government received the Vellore intelligence in the morning of July 11, 1806, by George Harcourt's letter. Before noon, it was confirmed by Marriott's and Gillespie's letters.[6] The Government, though shocked, remained cool and restrained. As the Commandant Fancourt had been slain, the Government immediately appointed Harcourt as temporary commandant.[7] It also ordered a commission under Major-General Pater to investigate the causes and nature of the melancholy event.[8] Later, when informed of the military court of inquiry, the Government ordered its closure, and added that the princes should not be removed from Vellore "unless the necessity of the case should render it indispensable."[9]

After the Government received the Vellore intelligence, the existence of the offensive regulation was brought to its attention. It was also said that the orders had produced considerable alarm among the troops and their countrymen. This belated revelation came as a great "astonishment" and "regret" to Bentinck.[10] He now felt that the sepoys indeed did have "just ground" for "alarm" and "dissatisfaction."[11] William Petrie and James Strange shared the President's grief.[12] Consequently, the Council sent an express to the Commander-in-Chief, whom it expected in Vellore at any time, expressing its ignorance of the regulations and recommending their immediate repeal and also of the new turban.[13]

The mutiny came as a benumbing shock to the Commander-in-Chief. Leaving his wife in Nundydrug, Cradock rushed down to Vellore, and he reached that station in the afternoon of July 14. When he arrived, Cradock found the garrison in a "proper state."[14] In their brief, Gilllespie and his colleagues attributed the mutiny to the princes. Cradock too was inclined to take that view. He concluded that the cause of the insurrection was "entirely to be looked for as having originated with the Princes."[15] Therefore, he immediately issued a proclamation to the *pettah* calling "upon every person to aid in the discovery of the horriod (sic) plot . . . to its very foundation."[16]

On the following day, the Commander-in-Chief received the Government's dispatches expressing its ignorance and the regulations in the Code and recommending the revocation of all the late orders. He also received the order to terminate the proceedings of the Military Court of Inquiry and the information about the appointment of the Mixed Commission. The Government's disavowal of the orders left the Commander-in-Chief in the lurch.[17] He began to wonder whether or not the late orders had been really offensive to the sepoy prejudice. On July 15, he wrote to Adjutant-General Agnew:

> I do, I confess, feel the most lively inquietude that it is in the power of possibility that infringement of the right and prejudices of the Natives, dear to them as life, should originate with me, who, I will say, as much as any man in India respect these immemorial usage.[18]

However, again, his lieutenants came to allay his apprehension. In a joint report, which was supposed to have been based on the findings of the Court of Inquiry, Harcourt, Gillespie, Kennedy and Munro stated:

> It has appeared from the evidences of the persons examined by the committees now assembled that the instigations of the Princes and their adherents constituted the principal cause of the formation and execution of the late conspiracy, that the authors of the conspiracy were all Moormen inhabitants of the pettah as well as sepoys, that the undoubted objects of their proceedings were to subvert the British and establish the Mussulman power by the elevation of one of the Princes to authority, that they took advantage of the temporary dissatisfaction excited in the minds of the sepoys by the introduction of the new turban to seduce them from their duty and engage them in the plot, that the Moormen attached to the Princes continue to employ similar means to corrupt the Native troops . . .

They further added that it was their "solemn conviction" that the insurrection in Vellore was "not the result of a momentary impulse but of a fixed and systematic plot, the success of which would involve our very existence in this part of India."[19] On this report, Cradock took his stand, from which he was never to recede.[20]

III

The Commander-in-Chief found the Government's recommendation to rescind the late orders quite unpalatable. He therefore resorted to a half-measure. He revoked the shaving, trimming and other orders fully but he rescinded the turban conditionally. In his circular letter to the commanding officers of the division, Cradock stated:

> . . . you will immediately give orders to the officers commanding corps in the Division under your command, to cause the turbans to be made up on the formerly established pattern, unless the Native officers and men should desire to wear that which it was intended to adopt; in which case they may be permitted to do so.[21]

The Commander-in-Chief also reacted very unfavourably towards the members of the proposed commission. He stated that they were neither daring nor intelligent enough to tackle a subject of "the greatest political importance." He proposed that either William Bentinck or William Petrie should preside over the commission and the members ought to be nominated from more intelligent and capable men.[22] Cradock's view was shared by many of his lieutenants.[23] While in Vellore, Cradock, without the Government's approval, instituted a court-martial to try the prisoners.[24]

When the Government heard about the conditional revocation of the turban order, it was sorely displeased. Bentinck felt that such a conditional revocation would create further problems. "It is possible," Bentinck said, "that Commanding Officers, seeing that a degree of importance is still attached by the Commander-in-Chief to this turban, may use an improper degree of influence in carrying its adoption." Furthermore, in an army composed of "men of different religions and prejudices," Bentinck apprehended that such an order would cause "much disunion and ill-blood."[25] Therefore, Bentinck demanded that the new turban should be removed entirely without any condition or qualification. Petrie and Strange without any hesitation approved the President's proposal.[26] The Commander-in-Chief subsequently acquiesced to the Council's demands.[27]

The Council also, when informed of the court-martial, ordered its suspension until the Commission completed its proceedings.[28]

Having removed the alleged cause of grievance, the Government issued a general order, on July 24, to re-establish the shattered confidence. It declared "that the late occurrences at Vellore have tended in no shape to diminish the confidence of the Governor-in-Council in that spirit of zeal, fidelity and attachment which the Native troops have so frequently displayed in the service of the British Government." The insurrection in Vellore, it asserted, "was excited by interested persons and was fostered by the deepest intrigue, in which the Native army of this Presidency had no part, with the exception of the two battalions composing the unhappy garrison." Therefore, it called upon the Indian troops to banish "from their minds all anxiety on account of any supposed diminution of confidence." The general order ironically made no reference to the late orders but it assured the troops of the Government's determination "to evince . . . sacred regard . . . for their religious principles and customs."[29]

Unfortunately, the general order did not produce the confidence it aimed at. Confidence is seldom re-established through high sounding declarations. It has to be effected through the operation of trust and good will. In the aftermath of the massacre, British officers expressed everything but trust and confidence.

IV

The British officers now regarded the once-harmless sepoy as a murderous monster. From the detached manner in which the troops were cantoned, the officers felt that they were "left to the mercy of traitors."[30] They urged one another to be prepared for the worst. They employed trusty servants and reliable sepoys to spy on the troops. In some garrisons, the British and Indian troops were realigned to make surprise attack impossible. Often British officers and soldiers slept with sword and pistols under the

114

pillows, some even with the boots on! Nearly all kept "a sort of feverish vigilance better calculated to create than to detect danger."[31]

On July 22, this sort of feverish vigilance produced a curious incident in Palamcottah where the first battalion of the third regiment was cantoned. At ten o' clock while preparing to go to bed, Captain James and his wife, through the window, in the dim moonlight, saw the sentry on the flag-staff "snapping his piece" and going through "some motion like priming" and "like firing bayonets." At once the terror of Vellore came rolling over the couple, and slumber instantly vanished. They sat quietly in their bedroom, and kept a long vigil over the sentry. At midnight another sepoy came, and both of them conversed awhile in low voice. Then the latter took the former's place, and the former went away. Welsh and his wife now became desperate, and they apprehended that some mischief was in the offing. Immediately, Welsh went and awoke the British and the Indian adjutants of the battalion and brought them to interrogate the sentry. The midnight inspection completely baffled the sepoy. Welsh's wife closly examined the firelock, and it was declared "clean and unloaded." Nothing more was done at that hour to embarrass the young sentry. However, a general inspection of the garrison was instituted, and it was found that the guard was absent from his post for more than an hour, and two sepoys for some unknown reason had run through the garrison once. These two trifling occurrences further augmented Welsh's apprehension. During the latter part of the night Welsh remembered that a few days earlier the Indian officers had told him that the Maravas, the caste to which the two sentries belonged, were "a treacherous race of men." He also recalled that many of the sepoys of the second battalion of the twenty-third regiment were Maravas. The more he brooded, the more firmly he became convinced that the Maravas ought not to be kept in the service. As soon as day broke, he contacted Lieutenant-Colonel Alexander Dyce, commandant of the Tinnevelly district, narrated the night's events and urged that all Marava sepoys to be immediately dismissed from the battalion. Dyce without any objection consented to the proposal. Consequently, that very day, 161 Marava sepoys,[32] including the two sentries, were discharged as "a political as well as military measure."[33] Interestingly enough, the Commander-in-Chief and the Government approved Dyce's action as "highly judicious and proper."[34]

V

The Palamcottah affair was only the beginning of such absurd affairs. A few days later, a more dramatic event occurred in Wallajabhad, where the second battalion of the first regiment, the second battalion of the fourteenth regiment, and the first battalion of the twenty-third regiment were stationed. The garrison was commanded at this time by Lieutenant-Colonel Ross Lang, who had just come from Hyderabad to succeed George Harcourt.[35]

On July 25, after the early morning drill, the first battalion of the twenty-third regiment was ordered to the barracks to clean its accoutrements. Due to an oversight on the part of the Adjutant, Lieutenant Richard Crew, the corps were not first dismissed to have their breakfast. Having given the order, Crew went away to the Commandant's house, and for some reasons he remained there till noon. Consequently, the sepoys too were detained without food in an "unpleasantly situated" barracks. As the morning wore on, the sepoys became hungrier, and they became noisy and tumultuous. With them, there was no officer except the Indian officer of the day. About noon, Lieutenant Crew heard that his men were tumultuous in the barracks. Crew immediately hurried to the barracks, and asked the sepoys what the trouble was. The sepoys responded that they were hungry and had not yet had their breakfast.

Without making any apology Crew simply dismissed them at once. The sepoys dispersed without causing any disturbance. But on their way home, in the burning sun, some of them uttered abusive remarks against their officers and declared that it would be better to kill them all and take the consequence rather than be held as slaves for seven rupees.[36]

Before long, in the afternoon, in an exaggerated form, the report of the tumult reached the Commandant's ears. The Commandant immediately summoned the commanding officers of the battalions and asked them to employ "confidential persons," to ascertain the disposition of the troops. Soon confidential persons came with their reports. A girl-servant, Catherine, reported that she overheard some sepoys say "that they would murder all their officers and then themselves."[37] Another girl-servant, Hussain Bee, stated that a bullock boy overheard his uncle advise "his women to collect all their property . . . [and] run off to Conjeeveram the moment the business should begin." "However mean" the informants might have been, it was observed, that their information ought not to "be despised in these eventful times."[38] Consequently, the officers doubled their vigilance during that night.[39]

Early in the morning, some confidential agents again returned with their reports. Their reports were scant and devoid of substance. The agents reported that they saw "several suspicious parties meeting together who seemed jealous of the approaches of any stranger, and whose conversations they could not overhear."[40] From these reports, the frightened officers concluded that their vigilance alone checked the progress of "conspiracy" during the night.[41] In the morning as they brooded over their situation, they became more deeply convinced that it was precarious. Therefore, they decided to take "immediate measures to prevent the execution of any project which might be meditated by the sepoys."[42] At one o' clock in the afternoon, Lang sent Captain Robert Hughes to Arcot to secure immediate assistance for "the preservation of many valuable lives,"[43] and at two o'clock as a preventive measure, he detached and marched off the corps under deepest suspicion—the first battalion of the twenty-third regiment—towards Poonamallee.[44] As soon as the order was given, the battalion got ready, and still with the possession of its arms and ammunition, marched out with willingness and alacrity as it would do under normal circumstances.[45] About twelve miles from Wallajabhad, it was halted and encamped for the night.[46]

The assistance from Arcot came promptly. About daybreak in the following morning, Gillespie arrived with the 19th dragoons. To his amazement, instead of murderous cry and bloodshed, he found the garrison as calm as ever. Gillespie's first reaction was that "the call was made without foundation."[47] He wrote to the Commander-in-Chief:

> I now on my arrival, thank God, find nothing to do. The alarm (according to Colonel Lang) has been great, but yet I cannot really see the source from whence the alarm originated when I find the folks here a little more tranquil and rational.

Then he added sarcastically, "I may perhaps gain some officer-like information."[48]

During the day, however, as the panic-stricken officers shared their alarm with Gillespie, the ghost of Vellore arose before him. By noon, he decided to march in and disarm the twenty-third regiment. "Seeing the fatal effects of too much security but a few days before at Vellore," Gillespie later observed that he consented to the "competent authorities ... on the spot."[49]

That afternoon the first battalion of the twenty-third regiment was marched back to the cantonment. Prior to its arrival, the other two battalions were assembled at the parade ground, and there Gillespie extolled them for their "steady soldier like conduct . . . in the midst of so pernicious an example," and charged them to remain loyal "to the British Government in India."[50] His brief address was translated into Hindustani and Tamil. Then the dragoons took their position, after which the twenty-third regiment was

118

marched in, "formed into a square and made to ground its arms. Gillespie then asked the Indian officers of the battalion "the causes of the mutiny." As he found "a diversity of opinions amongst the officers," and as he suspected them to be disaffected, he immediately ordered the commissioned officers "under close arrests," and the non-commissioned "into confinement." Then for the night, Gillespie moved the privates into tents pitched half a mile away from the cantonment, and surrounded them "with a strong chain of sentries and constant patroles."[51]

On the following morning, Gillespie ordered a drumhead court of inquiry to investigate the cause of suspicion entertained against the twenty-third regiment. During the next few days, the court interviewed numerous individuals, mostly children and women, and tried to incriminate the battalion.[52]

The Commandant, Ross Lang, from the first report of discontent, kept in touch frequently with the Commander-in-Chief. The intelligence of the alleged discontent came as boon to John Cradock.[53] The Wallajabhad agitation appeared to substantiate his argument that the late orders had little or nothing to do with the Vellore insurrection, The Government was a bit shocked at the report.[54] It seemed that the Commander-in-Chief's view was after all not to be totally discredited. However, it felt that the disturbance could be explained by the peculiar nature of the men who composed that particular corps. They thought incorrectly that the battalion was composed of "colleries and Southern poligars of noted enmity."[55] Petrie alone hinted that the sepoys might have a good reason for the "symptoms of insubordination" as they had been kept in the barracks "till noon without food after a long morning's drill."[56]

The Commander-in-Chief also insinuated that "the delay of military justice" was encouraging the troops to be insubordinate and urged a speedy trial and execution of the Vellore prisoners.[57] Furthermore, Cradock volunteered to go to Wallajabhad to evaluate the evidence promptly on the spot and punish the guilty "with every expedition and energy."[58]

The Government consented to the Commander-in-Chief's proposals. The military trials in Vellore immediately resumed[59]and the Commander-in-Chief repaired to Wallajabhad for personal investigation.[60] Meanwhile the Government, apprehending the unreliability of Indian troops, applied to the Supreme Government for the postponement of the embarkation of His Majesty's 19th dragoons and the 94th Infantry Regiment to Europe.[61]

The Commander-in-Chief arrived in Wallajabhad at daybreak of July 30. He spent the whole day and the next examining the evidence collected by the court of inquiry and interrogating the British and Indian officers. The findings indicated that the tumult in the barracks awakened suspicion, which was augmented by the reports collected from women and children who claimed to have overheard remarks of a hostile nature. Consequently, Commandant Lang applied for assistance and detached and marched off the suspected corps. The British officers furnished no positive evidence to substantiate the alleged disaffection. The Indian officers asserted that the tumult caused by the hungry sepoys alone was the cause of their embarrassing situation, and affirmed that no trace of disaffection existed in the battalion. They further pledged to manifest their loyalty even by embarking "upon foreign service if ordered."[62]

In the light of the battalion's behaviour on July 26th and 27th, in marching out and into the cantonment, in the most exact obedience and with alacrity, while in possession of their ball cartridges, the Indian officers' explanation appeared credible. Cradock concluded in the light of these forcible evidences that nothing like "a concerted plan or disaffection and evil design" existed in the battalion. The most that could be said against the battalion, the Commander-in-Chief observed, was that "there may be some evil disposition among individuals." However, Cradock went on to point out where the real cause of consternation lay. "I think your Lordship will observe," Cradock wrote to Bentinck, that "but for an evident alteration of sentiment in the minds of the commanding officers in respect to the behaviour of the regiments, and the confidence they would repose in them," they would not have made "their urgent representation" to Arcot.[63]

VI

While the Government was still in suspense, it received a report from Hyderabad, stating that only the timely revocation of the orders saved the capital from the horrors of mutiny.[64] The late orders produced in Hyderabad the same sensation they did in the Carnatic. Sepoys in Hyderabad had received letters from their friends and relatives in the Carnatic asking what they intended to do about the turban.[65] As in the Carnatic, the orders were interpreted to mean "a systematic design" to make the sepoy Christian. It was publicly stated that the British Government was going to make the sepoy Christian and that even the Nizam had protested to the Resident "against so abominable an innovation." [66]

In Hyderabad, the promulgation of the orders also marked a period of absurd rumours. It was stated that the British had built a church, and they were going to offer human sacrifice to sanctify it. Another purported that the British would massacre all the Indians except those who erected crosses over their houses. It was also rumoured that the British soldiers were out in the night cutting the heads off those who were found alone. It was again stated that the British needed about a hundred heads to appease the titular deity of a well near the British barracks to secure the treasure allegedly to have been in the well. A dead body found without a head near the Residency perhaps gave rise to these rumours and they were confirmed by an accident in which a drunken British artillery man shot a sepoy-sentry. It was also seriously stated "that a hundred bodies without heads [were] laying along the banks of the Moose River." The effect of these rumours, were indeed electrifying. The impact was as if a man-eater was on the move. People hurried home before sunset and did not leave their shelter until broad-day light. The atmosphere was charged with fear and tension, and people were on the verge of panic.[67]

These rumours no doubt augmented the notion that the turban was intended to proselyte the sepoys. Quite naturally, the sepoys resolved at all cost not to wear it. An order to wear the turban would be "the signal for a revolt."[68]

After the sepoys were alarmed, it was rumoured that Rajah Rao Rumba, one of sirdars of the Nizam, would erect a standard in the name of Buckshi Begum, and all the defected were to join him. It was also purported that Rao Rumba would entertain them all in his services at the same rate of pay and allowance as does the Company. There is no means of determining whether these offers were really made by Rao Rumba; however, they were certainly believed as such.[69] To the harassed sepoys, undoubtedly, Rao Ruma's offer came as a boon.

Fortunately for the British Government, the mounting tension was detected before the situation became desperate. On July 11, some officers of the eleventh regiment informed Thomas Montresor, the Commandant, about the sensational rumours and the mounting tension among the troops. Later that evening about eight o' clock "there was an uncommon disturbance and uproar in the rear of the cantonment." It was reported to Montresor that the troops "had meetings of their own," and were "now confident in their numbers. On the following morning, Montresor asked the commanding officers to investigate the cause of the alleged disaffection and agitation. The primary cause, it was reported, was "the intended introduction of the new turban" and the related regulations.[70] The secret agents further observed that the disaffection was "general and extensive" and if and when the troops were ordered to wear the turban, "a very serious mutiny" would occur. In case of disturbance, it was further stated, that no assistance could be expected from the Indian cavalry, although it might not join the mutineers.[71] Some Indian officers, however, assured Montresor that if he only revoked the late orders the sepoys would immediately return to loyalty.

Montresor weighed the different alternatives which he had at his disposal to preserve submission and obedience without countermanding the general orders. He thought of detaching the British artillery and infantry and keeping them in readiness to overawe the Indian corps, but he feared that any attempt in that direction would precipitate the very disaster which he wished to avoid. Fearing that, Montresor turned to exploit the intelligence of the Vellore insurrection. He tried to create "jealousy" between the cavalry and the infantry by pointing out and emphasizing the part the 7th regiment of Indian cavalry had played in the suppression of the Vellore insurrection.[72] But he did not succeed; his agents reported that the disaffection was "hourly increasing." It appeared that there was only one course to avert the impending catastrophe—the revocation of the orders. In this predicament, as there was no time to consult with the Madras Government, Montresor turned to Captain Thomas Sydenham, the Resident, who most enthusiastically approved the revocation of "everything that may be deemed a just, or at least a general cause of complaint."[73] Consequently, Montresor revoked the orders, assuring the troops that the Government had no intention to infringe upon their caste or religion. The effect was instantaneous. The mounting agitation dropped immediately. Every symptom of discontent at once disappeared. Every appearance of tranquility and good order immediately returned. Almost all the rumours too subsided.[74]

On August 1, the Commander-in-Chief submitted his final report stating that the alarm in Wallajabhad was much exaggerated. The Government was also pleased with the happy termination in Hyderabad. All appeared safe and secure.

VII

But the following day, August 2, brought new and unprecedented forebodings. On that day the Commander-in-Chief "in the most secret manner" and with a strongly worded preamble submitted two papers. The first one caused greater sensation than the second. In the first paper which was taken in Wallajabhad, Secunder Cawn, a subadar in the cavalry, deposed that the late disaffection was still mounting and, it was "entirely unprecedented in the Carnatic." He added that the cavalry too was disaffected, particularly the three regiments, the 4th, 5th and 7th, stationed in the Carnatic. The subadar alleged that the disaffection "arose principally from the intrigues of Tippoo's family and their adherents." A number of sepoys who were formerly in the Sultan's service were now in the Company's, and they were the "most active instruments of spreading disaffection." Secunder Cawn further added, "that the agents or the friends of the family were employed all over the country, that their intrigues extended to every place, and were carried on with activity above the Ghauts," and "that the country near Cuddalore was as much disaffected as Vellore."[75]

The second paper was Jemadar Sheikh Cassim's deposition. After Cassim had been sentenced to death, he voluntarily called his commanding officer Lieutenant-Colonel Forbes and gave him a narrative account of the events that led to July 10. In his deposition, Cassim alluded that the cavalry regiments both in Arcot and Connatore had been sympathetic to their plans.[76]

In the accompanying minutes the Commander-in-Chief demanded that the Government must "at once avow the just suspicion that attach to the descendants of Tippoo at Vellore and its fatal *pettah*." He asked, "Can it [the alleged disaffection in the cavalry] be imputed to another cause, than the attempt to restore the Mussalman Government, certainly in the Mysore, perhaps even in the Carnatic?" Unless "acted upon with promptitude, energy and judgement," he added, "our Dominion in this part of India" might be lost forever.[77]

The Commander-in-Chief's two papers made a deep impression on the Government. Cawn's and Casim's depositions taken "at distinct times and distinct places" and "unconnected with each other" appeared to give credit to Cradock's warning about Tip Sultan's sons. The Military Court of Inquiry as well as Colonel Alexander Campbell, who had interrogated many deserters in Trichinopoly, expressed the view that the late Sultan's sons were the real instigators of the insurrection. Quite ironically the disturbances in Wallajabhad and Hyderabad now seemed to suggest that they were only parts of a general conspiracy. Consequently, the Government accepted Secunder Cawn's deposition at face value.[78]

Once the Government conceded to the Commander-in-Chief's interpretation, it panicked. It now saw everywhere intrigue, conspiracy and treason. The alleged disaffection in the cavalry appeared "particularly alarming." Until now next to the British corps, the Government placed its "chief reliance" on the cavalry. The very tower of strength now appeared to have become the source of weakness. The Government apprehended that, as the cavalry was largely composed of Muslims, it would show itself "forward in support of the Mussalman interest." It was sure that the sky was overcast and a terrible storm was in the brew, but it had no clue whether the storm would dissipate calmly or descend furiously.[79]

VIII

Therefore, the Government resolved to avert the storm which it felt was impending. As a preventive measure it decided to remove the princes "from the Coast with the least practicable delay." In so doing, the Government believed that it would eliminate the very source of sedition. It also sought to strengthen its British force. An express was dispatched to the Supreme Government asking for "immediate reinforcement of European troops, to the extent, if possible of one regiment;"[80] another was sent off to Ceylon requesting the Governor to convey to Coast "as large a detachment as may be practicable of European troops."[81]

Since some of the princes were very tender in age, and the families of some elder princes were extremely large, it was decided to deport only the first ten princes and a few other immediate relations of Tipu Sultan. They were to embark immediately for Calcutta. Each deportee was allowed to take a few attendants with him, but not his family. The families and the other two princes were to follow them after the monsoon by land.[82]

In the Government, more than others, Bentinck became obsessed with the dread of general sedition. He wrote to Major Mark Wilks, the Acting Resident in Mysore, that the princes' intrigues had produced "a dangerous indifference" both in the cavalry and infantry.[83] He told the Supreme Government that his confidence in the army was "for the present deeply shaken."[84] To Thomas Maitland, governor of Ceylon, he described the situation as "very critical."[85] He wrote to Thomas Munro, who was in the Ceded District at this time, "Let me advise you not to place too much dependence on any of the Native troops. . . But, believe me, the conspiracy has extended beyond all belief, and has reached the most remote parts of our army; and the intrigue has appeared to have been everywhere most successfully carried on."[86] Bentinck apprehended even a surprise slaughter in the Presidency town. He confessed later on, "For many nights together (sic) shortly after the mutiny at Vellore I and every individual went to bed in the uncertainty of rising alive."[87] In the gloom of suspicion, apprehension and dread, Bentinck longed for a ray of light to guide his path. Therefore, he sent confidential letters to collectors, magistrates and commanding officers to ascertain the depth and width of the suspected conspiracy.[88]

Because of the fear of conspiracy, the Government felt that the Indian troops might resist the deportation of the princes. Therefore, it first made "the necessary military preparation," and then it disclosed its plan.[89] Fear was also expressed that the Muslims of the Presidency might offer resistance at the embarkation. James Oakes, who had just taken his seat in the Council, proposed that the embarkation should take place in Sardas, instead of Madras. He stated "that the present calm" in the Presidency was an attempt "to lull suspicion of meditated mischief."[90] Oakes' recommendation was however overruled, as others felt that such a move would indicate unwarranted apprehension.[91]

Events proved that the Government's apprehension was unfounded. On August 15, Thomas Marriott informed the princes of the Government's intention to move them to Calcutta. He told them that they were to leave by sea in three or four days and their families would follow them overland, after the monsoon season. Marriott assured them that they would receive the same treatment which they had been receiving and that during their absence their families would be properly taken care of.[92] The intelligence came to the princes as a surprise. However, some were "well satisfied, especially Moi-udeen, that his life was saved." But others were shocked, especially Fatteh Hyder. He was especially "very violent." Fatteh declared that he would not go unless his family accompanied him, and he even threatened to commit suicide if the Government adopted physical coercion. Nonetheless, due to Marriott's relentless persuasion, Fatteh eventually submitted to go. The princes' mothers were "most distressed" at the thought of separation from their sons. They had never before parted from their sons, and they looked upon the proposed voyage "as little short of certain death." The two mothers of the last three princes, who had been ordered to embark, insisted on accompanying their sons even "as common attendants should there be no accommodation."[93] In consideration of the princes' tender age, the Government permitted the mothers to accompany their sons.[94]

In the morning of August 20, under the command of Lieutenant-Colonel Gillespie, a very strong escort of British troops assembled at the palace. At the appointed time, palanquins were brought, and as soon as the princes were seated, "the whole moved off with perfect regularity and good order." At that time, an "immense" crowd of people was outside the fort hoping to have the last glimpse of Tipu Sultan's sons, but the princes "were not exposed to public observation, [or] idle curiosity."[95] Thomas Marriott adds, "The male part of the family observed more fortitude and resignation than I expected . . . but their families made terrible wailings."[96]

After a slow march of nine days, the princes' party arrived at the Presidency on August 29. On the following morning, the princes embarked on board His Majesty's ship *Culloden* as twenty-one guns boomed. The solemn occasion was unmarred by any degree of commotion or disturbances.[97]

The apprehension of general sedition also induced the Government to take quick measures to dispose of the prisoners. Their number had steadily grown. The original seventy-five had swelled to nearly six hundred. Many of the prisoners were taken by villagers and police peons in different parts of the Carnatic; and some returned voluntarily. The largest portion of prisoners was confined in Vellore; but others were detained in St. Thomas Mount. In August, under the Commander-in-Chief's instruction, Lieutenant-Colonel Forbes attempted to categorize the prisoners in Vellore into three groups: Innocent, and above suspicion; Guilty, but not charged with specific and capital crime; Guilty "beyond pardon." On August 5, the Commander-in-Chief recommended to the Government that the innocent "should be protected," the guilty "beyond pardon" should be executed, and the remainder should be punished beyond the seas "for the safety of the state."[98] Bentinck approved Cradock's recommendation, and even described the banishment as "a just, necessary and merciful punishment."[99] However, he observed that all the prisoners must be heard personally. "As a measure consistent with justice, with the spirit of our regulations and laws and with the general character of our government [and] as satisfactory to that part of the publick (sic) who may be friendly to us," Bentinck stated, all the prisoners must be reviewed by "a regularly constituted tribunal." Therefore, he recommended that the prisoners from all parts of the country should be marched down to St. Thomas Mount, and they should appear before a special commission and try to acquit themselves if possible.[100] The Board accepted the President's suggestion unanimously, but for some unknown reason the adopted measure was not implemented immediately.[101]

IX

The panic which seized the Government did not last long. In a fortnight's time several evidences came to the Government suggesting that its alarm was ill-founded. Several commanding officers reported their satisfaction with their corps. Major-General Dugald Campbell, commandant of the Northern Division, stated that a "most perfect tranquility and good order" prevailed throughout his district.[102] From Vellore, George Harcourt reported that the cavalry was performing "hard duty with pride and willingness." He also added that the sepoys of the eighteenth regiment, who had just come from Trichinopoly, were "so much dispirited and hurt" at the Vellore insurrection and they obeyed their officers "more like servants than sepoys."[103] Resident William Blackburne in Tanjore assured that the "fidelity and attachment of the provincial battalion of Tanjore" was "undiminished", and could be "entirely depended on."[104] Encouraging intelligence came from Mysore too. "The Dewan's confidence in the troops of the Rajah," Wilks wrote to the Government, "is perfect." Wilks further stated that there was no fear of intrigues in Mysore.[105] Major-General Hay MacDowall, commandant in the Mysore district, also expressed his "favourable opinion

129

of the troops under his orders."[106]

Further encouragement also came from the Mixed Commission, which had been in session from July 21. In its report, the Commission attributed the insurrection not to a general conspiracy but primarily to the apprehension caused by the military regulations. The report observed:

> On the whole, we draw from the evidence now before us the following conclusions: That the late innovations as to the dress and appearance of the sepoys were the leading cause of the mutiny, and the other was the residence of the family of the late Tippoo Sultaun at Vellore.[107]

If further explanations were needed, they came from Thomas Munro and the Supreme Government. In his reply to Bentinck, Thomas Munro denied that the princes had extended their intrigues beyond Vellore. He stated that if the princes "had extended their intrigues beyond Vellore, the most likely places for them to begin were Chittlledroog, Nundidroog, Gurrumcondah and Seringapatnam," and he added that his investigation did not find any trace of intrigue or conspiracy. Munro then proceeded to explain that "the restoration of the Sultan never could alone have been the motive for such a conspiracy. Such an event could have been desirable to none of the Hindoos, who form the bulk of the Native troops, and to only a part of the Muslims." He then stated that it was irrational to assume that the very troops who had refused to be enticed by the tempting offers of Hyder Ali and Tipu Sultan would betray the same Government without strong reasons. "The extensive range of the late conspiracy," Munro pointed out

> can only be accounted for by the General Orders having been converted into an attack upon religious ceremonies . . . it must be confessed that the prohibition of the marks of caste was well calculated to enable artful leaders to inflame the minds of the ignorant—for there is nothing so absurd but that they will believe

when made a question of religion . . . The rapid progress of the conspiracy is not to be wondered at; for the circulation of the General Orders prepared the way, by spreading discontent; and the rest was easily done by the means of the tappal, and of sending confidential emissaries on leave of absence. The capture of Vellore, and, still more, the rescinding of the offensive parts of the regulations, will, I have no doubt, prevent any further commotion—for the causes being removed the discontent which has been excited will soon subside and be forgotten. The Native troops, sensible of their own guilt, will naturally for some time be full of suspicion and alarm; but it is hardly credible that they will again commit any acts of violence.[108]

The Supreme Government began by challenging the inference the Madras Government had drawn from the evidences it had. It also questioned the validity of Subadar Secunder Cawn's deposition—the prime evidence that drove the Madras Government to consternation. It observed the Secunder Cawn's statement that the disaffection was "entirely unprecedented in the Carnatic" was "nothing more than a description of the disaffection produced by the General Orders, and fomented by the agents of the Princes." The disaffection of the cavalry too was directly caused by the obnoxious orders. For "to invade the sacred prejudices of one portion of a community," the Supreme Government commented, "is to invade the prejudices of the whole." Furthermore, it pointed out that except for those relating to the turban, the other regulations were applicable to the whole army. It further added that Secunder Cawn's assertion about the intrigues beyond the Ghauts and in other places could only be mere conjecture, as it was impossible for any one man to have had personal knowledge of such affairs in such a short time over such an extensive area. And it concluded that there was no basis for assuming the existence of a general conspiracy, and that the orders in themselves were notorious enough to create the late disaffection and agitations.[109]

The Supreme Government then proceeded to advise the Madras Government to avoid precipitating but adopt conciliatory measures. It suggested that the "principal perpetrators of the massacre at Vellore alone, should be brought to exemplary punishment," and others should be reprieved. It also urged that investigations should cease immediately. The Supreme Government also declined to send the troops which the Madras Government had asked for, and expressed great alarm over the application to Ceylon. It was apprehensive that the reinforcement of British troops would indicate "mistrust and suspicion" and make reconciliation impossible.[110]

X

The Madras Council now felt that it had been wrongly swayed by the Commander-in-Chief's manoeuvre. Bentinck particularly felt embarrassed over his loss of composure. He now fully believed that his alarm had no foundation at all. The pendulum began to swing to the other extreme. On August 26, Bentinck submitted to the Board a proposed general order. The recommended order revoked all additions which might have been made to the sepoy's uniform by his commanding officer and it gave "full liberty" to the sepoy to wear all his "joys and ornaments" as he liked. The order also expressed in the strongest language "the utmost displeasure of the Governor-in-Council" upon any commanding officer who might deviate from the established regulations "in the most trifling particular."[111] The other members of the Board considered the proposed order as being couched in severe language and they declined to give their assent. They argued that the publication of the proposed order would encourage the sepoy to be presumptuous and it would lead to the breakdown of military rapport.[112] Their unanimous disapproval infuriated Bentinck. He first threatened to publish the order upon his own authority, and declared that such an order was "so necessary and indispensable to complete satisfaction of the sepoy and to the prevention of similar calamities."[113] However, after some reflection, Bentinck calmed down, and he later presented the Board with another order couched in milder terms. The Board gave its approval; and it was published on September 24.[114]

Bentinck's recuperation from the panic terminated his brief honeymoon with Cradock. As he now reversed his view, necessarily his interpretation of the event and his suggested remedy ran contrary to the Commander-in-Chief's. "It has been unfortunate," Bentinck wrote to Bosquet, "that the Commander-in-Chief and the Government should have taken a different view of these transactions . . . Differing as to the causes of the distemper, our opinions necessarily differed upon the remedy."[115] The disagreement was also very bitter. "We have differed very much and very unpleasantly," Bentinck confessed to his father.[116]

The chief area of bickering was the disposal of the remaining sepoys and Indian officers of the mutinied battalions. Besides the prisoners who numbered nearly six hundred, there were also others numbering 15 officers and 516 sepoys, who voluntarily returned. They were not kept in confinement, but continued to do their work as usual. These men were also "generally implicated in the mutiny as those who were actually under imprisonment."[117]

On September 2, 1806, the Commander-in-Chief revived the question of prisoners. Nineteen of the prisoners had been tried by court-martial and sentenced to receive capital punishment. Cradock recommended that these prisoners should be executed in three batches at three different places—Vellore, Trichinopoly and Mysore.[118] He also repeated that the other prisoners should be banished *en masse*. Cradock further added that the number of the regiments to which the mutinied battalions belonged to should be also expunged from the army list.[119] Bentinck squarely negated all three proposals. He declared that the proposed execution in different places would denote "a sentiment of general distrust, the belief of general disaffection, and the determination to coerce the feelings and opinions of the sepoys." Bentinck further added that such an act would produce the very effect which the Government was strenuously trying to avoid.[120] Petrie and Oakes supported Bentinck in his assertion.[121] Consequently, in accordance with the majority decision, the execution took place in Vellore alone.

In the morning of September 23, the nineteen prisoners were executed "on the western glacis of the fort." Six were blown away from guns; eight were hanged; and five were shot by a detachment of their own colleagues. Later in the day, George Harcourt reported that "the painful duty was performed without a single failure or accident."[122]

Bentinck now found the banishment *en masse* extremely repulsive. He roundly condemned it as unjust as well as impolitic. It would be unjust, Bentinck argued, because not all the prisoners were equally guilty. There were undoubtedly degrees of guilt, ranging from perhaps active cooperation to mere passive sympathy. Furthermore, Bentinck pointed out that though the sepoys' behaviour might have been outrageous, "the origin of the feelings which led to the commission of these crimes must never be lost by this Government in the measures to be taken." Therefore, he argued, the prisoners could not be punished as traitors. "We are punishing murder rather than the resistance to orders," he went on, "we are vindicating the law and justice, rather than gratifying revenge." Bentinck further stated that "in calculating the effects of punishment, the numbers that have already suffered must not wholly be excluded." Banishment *en masse* would be impolitic, for such a measure would alienate the army, Bentinck added. Moreover, he proceeded to state that "the judges of our actions" would be the same army which at one time was more or less agitated by the same feelings.

The horror and detestation which they would feel at any other time against the acts of these mutineers, will be softened by the sympathy which men originally engaged in the same cause, must entertain for each other . . . my opinion is, that a punishment of extraordinary severity, as would be the exile of 600 persons without trial, might excite compassion, might revolt the general sentiments of the Army, and would tend to alienate rather than to recall their affection.[123]

Bentinck preferred a general amnesty to the prisoners, but he feared that such a measure would be dangerous in practice. For he observed:

. . . At no time would it be safe to turn adrift so many hundred men bred up to arms, unaccustomed and unable to obtain subsistence by any other honest means. But in the present moment, their liberty might be greatly injurious to the Service, while the late transactions are still fresh in the minds of the people. Hatred to a Service from which they are deprived of the benefits they have long enjoyed, might induce them to spread in every part of the country a disgust which might impede the recruiting service. Living in poverty and distress, they might perhaps communicate [to] the other parts of the Army, and keep alive the dissatisfaction which all our endeavours were directed to allay.[124]

Therefore, Bentinck recommended temporary confinement of all the prisoners.[125]

Bentinck's proposal found a cordial reception in Petrie and Oakes.[126] But Cradock found it extremely galling. "I will compromise for any measure rather than confinement," he declared.[127] Confinement, he asserted, would positively perpetuate the memory of the ghastly night and destroy all possibility of reconciliation and harmony. "To men, who have forfeited their lives, under every principle," Cradock mournfully declared, "I give my solemn voice for banishment . . . as a gift to humanity and generous feeling."[128] Despite the Commander-in-Chief's stern protest the majority decision was effected. The prisoners were kept "for the present in confinement as a temporary measure."[129]

On the third recommendation, to expunge the number of the mutinied regiments, Petrie and Oakes supported the Commander-in-Chief's proposal. "The horried (sic) scenes of perfidy, cowardly assassination and inhuman cruelty" demands, Petrie declared, "that the battalions which committed such outrages should be reduced to oblivion."[130] "The honour of the Army," Oakes stated, "requires their being expunged from the list."[131] But Bentinck would not yield to the majority. The expungement, he declared, would immortalize the battalions as "martyrs to religion." Such an impression should never be allowed to be given, he asserted. Therefore, he vetoed the majority decision upon his own authority.[132] Subsequently, however, the Supreme Government intervened and demanded the expungement.[133] Bentinck had to submit.[134] Consequently, on January 1, 1807, the first and twenty-third regiments were expunged, and their places were taken by the twenty-fourth and twenty-fifty regiments, which were newly introduced. The second battalion of the first regiment became the second of the twenty-fourth; the first of the twenty-third became the first of the twenty-fifth. The loyal sepoys and Indian officers of the mutinied battalions were incorporated into the first of the twenty-fourth and twenty-fifth.[135] The two regiments however were completed by recruits from the Carnatic and the Circars. At this time, upon the recommendation of the Supreme Government, the men who had returned and were serving were also dismissed from the Service. Only those who proved themselves as having dissociated themselves with the mutiny were incorporated into the new. [136]

XI

During the months of August and September, the panic to which Bentinck himself had been once victim, continued to gain momentum among many British officers. Exaggerated reports were circulated. The Wallajabhad incident was spoken of as "insurrection."[137] The existence of a general conspiracy was simply assumed. Even the absence of agitation was construed as prelude to disaster. "When the lull is greatest," it was declared, "the most dangerous progress is made!"[138] "Look well after them [Indian troops]," some commanding officers advised their colleagues, "perhaps something may be in train."[139]

A feverish watch was kept over the Indian troops. In Bangalore, the Commanding Officer Lieutenant-Colonel Samuel William Ogg prohibited some Muslim officers from attending a religious ceremony, since it was performed by a fakir, who had been Tipu Sultan's pir.[140] In Madras the Indian Adjutant, Jemadar Sheikh Hussain, of the first battalion of the twenty-second regiment, was taken and tried on a charge of holding "arguments of a seditious tendency."[141] Little things which under ordinary times would go unnoticed signaled dark forebodings. The three-piece cloth found at the flagstaff in Seringapatam was rumoured as the French "Tricolour flag."[142] Some absurd and obscene teachings of two fakirs in Bellary were seen as "part of that general system of corruption," which pervaded "the whole country."[143]

In the Presidency Town too, there was an obsession with the dreaded general massacre. When the Nawab invited the leading men of the British community for a nautch on August 15, it was rumoured in the higher circle that it was a sinister move "to collect all the principal Europeans into the palace" and wipe them out in one blow. Many met in secret consultation, and decided to decline the invitation. William Bentinck, however, rose to the occasion. He decided on his part not to show any suspicion towards the Nawab. Bentinck's example was at once followed by many others.[144] "The nautch," states Edward Hawke Locker, who was present on that occasion, "went off extremely well." He adds, ". . . the poor Nabob, so far from meditating slaughter, was alarmed even at the suspicion, and dreaded it as much as the [Madras] council."[145]

While the Britons on the Coast dreaded slaughter, the Indians were tortured with a terror of their own brand. Rumours of coercive proselytism and attack on caste were still rampant. They pestered and plagued many Indians. Near Wandiwash, it was stated that "the Europeans intended the Natives should become Christians, and wear the cross."[146] In Seringham, near Trichinopoly, it was observed that Napoleon Bonaparte would be soon arriving, and then everyone would be made Christian.[147] In Palamcottah, it was rumoured "that five companies of Europeans were on the road to make Christians of all the Natives."[148] One of the battalions in Hyderabad, it was circulated, was going to be marched down to the south, and there the sepoys would be made Christians.[149] In many towns and villages, it was rumoured that the famous temple in Trivanamalli was going to be erased and a church would be erected instead. It was also commonly reported that the Government had mixed cow's or swine's blood with the salt which it manufactured, in order to defile both Hindus and Muslims. The reports and rumours, however absurd they might sound were "attentively listened to" and "firmly believed" by many credulous Indians.[150]

The Indians had their own interpretation of the Vellore insurrection. "Except for them [mutineers]," many sepoys declared, "by now we would all have become infidels." The insurgents were regarded as martyrs to their religion. Subadar Sheikh Adam, the insurgents' leader, was highly eulogized. The insurgents were thought to have begun well but failed to have carried out their good work. If they had only pulled up the draw bridge and locked up the gates, and refrained from drinking, it was commonly spoken, they would not have succumbed to the cavalry attack.[151]

XII

In October, the existing tension precipitated a dramatic event at

Nundydrug which in turn triggered a series of melancholic incidents elsewhere on the Coast. In Nundydrug at that time, a small detachment of four companies of the second battalion of the eighteenth regiment was stationed. The remainder of the battalion was forty miles away in the main garrison at Bangalore. Many of the sepoys on the battalion had been formerly in Tipu Sultan's army. The Nundydrug garrison was commanded by Lieutenant-Colonel Alexander Cuppage, but he was assissted by Major Alexander Muirhead.

On October 9, Subadar Custory, one of the secret agents, reported to Major Muirhead that a few days back, on September 28, about eight o' clock in the morning, in front of the main guard, some Indian officers held a conversation of hostile nature. In the course of the conversation, one of them, Venkatachellum subadar stated "that the Malabars [Tamils] were the first . . . next to them were Mussulmans, the next [the] French, and that the English were the last. . ." Other officers listened to him with an air of approval. After a while, another officer, Cawder Beg Havildar, added that "according to the Mahomedan astrology the Europeans are to perish by the sword of the Mahomedans, notwithstanding their present power and government." At this Subadar Custory, who was also there, intervened saying "that they were formerly sepoys of five rupees, and were gradually raised to their present rank through good conduct in the English service, and it would be ingratitude to speak against them." To Custory's admonition, Venkatachellum and two others, Subadar Muhammad Razza and Jemadar Decca Ram, retorted, "The Europeans seized all the country in their possession by treachery, that they heap money in great plenty, while they give them only trifling allowance." Then they defiantly asked Custory, "What the English could do against three powers, the Malabars, [the] Mahomedans, and the Mahrattas when they unite together." To their haughty query, Custory related a fable. Once upon a time, he began, there was a huge fish, which all other fishes in the sea conspired to destroy. While they conspired, God disclosed the plot to the huge fish and gave it also a celestial wheel for protection. The huge fish affixed the wheel in its tail, and at the approach of its enemies, it stirred the ocean and caused a giant whirlpool. As the enemies were thus confounded, the huge fish opened its mouth and swallowed all the conspirators into its belly. Brushing aside Custory's fable, Venkatachellum again stated "that the Hindoos, Mussulmen and Mahrattas are one; the French have a country of their own, but the English only got their . . . merchandize." At this everyone, except Custory and another officer, Jemadar Murlieu, "laughed heartily," confessing that "they were of the same opinion." Observing that Custory and Murlieu did not join in the laughter, Venkatachellum said that if they presumed to argue, he "would trample them under foot." At that Custory stated, "as he had served the Company during a long period, he would not be so ungrateful as to be against them. . . Should the conspirators kill him, he would leave his seven children to the mercy of the Company, with full assurance of their generosity and protection." At this remark, the men arose and went on their way.[152]

Subadar Custory also added that in the afternoon about four o' clock, while coming from Sultanpet, he met a lad, a relation of Subadar Muhammad Razza, carrying "a large book wrapped up in a cloth under his arm, a small part of which was uncovered." It was like one of Major Muirhead's books. Therefore, Custory stopped the boy in order to examine the package. But the lad refused to let Custory touch the book "affirming that it was sacred . . . brought from Mecca . . . and . . . it contained [a prophecy about] the downfall of the Europeans by the sword of the Mahomedans."[153]

Subadar Custory further stated that in the evening an entertainment was given to many officers and sepoys at Subadar Muhammad Razza's home, from which he was excluded.[154] He insinuated that the party was held for seditious purpose. Custory also added that while he was in the picket room in the same evening, he overheard a Muslim sepoy say that "we are only waiting for an order, which when issued we will destroy our commanders, and all other Europeans and their offspring in this neighbourhood."[155]

From these reports, Major Muirhead concluded that a murderous conspiracy was truly underway. Therefore, to arrest its progress he imprisoned Venkatachellum and Muhammad Razza subadars, whom he considered as the leaders of the supposed plot. He also doubled his vigilance over the corps.[156]

The subadars' imprisonment generated severe criticism among the sepoys. They rightly blamed Custory as the author of the subadars' arrest. They also criticised him as making too many rules and being too strict. As sepoys became more restless, the secret agents returned with more allusions to conspiracy. So much so that on October 16, Major Muirhead reported, "It is now my opinion that disaffection has gone to a great extent in the detachment."[157]

Understandably, the Commandant Lt. Col Cuppage agreed with Major Muirhead's assessment of the situation, and they panicked. On the following day, the 17th, Cuppage marched off the two companies of the imprisoned subadars towards Bangalore. He also sent an express to Bangalore asking for a detachment of dragoons.[158]   The next day, the 18th, Cuppage wrote to Hay MacDowall asking whether another company could be marched off from Nundydrug.[159]

During that afternoon, to the suspicious men, things began to move from bad to worse. Custory stated later on "that from about 4 till 5 o'clock . . . he saw [that] something was wrong . . . the sepoys were in constant movement in small parties. They seemed to consult frequently, turn their whiskers, and show every mark of disaffection." Custory further added that about seven o' clock a sepoy informed him that he saw "a greater number of sepoys' families go away . . . in parties, chiefly of ten or twelve." Half an hour later, at 7:30, another waited on him with a similar report.[160] About 8 o'clock Arnasum came to him and reported that four sepoys, two lascars and one fakir were conversing near the pagoda, and he overheard one of them to say in Hindustani, "This Pariah Subadar has made all our secrets public, but wait and see what will happen in two hours (2 gurries)."[161] Arnasum's report, in the light of his earlier observations, seemed to suggest that the sepoys were planning to murder the British officers in two hours' time. Consequently, Custory dashed off to the nearest British officer, Captain Baynes, to announce the impending disaster. Baynes immediately rushed down to the pagoda with the intention of tracking down the sources of the supposed plot. But at the pagoda, he found only the fakir. And the fakir refused to divulge any information at any cost. Then Custory and Baynes hurried to Cuppage's quarters with their intelligence. Soon other officers were summoned for consultation. It was decided that they should immediately send an express to Bangalore for relief and that they barricade themselves at Captain Baynes' house until the arrival of assistance.[162] Without a moment's delay, the express was dispatched, and the officers marched to the place of their shelter. While they were on the road, another secret agent, Subadar Abdul Cawder, met them with what they considered unmistakable evidence. A few minutes ago, he said, one of his agents called at his home saying, "Something will happen tonight. You had better remain quiet and take care of your family in the house."[163] Abdul Cawder's intelligence fully confirmed their fears. They quickly barricaded the house, and having armed themselves with necessary weapons of defence, remained quietly awaiting the assailants' attack.

However, the storm did not burst. The evening wore on, midnight passed, and still the assailants had not attacked. The dawn came, and also the broad-day light. The morning sun too gradually reached its perpendicular height, and yet the sepoys had not commenced their murderous work. The calm of the previous evening still remained undisturbed. The noon too passed away. Just about two o' clock, Lieutenant-Colonel Henry Davis, with a detachment of His Majesty's 22nd Light Dragoons and a gun, galloped into the garrison.[164] "I. . . arrived here before two o' clock and found all quiet," Davis observed, "but really and truly they had a narrow escape of or from a 'Vellore fever.' You know Baynes' house in the barrack square . . . I found them all snug." "The sepoys are now dismally quiet in their barracks," he added.[165]

On the following day, October 20, Lieutenant-Colonel Davis instituted a court of inquiry.[166] The court sat for a few weeks. In all its proceedings, no positive evidence was advanced to prove the existence of a plot to murder the officers. But much was deposed to make the officers nervous. An Indian lady alleged that on October 17, she overheard some sepoys say that "it was their intention to kill the Europeans and afterwards to stand or fall under the Moorish colours."[167] A fakir observed that he overheard some other sepoys say that "two companies are gone away, and we must do the best for ourselves."[168] At least three witnesses asserted that they saw sepoys' families going away in the evening of the 18th, but several testified that the families were all found in their huts about ten o' clock in the morning. [169] The court made no attempt to question the families about the alleged flight. Lieutenant-Colonel Davis added that while he was marching towards Nundydrug, "he was frequently informed" that there was trouble in Nundydrug.[170] References to various and diverse kinds of rumours were made. Some purported to have heard that the "Vellore affair" would be "repeated here."[171] Others said that they had heard that Marathas and the French would soon invade the Company's territory, and that they would be assisted by all the poligars and former sepoys of Tipu Sultan.[172] It was also mentioned that fakirs from Hindustan were in Nundydrug exhibiting puppet shows, acting out French victory over the English and displaying the former splendor of Moghul Court.[173]

Among all the evidences deposed before the court, the one by the acting Indian Adjutant Jemadar Sheikh Dowd was most exhaustive and, to British officers, most disconcerting. Dowd made his depositions after he was promised full pardon if he disclosed all that he knew. Dowd began by saying that prior to the revocation of the turban order that battalion had sworn to do as the oldest one would do. But he denied any knowledge of the alleged conspiracy on October 18, as he had returned from Seringapatam only few days earlier. However, he added that in the afternoon of the same day he heard two sepoys say that "something" was to happen that night. Dowd confessed that he did not know exactly what the sepoys meant by "something," but he supposed that "they intended to kill the Europeans, plunder all they could and then run off." Dowd also proceeded to give his opinion of the corps. He observed that in his view, on the 18th, three fourths of the troops "would have certainly joined the undertaking." He also stated that the detachment in Bangalore too was "equally disaffected," and that "constant communication" was maintained "between them and the people here, both verbly and by letter."[174] But later on, he added that "he cannot advance proof of it, but he believes in his heart that such was the case."[175]

Sheikh Dowd also declared that the whole country was ripe for rebellion, and was waiting only for an opportune moment. He stated that an invasion was ever expected either by the Marathas or the French. When that happened, he added, the poligars, the amildars, and the sepoys would arise as one man and overthrow both the Braminy and British governments. He further added that the subadars constantly told their companies that the moment the army revolted, "the different amildars, Mussalmen and ryotts would join and assist" them to drive the British into the sea.[176]

The court of inquiry strangely presented no formal report. But Hay MacDowall, who arrived in Nundydrug on October 29, and Henry Davis submitted their conclusion of the findings in their official letters. MacDowall's letter took the form of a nine-point report. In brief, he observed that persons of various descriptions, "with a treacherous design," were wandering all over the peninsula, and they "in the most secret manner endeavoured to seduce and alienate" the troops. In Nundydrug, he concluded that these "insidious artificers" altogether succeeded in inducing the troops "to commit the most daring and atrocious acts," but the timely discovery of the plot and the measures promptly adopted alone completely frustrated their diabolical design and saved the officers' lives. MacDowall further added that the country had been worked up to believe that "wonderful changes" were around the corner, and the British would be "expelled from India" and with great ease. He further remarked that the Indian officers, amildars, poligars and other chieftains were the main agents of sedition.[177]

Davis' letter was equally alarming. Davis declared that these were "the times of trouble." He felt that "a considerable degree of disaffection" had been produced by the seeds sown by the "avowed enemies of the British Government." Very ingeniously Davis concluded that these enemies were the Holkar and Fetteh Ali, Tipu Sultan's nephew. "That Holkar, Tippu's nephew and others have sent hundreds, perhaps thousands of commissaries into Mysore and our own provinces cannot be doubted," he claimed.[178]

Like MacDowall, Davis too concluded that Cuppage's prompt measures alone thwarted the massacre. ". . . in my humble opinion," he wrote to Cradock, "had he not done so, another butchery would have taken place, and the consequences might have staggered to the very foundation the Empire [in] this Peninsula."[179] In his reasoning, Davis, was, however, completely obsessed with the Vellore ghost. "It is allowed," he observed,

> by every British officers (sic) in India that Colonel Forbes was too incredulous . . . in not paying proper attention to the intelligence he received from the sepoy . . . If Colonel Forbes was blameable, Colonel Cuppage would have been highly culpable, nay criminal, had he not resorted to the measures he adopted.[180]

Hay MacDowall, after his arrival, marched back the two companies to Nundydrug. In the evening of October 30, he paraded all the four companies, and harangued them expressing his "regret and astonishment" at their "abominable projects" though they had no "cause for complaint." Then he asked the sepoys to quit the service if they so desired. Consequently, eleven asked for discharge, which was subsequently granted. The vast majority, however, according to MacDowall, expressed their contrition, "promised an entire reformation and avowed their willingness to die for the Company."[181]

XIII

Down in Bangalore too, where the rest of the battalion was cantoned, a careful watch was kept. Early in October, Lieutenant-Colonel Samuel William Ogg, the Commandant, complained that a large number of people from Colar Sera were "passing and repassing . . . without any ostensible object in view."[182] Ogg's suspicion of strangers bordered on frenzy. A few days later, he jailed a naigue's relation because he appeared "to avoid observation."[183] The poor man remained in confinement several days until his relation discovered his plight and secured his release. The disturbance in Nundydrug made him suspect a plot in Bangalore too. "The late accounts," he wrote to Cradock, "have revived in my mind the opinion that some plan is in agitation . . . the peers and fackirs . . . are blowing the coals in the quarter."[184] Though he was tortured with the fear of plot and conspiracy, he found no overt cause for suspicion. "With respect to the part of the corps at headquarters," Ogg wrote on October 20, "I can say, that it is impossible for people to behave better or appear more satisfied."[185] Yet, fear haunted him. He suspected two Indian officers just because, as he put it, they appeared "cautious, reserved and gloomy."[186]

Once Ogg became obsessed with suspicion and fear, he mistook dawn for dusk. Even the appearences of goodwill and confidence were interpreted only to mean hypocritical gestures to delude him into complacency. Though he found the troops "perfectly happy and contented,"[187] and "everything" in the garrison "perfectly orderly and quiet,"[188] he entered into a ruthless and violent campaign of fact-finding. On October 22, he invaded a munshi's house and brought "a bundle of papers for examination. Nothing of importance was discovered except one letter. From that letter, Ogg concluded that the liberation of the Mysore princes had been "in contemplation for six years."[189] On the following day, Sied Mahomed Cawdry's temporary residence was attacked, and his papers examined. From one of his papers, Ogg concluded that he was an emissary of sedition.[190]

A few days later, Ogg felt that he had found evidences of a plot. On October 24, a letter was found in the garrison, which stated that with the exception of five men, all other sepoys and Indian officers had conspired to murder "the principal European officers."[191] At this information, Ogg incarcerated Secunder Cawn and Narsu, whom he had earlier described as suspicious, and four others, including the poor stranger, whom he had previously confined, and his relation, who had secured his release. Two days later, on October 26, Sheikh Dowd deposed in Nundydrug, that the detachment in Bangalore too was as culpable as the one at that station.[192]

Three days later, Ogg received MacDowall's letter ordering him to institute an inquiry in order to trace "the cause of the extraordinary commotions."[193] Ogg immediately converted his informal inquiry into a formal one. A systematic house to house search commenced. Several civilians were arrested, their houses invaded and searched without any reference to the Mysore authorities. In fact, Ogg suspected the Mysore officials too. He simply assumed that a plot to murder him and his associates truly existed in Bangalore and he then went so far as to accuse the Mysore officials as either conniving or participating in treasonable activities. Naturally, the Mysore officials were stunned and shocked; and at Ogg's treatment they felt extremely insulted. When Ogg's behaviour was reported to Purniah, the Dewan of Mysore, he too was deeply hurt.[194]

Despite the relentless and ruthless investigation, no discovery of "great importance" was made. Therefore, the court, on Novemember 1, issued a proclamation promising a reward of Rs. 350.00 to any who would furnish evidences of a plot in Bangalore. The proclamation further stated that an additional reward of Rs. 1,750.00 would be granted if the information given led "to a complete discovery of the whole." It also promised a full and ample pardon" to the witness if he had any part in the misdemeanor.[195]

The lure of reward soon brought many witnesses. The evidences deposed seemed to suggest that the troops, despite their ostensible contentment, did indeed plan to mutiny in collaboration with their colleagues in Nundydrug. A sepoy stated that another told him that in about ten days "all the Europeans would be put to death."[196] A woman asserted that a sepoy told her that "we shall destroy them [the British officers] in two or three days."[197] A fakir affirmed that a sepoy carried messages of assurance from Subadar Secunder Cawn of Bangalore to the two incarcerated subadars in Nundydrug.[198] A person also stated that a citizen of Burra Balapore incited the Muslims to unite and destroy the English.[199] Further evidences also were deposed suggesting a general conspiracy. Some stated that fakirs were preaching that the English Government would be soon destroyed. ". . . how many sovereigns have fallen? . . . Can the European Government possibly remain? This is only for a few days," thus a fakir was alleged to have preached near the Macan. Another fakir was reported to have stated, "They [empires and kingdoms] are birds of passage like the swallow . . . the noonday remains with no man. . . This [too] is going likewise."[200] A school teacher, Sheikh Anser, was accused of teaching seditious songs to his pupils and several others.[201] Evidences also were advanced to implicate the Amildar of Bangalore, Madha Rao, and the Dewan, Purniah, in hostile activities towards the British.

The allegation against the Amildar and the Dewan was of a strange kind. It was made by two sepoys and an officer. They stated that an ex-commandant of the peons, Timnaig, told them that Madha Rao and Purniah were secretly planning to overthrow the British Government and they were patronizing a nawab in secret who was to succeed the present government. The witnesses also stated that Timnaig alleged that the Amildar knew of the Vellore massacre about fifteen days before it occurred and that he recruited many men with the plan of annihilating the British authority if the insurrection succeeded. Timnaig also stated that the Amildar divulged his plan to him and asked him to cooperate with him, but he refused. Consequently, the Amildar put him in irons. Timnaig declared that he would positively prove these allegations, or he would consent to be hung with his family in the gateway of the Bangalore fort. The witnesses also stated that after a long search they found the nawab who was to be the future king. The nawab told them "that God had taken the form of a man, and is at this present time in Bangalore and that he is the author of all these things." Furthermore, disturbances would first commence at Nundydrug, it would then spread to Bangalore, to Seringapatam, and then all over the country. [202]

A letter was also produced to accuse the Dewan. It was written in Telugu and it was picked up in the fort. The letter stated that the Dewan was determined to massacre the officers, and it urged the British Government to take prompt measures to thwart his plans. "If there is any delay," it

149

declared, "the officers will be murdered and Poorniah will seize the country." The letter concluded saying that "of this there is no doubt. If it is not true, may the writer perish miserably. . ."[203]

The court sent a report of these allegations to Hay MacDowall, who subsequently referred them to the Resident, Mark Wilks. The Resident immediately knew that the allegations were absurd, and prompted by base motives. He was indignant that such silly and malignant charges had been received in official records. However, inasmuch as he was obliged to, he disclosed the communication to the Dewan. "The Dewan," Wilks observed, "received the communication with the temper, and extraordinary good sense which so peculiarly distinguishes his character." Soon the Resident and the Dewan agreed "with regard to the proper course of proceeding." Madha Rao was immediately suspended; and his office was assumed by Butcherao, a distinguished public servant; and at the request of Mysore Government two British officers, Lieutenant-Colonel Henry Davis and Major Robert Barclay, the town major of Fort St. George, repaired to Bangalore to investigate the charges against Madha Rao and Purniah.[204]

Davis and Barclay spent three full days investigating the validity of the allegations. The inquiry only confirmed the commonly known facts: that Timnaig was in iron not for attachment to the Company but for repeated thefts. When Timnaig was directly questioned, he completely denied what he had told the sepoys and the officer. Furthermore, he solemnly appealed to heaven and declared that Amildar Madha Rao did not know "one hair's breath of the matter."[205] The nawab too was a farce. He was found to be a lame and pitiable creature, living in filth, in a corner of a cattle-shed, and was supported by charity.[206] "The Nawab," wrote Henry Davis to Wilks, "is a most miserable looking devil—a withered arm and delibitated (sic) limbs. . . He seems to live in his filthy basket. Your nose and eyes would revolt at the first view."[207] The letter was totally anonymous. The whole allegation, Davis observed, originated "in a littleness of mind."[208] After pursuing the proceedings, Hay MacDowall confessed "that the accusations have been made with the most malicious and vindictive intent, by a desperate and infamous vagabond."[209]

The court of inquiry too, after weeks of strenuous exertions, concluded that the earlier alarm was groundless. "After every effort of this court to ascertain the fact," Ogg reported, "nothing beyond suspicion can attach to this part of the corps, and even that is confined to a very small number." Even the suspicious ones, he stated, could be accused only of "seditious" talks, but he added that "the bad characters of many of the witnesses" made him "incredulous of the truth of some of the allegations against some men accused of seditious language." Ogg expressed deep sorrow for his earlier unfounded suspicion and stated, "I firmly believe that this part of the battalion has been and still is steady in its fidelity and allegiance.

XIV

The Government, particularly the Governor, viewed the Bangalore proceedings with particular concern. Bentinck thought that Ogg's ruthless action made the Mysore Government feel "insulted and degraded in [the] eyes of its subjects," and that it was indispensable to make "the most complete reparation."[211] Upon Bentinck's recommendation, the Government apologized to Purniah for Ogg's improper conduct and requested him to reinstate Madha Rao in his former office.[212] The Government also expressed its displeasure by removing Lieutenant-Colonel Ogg from his command in Bangalore.[213]

On the Nundydrug affair, the Government reached no conclusion. The Commander-in-Chief alone expressed his opinion, while others preferred to remain silent. The Commander-in-Chief, after the perusal of the proceedings, declared that his alarm of the general conspiracy had been again proved. He accepted Davis and MacDowall's conclusion that the corps were ready to massacre their officers in that night. It "leaves me without the doubt," he stated, "that the detachment of the 18th regiment at Nundydrug were brought up to the last stage of disloyalty, that they were prepared for any extremity and without pretext, or known cause, were ready to renew the scenes of Vellore."[214] The Vellore insurrection, he proceeded to state, then appeared "unusual," but in reality it had inaugurated a "systematic" rebellion. He now called upon the Government to admit the existence of an insidious enemy and take all possible measures to expose and seize him. Cradock went on:

> That there is an enemy, somewhere to the British name, to their very existence in this country, I believe is now acknowledged, and it becomes a sacred duty to detect the demon under whatever shape he may assume. It may be the Mussulman spirit; it may be other causes, in which we ourselves are not without a share . . . it directs all its force to corrupt the native army. . . it attacks our Empire of Opinion, and boldly prophecies the English downfall . . .
> . . . Whoever are the emissaries throughout the country whether foreign, or domestic, their origin should be traced, they should be watched, or taken up. I would throw aside reserve, or delicacy; for such hesitations, after the late rude assault, will not heal the wounded ascendancy of the British name.[215]

Bentinck refrained from making any comments. Later on, he denied the alleged plot and asserted "the alarm as groundless and the appearances of danger as insufficient to justify the conduct of the commanding officer."[216] Bentinck's assessment was largely conditioned by Purniah's and Wilk's views.[217] Purniah was quite cynical of the officers' proofs of conspiracy. He stated that the so-called evidences were "swaggerings of bang smokers [rather] than any serious conspiracy."[218] Wilks maintained that the officers' alarm was really due to their "gross ignorance of the manners, the customs and the forms of expressions of the Natives."[219]

Quite ironically, the Supreme Government found an "actual formation of a plot for the destruction of the European officers at Nundydrug." However, it did not attribute it to a general conspiracy, rather to the nature of the men who composed the battalion—that they were Mysoreans and who had actually fought against the British in the Mysore wars.[220]

The Nundydrug and Bangalore affairs were grossly exaggerated among the British officers. They were whipped up as the intelligence passed from one station to another. Lieutenant-Colonel Dyce's letters to James Welsh, who had just become a major, could be perhaps taken as a sample. He writes:

A horried conspiracy at Nundydrug of 5 companies of the 18th reg. has been detected in which the com.n.[commissioned] officers were the ringleaders. They intended perpetuating the horrors of Vellore, but the arrival of Colonel Davis with two squadrons from Bangalore saved the officers.[221]

From the various important and authentic manner which came out in clear evidence at the enquiry into the plot at Nundydrug the most serious and well grounded apprehensions may be entertained of the fidelity of our n.[ative] army in general. It would appear that all the n.o. [non-commissioned officers] except one subidar and nearly the whole of the 5th (sic) companies[222] at that place (Hindoos and Pariars as well as Mussalmen) had engaged in the conspiracy under the direction and instigation of fackir's (sic) from the north of India, many of who are spread all over the country promoting the same cause, the accomplishment of a prophecy foretelling the total extirpation of the Europeans from India in this year.

. . . on the eve of . . . [this] taking place at Nundydrug, the other 5 companies at Bangalore completely deceived Lt. Col. Ogg by their respectful behaviour and appearance of *happiness* and *content*

among them, and he wrote to Headquarters to say he had no
suspicions of the loyalty of his people, but *these very men had then
sworn to support the insurgents at Nundydrug by a similar
conspiracy at Bangalore.*

The n.o. [non-commissioned officers] were the leaders and first
conspirators.

The plan is supposed to have been traced in (sic) Holkar's camp
and to include the Nizam's brothers, Tippoo's sons and some
others.

It appears in evidence that the agents were at work six months
before the publication of the code of regulation. Consequently, the
turbans were brought in as auxiliaries and not principles in the
cause.[223]

Such devastatingly alarming letters, packed with profound inaccuracies and
gross exaggerations, had precipitating effects. At least one commanding
officer, Lt. Col. Alexander Baillie, became insane due to strain of fear and
dread.[224]

In consequence of the Nundydrug affair, on the Commander-in-chief's
recommendation, the Government took measures to trace the alleged
emissaries of sedition. It sent out circular letters to magistrates asking them
to "watch with attention" the movements of wandering fakirs, pandarums
and other religious mendicants with the aim of probing into their probable
aims and objectives.[225] The commanding officers too were given similar
notification.[226] The Government also introduced its own brand of fakirs—
spies who were disguised as fakirs—to associate with the suspicious
characters and discover their motives and intentions.[227]

XV

This extreme vigilance triggered the most ludicrous and absurd event of
all the ridiculous episodes of the aftermath. It occurred in the Palamcottah

fort, where James Welsh was still commanding his first battalion of the third regiment. His superior, Lieutenant-Colonel Alexander Dyce, at that time had gone away to the pleasant hills of Kuttallum.

To understand Major Welsh's action, it is essential to trace briefly the immediate prelude. Like many officers, Welsh too had gradually become obsessed with the dread of Muslim conspiracy. In the middle of November, he received from Dyce, the above cited, grossly exaggerated accounts of Nundydrug and Bangalore affairs.[228] Quite naturally the accounts disturbed him. He realized that it was indispensable "to watch over even the Native officers."[229] Consequently, he asked some of his trusted domestic servants to spy on the officers, promising rich rewards if they brought relevant intelligence.[230]

On Sunday, November 16, Major Welsh was informed that "some blood" was found sprinkled "at the church door." Upon observation, it was discovered that there were "two large stains on each side of the threshold and then drops of blood, leaving from them through the railings of one grave and completely round another." Farther than that no stain was found. In the following morning, November 17, Welsh was reported that during last few nights a ghost[231] appeared in the fort demanding whomever it met "bread and water." Welsh insinuated that the blood at the church door and the ghost asking for bread and water were the devices of the seditious emissaries to stir up the mind of the ignorant and superstitious sepoys, and he considered the reports "as a friendly warning of danger."[232]

The next morning, one of Welsh's favourite sepoys, Aitwar Singh, who was under order to proceed to Shivilputore, near Shankarancoil, came to take leave of him. While conversing, Aitwar said:

> Sir, the battalion has been in a state of mutiny. Be on your guard. If
> I stay [here] I should die near you. If the Gentlemen introduce this

turban again in the battalion or any way do any oppressive act, they will kill all the Gentlemen.[233]

In Aitwar Singh's remarks, Welsh saw not a sentimental expression, but an affectionate hint of an impending disaster. He took no note of the "if", but simply concluded that the battalion was in "a state of mutiny."

After sending away Aitwar Singh, Welsh waited on George Stratton, the magistrate. While conversing, Stratton placed in Welsh's hand the circular letter which he had just received from the Government, warning him against religious mendicants. Welsh's fear of emissaries now appeared well grounded.[234]

That evening, at the parade, the sepoys appeared extremely "inattentive and careless in their movements." "They seemed," according to one of the officers, Lieutenant Ralph Gore, "as if they were all drunk."[235] The officers interpreted the sepoys' inattentiveness as prelude to mischief, and it increased their "uneasiness" during that night.[236]

In the following morning when Major Welsh was at the breakfast table with Captain George John Pepper, his wife whispered to him that their butler had discovered a plot to murder them all in ten days. All the Muslims were involved in it, and if they suspected that their plot had been leaked, she added, the conspirators would perpetrate it at once. She further stated that Tymann Tindal, one of Welsh's favourites, and their boy Ramaswamy were also party to the plot.[237] In the butler's evidence, Welsh saw "an undeniable proof of a conspiracy."[238] While they were eating, they felt that they were being "narrowly watched."[239] Their boy Ramaswamy "disappeared for some time," and then returned while they were still at breakfast." This further confirmed their apprehension.[240] Having nervously taken breakfast, Welsh and Pepper hurried to magistrate Stratton's place. There they were joined by some senior officers who had been summoned. They immediately began to discuss the measures they ought to take in order to avert the impending blow. But fearing that they might be overheard, they moved to Deputy Commercial Registrar Robert Douglas' quarters, as they felt it to be "a more private place." While they moved from one place to another, it appeared to their jaundiced eyes that "the eyes of all" were upon them. They became fully convinced of their precarious and desperate situation. "This combination of circumstances," Welsh stated later, "left not a doubt in my mind as to the *immediate* danger."[241]

In the consultation, Welsh manifested tremendous magnanimity and heroism. He proposed that all the twenty Europeans who were in Palamcottah should immediately quit the station and ensure their safety, but he would "remain with his corps and let things take their course." But the magistrate Stratton and the Collector James Hepburn objected to the idea asserting that the battalion could and should be surprised and disarmed. They contended that since the insurrection was to take place in ten days, "at least a great proportion of the corps must be ignorant of it;" therefore with safety, it could be attempted. Consequently, Welsh acquiesced to their proposal.[242]

Having agreed to disarm the battalion, the officers decided to execute it promptly. Immediately, they decided to detach Sheikh Hyder Subadar[243] and Muhammad Essack Havildar Major, whom they suspected as ringleaders, from the battalion. Welsh sent for these two men and ordered them to go to the magistrate's office in Tinevelly to give evidence on the death of a sepoy who had been poisoned by his wife a few days earlier. Sheikh Hyder and Muhammad Essack "seemed much flurred (sic) but assented."[244] However, they did not leave the fort immediately but lingered a while.[245] While they were still in the fort, Welsh dispatched an express to Dyce informing him of the discovery of the plot and his resolve to defeat it or to perish in the attempt.[246]

As soon as the officers observed that Sheikh Hyder and Muhammad Essack had left the fort, they, having armed themselves, marched to the sepoy barracks. The time was near eleven o' clock, and the sun was getting hotter. At the barracks, Welsh made the drummer beat "the long roll," and as the Indian officers and the sepoys came running, he ordered them to deposite their arms in a corner and line up. Having lined them up, Welsh told the sepoys, that treason was in the corps, and he had come down "to put it to the test," and he and his lieutenants were ready to sell their lives "dearly if necessary." Obviously, the sepoys were flabbergasted. He then marched the dumbfounded corps to the general parade, keeping all the Indian officers ahead and "beating the long roll all the way." At this time, to the British officers' astonishment, Sheikh Hyder and Muhammad Essack appeared in the distance. However, without losing his manliness, Welsh commanded them simply to join the corps. He then ordered everyone except the Muslims "to fall out and form in front," and gave some of them loaded arms. Welsh then turned to the Muslim sepoys and said, "By the blessing of God, I hope I have defeated a plot to murder me and their European officers . . . I found it absolutely necessary for my own safety to disarm you all until the business is investigated." Having said this, Welsh marched the Muslim officers to his quarters, and confined them all in one of his rooms, putting sentries over the door. Meanwhile, some Hindu sepoys, under British officers' command, went and took possession of the gates. Returning from his quarters, Welsh gathered all the Muslim sepoys and marched them out of the fort.[247]

The afternoon wore on without any ostensible disturbance. The expelled Muslim sepoys, who numbered about four hundred and fifty quietly returned home or dispersed into the neighbouring villages. The Hindu sepoys who were inside were quite naturally elated by the apparent confidence which their commanding officer had placed in them. However, in their fidelity, too, the officers entertained "strong suspicion."[248]

Later on, in the evening, the defending force was strengthened by the arrival of the collector's peons. After that addition, there were about five hundred men in the fort. Among them only a hundred and fifty were given arms.[249]

Towards the evening Major Welsh dispatched two expresses, one to Trichinopoly and another to Madura imploring immediate assistance. To the commandant in Trichinopoly, Alexander Campbell, he wrote, "I have now with a handful of men quiet possession of the garrison. . . We look for immediate succor and shall defend our present position with our lives."[250] To Captain John Lindsay, the commanding officer in Madura, he wrote, "I am at a loss what steps to take in this insulated (sic) [isolated] situation . . . A wife and child are with me, and God alone must direct my steps right."[251] In the same evening, Welsh sent "a small guard" towards Kuttallum to meet Lientenant-Colonel Dyce, whose return was anxiously awaited, and escort him back to Palamcottah.[252]

At sunset, Welsh divided the Indian officers, who were in confinement, into two groups and placed one party in the godown and another in the general store for the night. Not unnaturally the Indian officers were rudely shocked by the day's events. They neither could understand nor explain their officers' behaviour. Alas, the phantom of Christianity alone arose before them. "After the Native officers were removed from my house to the general stores," Welsh stated later, "they assured Captains Wilson and Pepper and myself that they were ready to embrace our religion . . . topics and crosses to *convince us of their fidelity* !!!"[253]

XVI

During the night, Welsh brooded over the general situation. As he brooded, it appeared that the situation was extremely menacing. In his wild imagination, he saw the Vellore ghost not only in Palamcottah but in many other garrisons throughout the Coast. The plot in his garrison, he thought, was only part of the general Muslim conspiracy.

Early in the morning, he shared his alarm with his countrymen. They too thought the situation was desperate. With their consent, he sent a request, couched in graphic language, to Colombo, across the Manor Strait, for immediate assistance. "By a miraculous effort," he began his letter to Sir Thomas Maitland:

> We have discovered and quelled a mutiny at this place. An express has been sent off to Trichinopoly, but from the nature of a plot understood to be in great forwardness all over the Coast, we think it absolutely necessary to apply to you for immediate succor by Tutacoryn. A few companies of Europeans for a rallying point, at this period, may prove the means of saving the Company's territories all over the Coast. . . all Mussalmen are concerned in this plot . . . A European succor alone can complete the work which under Providence we have so fortunately begun.
> . . . we will sell our lives most dearly before any force shall conquer us. . . we have four ladies in the house with us. . . Col. Dyce commands this district if alive, and will be here tomorrow. We keep possession of this fort, but rely only on our citadel, a large house.[254]

Welsh sent this letter to John Baggot, the master intendant of Tuticorin, to be transmitted to Ceylon. The covering letter to Baggot was equally or more sensational and electrifying. "Send off this immediately as you value life," he wrote. "God has done wonders by our weak hands. . . Hundreds of pagodas will be paid for a conveyance if a cheap one cannot be procured . . .," he added.[255] According to the instruction, Baggot immediately dispatched the letter with an express boat at the cost of three hundred star pagodas.[256]

The same morning, hearing that a fakir who lived in Palamcottah had left for Quilon, Major Welsh sent an express to Lieutenant-Colonel Robert

M. Grant, commandant of that station, asking him to disarm his corps promptly. "We have discovered and defeated a plot of Moormen to murder us all," Welsh wrote, "and you may rely on the same fate intended you." ". . . do not rely on appearances. They are certainly false," he warned. "I know that agents are gone your way . . . the followers of the False Prophet are unanimously corrupted," he added.[257]

After dispatching these desperate letters, Welsh and a few other officers, constituting themselves a committee, proceeded to elicit information, which could be construed to substantiate the alleged plot. Among the witnesses who came forward two alone deposed something which could claim to have any reference to plot or hostile intention against the British.[258] The first evidence was that of Welsh's boy Ramaswamy. He stated that four or five nights ago while returning home he overheard some sepoys say, ". . . the French would give double pay . . . it would be well to kill the White people . . ."[259] The second evidence was that of Welsh's butler, Iyen Permaul. It was primarily on his evidence that the corps were disarmed. Therefore, it is appropriate to cite the deposition at length. "Two or three days ago," Permaul began:

> Mr. Welsh gave me orders . . . that if I would bring the news in the village, my master would give me a handsome reward. Having heard that the Mussalmen were consulting together, I accordingly, on the 18th November, went secretly to the place where the fackir lived, who come from Vellore[260], having taken off my clothes and put on the resemblance of a beggar. Hyder Sahib Subadar first came to him, sat down and said as follows: '. . . I received a letter from the South. The White men will be all destroyed (or as literal as possible be spoilt) in ten days. . . We are now to receive double pay, and a letter has been written and received from the French, Mogul, and Nawab and other people to kill the Gentlemen in ten days. He then sent for three subadars and mentioned it to them.

They said let it be so. The Major Havildar came last. He told him the same. . . I will in ten days gather all the Mussalmen and kill the gentlemen. Saying this they separated after agreeing to meet the next morning. I came to the lady who gives me victuals and told her this. Besides this I know no more.[261]

Permaul further stated that the conversation took place in Tamil, not in Hindustani, which he understood very little. He also said that he suspected Tindal Tymann and Ramaswamy because they seemed to be Subadar Sheikh Hyder's "great friends."[262]

In the court, many testified, and Permaul admitted, that just two days earlier he had beaten a fakir, and consequently he had a bitter quarrel with Subadar Sheikh Hyder and several other Muslims, who threatened to beat him up.[263] Permaul however asserted that the fakir whom he had beaten was different from the one with whom Sheikh Hyder held the alleged conversation.[264]

The committee also reissued the proclamation promising a reward of Rs.1,750 to any who would give proof of or evidence to the alleged conspiracy. But none came forward with any intelligence.[265] Only some "anonymous letters" were thrown in the fort stating that "disastrous changes" were "about to take place," and alleging that Ramalinga Mudaliyar, a leading local inhabitant, and the Dewan of Travancore were "parties in the conspiracy."[266]

In the following morning, November 21, Lieutenant-Colonel Alexander Dyce arrived at Palamcottah. He found "the garrison in a state of the greatest alarm and consternation."[267] Upon Welsh's word, Dyce implicitly accepted the existence of conspiracy.[268] He therefore felt that it was his "primary duty" to ensure the safety of the Europeans and the fort. He too suspected the fidelity of the Hindu sepoys, who were within the fort. Consequently, Dyce decided to instill and cement the loyalty that might be in the Hindu breasts. He ordered the Hindu sepoys to the general parade and harangued them stating that he had returned to Palamcottah "expressly to support the authority of the English Government, or to perish in the attempt," and challenged them to follow his example by stepping forward to "take an oath of allegiance to the British Government under the colours." The response was unanimous and most enthusiastic. At once the oath of fidelity was administered to all according to the forms of their respective sects. To deepen their apparent loyalty, Dyce immediately, on the spot, promoted five to rank of subadar, another five to that of jamadar, twenty-five to that of havildar and another twenty-five to that of naique. These promotions produced the calculated effect. After the general salute, the men themselves "voluntarily gave three cheers."[269]

In one respect, the parade and the oath-taking ceremony had an adverse effect. That is, when the Muslim sepoys, who were outside the fort, heard of the ceremony, they concluded "that the Hindoos had renounced the faith and the worship of their forefathers."[270]

Despite the positive manifestation of loyalty by the Hindu sepoys, Dyce's apprehension did not cease. That evening about seven o' clock at the report of some "inflammatory exclamations" by the Muslim officers who were still in confinement, he put them all in irons though Welsh and some other officers objected to such a measure.[271] They remonstrated saying that if necessary they would blow some of them from the mouth of gun but would not consent to humiliate the gallant fellows whom they had often led into heroic actions.[272]

Dyce's apprehensions, however, did not remain long. The moment he paused to reason his fear melted away. His investigation into Welsh's evidences indicated that they were spurious and of "doubtful veracity."[273] He wrote to Alexander Campbell on November 22, "Our danger in the present posture is not so immediate as I imagined on my arrival yesterday."[274] Dyce's fear was also decreased by the assurances given by some leading and wealthy people. ". . . a most loyal and satisfactory address has been made to Mr. Stratton and myself," Dyce reported, "by all the principal and wealthy inhabitants of Tinnevelly and neighbouring districts strongly pressive (sic) of their attachment to the British Government for the protection it affords to their religion, their persons and their property."[275] They also denied the existence of any conspiracy among the troops.[276]

Whether there was a plot or not, the battalion has been treated as if it had conspired against and thirsted after its officers' blood. The act had been done, the clock could not be put back. It only remained for the truth to be investigated and exposed. If guilty, the corps had to be punished; if innocent, the author of humiliation had to be brought to condign punishment.

XVII

Major Welsh's dispatch to Lieutenant-Colonel Grant reached Quilon in the evening of November 21.[277] In Quilon, at that time, a detachment of the Travancore subsidiary force, consisting of two battalions of Indian infantry and a small company of British artillery, was stationed.[278] As soon as Grant received the intelligence, he summoned his senior officers, disclosed the unexpected and shocking news and "requested their advise (sic) and assistance as to the line [of] conduct that ought to be pursued."[279] At the consultation, the officers decided to adopt immediately some temporary measures to prevent surprise assault in the night. An alarm post was installed, where the officers, artillery men and two companies of trusty sepoys were lodged. Guns were planted against the sepoys' barracks and their huts, and a captain and six subalterns took charge of them. A party of picked Hindu sepoys, under a British officer, took charge of the magazine.[280] Apparently, these precautionary measures made no effect upon the unsuspecting troops. These measures, wrote S. McDowall to James Welsh, "seemed to create no alarm nor did the motive seem to be understood."[281]

The Indian troops went to bed as usual. The night passed away without any distraction. However, in the morning despite the peace and tranquility, the British officers met together and decided unanimously to disarm the corps. In the afternoon, they ordered the battalions to proceed to the artillery barracks company by company and surrender their "side arms and pouches of ammunition." The sepoys obeyed "without a murmur."[282] Subsequently, Grant assembled the Indian officers, explained to them the intelligence he had received from Palamcottah, observing that he had "entire confidence in their fidelity," and if there were any disaffected among the sepoys, they must be indeed "very few." He then as an expression of his confidence assigned them "a station along with the European officers at the alarm post." The Indian officers appeared quite pleased with this "apparent mark of trust and professed their fidelity warmly." However, at the same time Grant gave "secret instructions to the captain of the day to secure them on any alarm."[283]

On the following day, November 23, Grant issued a proclamation offering a reward of five hundred star pagodas "for the discovery of emissaries or any disaffected persons." Curiously enough, no one came to claim the reward.[284] In this state of suspicion and caution, the garrison remained till November 25, when a recommendation to rearm the corps arrived from Palamcottah.[285]

Major James Welsh's cry for help was promptly answered from Trichinopoly and Ceylon. From Madura, Welsh received no assistance as the resources there was scare and also the commanding officer, Captain John Lindsay, suspected the fidelity of his own corps.[286] In Trichinopoly, Alexander Campbell received the express on November 21. That very night, he dispatched a detachment of the sixth regiment Indian cavalry, two hundred and fifty strong, under Lieutenant Smith's command.[287] Ironically after sending it, Campbell lamented that the whole detachment was comprised of Muslims and it might defect.[288] Furthermore, on the following day, November 22, "after the most mature reflection," Campbell decided to dispatch a strong force to Madura to intimidate the poligars, who might be tempted to take advantage of any disturbance in Palamcottah. From Madura, Campbell felt, it could be moved any direction as Welsh or Dyce might think necessary.[289] Consequently, the first battalion of the fourth regiment, the light company of His Majesty's 69th Regiment and a detail of artillery left Trichinopoly in the morning of November 23.[290]

While sending these troops, Campbell, perhaps knowing the person, feared that Welsh might have misjudged the situation and taken an injudicious measure. Soon after receiving Welsh's message on Novemember 21, he wrote, "I fear he has been precipitate. But I cannot judge correctly."[291] On the following day, he wrote to Dyce urging him to use his judgement and discretion, and if necessary even to disavow Welsh's action though it might be "repugnant to your private feelings."[292]

Major Welsh's alarm reached Colombo in the forenoon of November 23.[293] As on the previous occasion, Governor Maitland responded promptly and with alacrity. He dispatched a detachment of picked men,[294] under Captain Mercer, to Tuticorin and ordered another to Jaffna.[295] The latter was done with a view to transport that detachment to any part of the Coast without loss of time in case another request should come.[296]

Maitland's assistance was prompt, vigorous and commendable, but most uncharitably, he did not stop there. With no fewer promptitude, Maitland chartered the *Brig Ariel* and sent off Welsh's two letters (to Baggot and to himself) to William Windham, the Colonial Secretary. In his covering letter, Maitland wrote:

> I have great disinclination to send to England accounts of an
> alarming tendency, without being more thoroughly informed on

the subject than I am at present but. . . I think there is quite sufficient grounds for adopting the measure I have taken. . . The nature of the information is of sufficient magnitude to warrant the measure. . .

Enclosed you will find the two documents [for] which I have sent the *Brig Ariel,* and that you be thoroughly apprized of the exact character and description of the situation in which things stand as far as I myself know them. I send you the originals as I received them, inaccurate no doubt and evidently written under the pressure of the trying situation in which Major Welsh is placed but perfectly descriptive of his situation and leading to the supposition that it is not partial and a general feeling and a general conspiracy against His Majesty's Government in India . . . I shall be most happy indeed if this reaches you in time to prevent by the wisdom of His Majesty's ministers the fatal effects that I fear are to justly to be apprehended from the actual state of things on the continent of India. It may be proper to add . . . a similar conspiracy was discovered and for the time quelled at Nundydroog since the original one at Vellore.

The only further information I can give you upon the subject is that I understand Major Welsh to be an officer of considerable reputation and character.[297]

In a private letter on the same day, Maitland noted:

. . . of course you will perceive that we have no positive data to go on with regard to the actual extent of this new insurrection . . . but we certainly have grounds sufficient to ascertain that the late spirit of rebellion is still in full vigor, which in itself I apprehend to be of infinite more importance than any detail with regard to its immediate extent or effects . . . [298]

After transmitting "the panic, yet warm and with all the exaggeration" to England, Maitlland made no effort to verify the accuracy of the account which he had dispatched. He also did not inform the Madras Government of his dispatch to England, a common courtesy required at all time.[299]

XVIII

On November 24, from Colonel Alexander Campbell, the Madras Government received the intelligence of the Palamcottah affair. The limited information the report furnished was too meagre to draw any conclusion. However, from the previous experiences, the Government rightly suspected that the report must be grossly exaggerated. With good reason, it condemned Welsh's measure in "separating the Mussalman from the Hindoo troops" as "highly injudicious." The Government merely observed that unless Major Welsh furnished "grounds of the strongest necessity" for his action, he would "incur His Lordship's dissatisfaction."[300]

While the Government was awaiting for further information in anger and suspense, intelligence arrived from Quilon. It stated that Lieutenant-Colonel Grant disarmed his two battalions merely on the recommendation of James Welsh, though there was no ostensible cause for suspicion in Quilon. Such an intelligence was even too much for the Commander-in-Chief. "I conceive," John Cradock commented:

> I only anticipate the indignation of Government when I call their attention to the communication from Quilon . . . that Lieutenant-Colonel Grant. . . without other foundation than the knowledge of the occurrence at Palamcottah. . . disarms the two battalions under his command. It will scarcely believe that this officer, on the same day, writes to the Adjutant-General that upon hearing of the circumstances at Palamcottah, he had taken the common precautions, but had the pleasure to feel that no symptom of disaffection had appeared.[301]

On his own initiative Cradock ordered Grant's removal. Grant was asked to resign his command immediately to the next senior officer and proceed to the Presidency "to answer for his conduct."[302]

The Quilon-Palamcottah affair deeply impressed the Commander-in-Chief. He rightly felt that there was a deep suspicion "in the breast of almost every officer towards the Native troops." ". . . all the course [of] late events," he observed, "too fully proves the persuasion." The precipitous suspicion was "better disguised by some than others." If the trend continued, he feared, "the most respected class" of the army would be alienated. Therefore, he resolved "to recall the military mind," risk suspicion, and apprehension, and make it "a point of honor."[303] To that end, on December 2, Cradock issued a circular letter to the commanding officers asking them to eschew "the belief of latent treachery," refrain from admitting vague and malicious reports and show "manliness" in their conduct.[304]

The Government was enraged when fuller reports arrived from Palamcottah and Quilon. It flatly stated that "Major Welsh was not justified in the measures which he ordered," and commanded that he too should proceed to the Presidency to answer for his conduct. Immediate order was also sent for the rearmament and incorporation of the Muslim troops.[305] Furthermore, in addition to confirming the Commander-in-Chief's action towards Lieutenant-Colonel Grant, the Government apologized to the troops in Quilon.[306]

Even prior to the arrival of the Government's formal order, the work of redress had commenced at Campbell's initiative. However, it was done with extreme clumsiness. In Pallamcottah, Dyce took more than a week to incorporate the Muslim sepoys. Despite the humiliation they had suffered, the sepoys with few exceptions behaved amazingly well.[307] "They have committed no sort of irregularity," Dyce reported, "and profess implicit obedience to anything short of abjuring their religion and wearing hats." "The commissioned native officers in confinement," he added, "make the same declaration of loyalty." "But they have all asserted," he further added, "if it is absolutely required of them that they will embrace Christianity and eat our food."[308] The phantom of Christianity indeed still lurked behind them. After incorporating them, Dyce marched the battalion off to Sankarancoil en route to Trichinopoly. Its place was taken by the first battalion on the fourth regiment which had just come from Trichinopoly to Madura.[309]

In Quilon the restoration began in the evening of November 25. About five o' clock, Grant received a letter from Dyce instructing him to rearm the corps if he had disarmed them merely on the basis of Welsh's letter, "*without* any proof, direct or presumptive, of treason or disaffection in the corps."[310] Consequently, Grant rearmed the troops that very evening, but he retained the steps adopted in the first evening for the night. On the following day, Grant ordered the troops to take the oath of fidelity. He then issued a garrison order expressing his regret for suspecting their fidelity and assuring them of his full confidence in them.[311]

Grant received the intelligence of the Government's displeasure in the second week of December. Consequently, he resigned his command and proceeded to Madras. About the same time, Lieutenant-Colonel Colin Macaulay, the Resident in Travancore, received a draft of the Government's proposed apology to the troop. On December 18, at the evening parade, the apology was read to the troops in Tamil and Hindustani. The troops had the pleasure of knowing that the author of their humiliation was not spared.[312]

During the months of February and March, 1807, Major Welsh and Lieutenant-Colonel Grant were court-martialed. Three charges were proffered against Welsh and two against Grant. Welsh was accused of disarming the troops "without any justifiable cause," expelling the Muslim sepoys merely on "a vague suspicion," and sending alarming letters without foundation.[313] "Unofficerlike" conduct in disarming the corps without previous investigation and "conduct highly disreputable to the military

170

character and injurious to the public interests" in humiliating the troops were the charges against Grant.[314]

Welsh and Grant quite naturally pleaded not guilty. Welsh's defence was extremely well written and logically argued, however spurious and faulty his evidences and assumptions might have been. Banking on the prelude to Vellore, Welsh noted that in no plot was it possible to arrive at positive evidence. In Palamcottah, Welsh declared there were adequate circumstantial and presumptive evidences to convince that "a dangerous conspiracy" indeed existed. Thus, having detected the conspiracy, Welsh asserted, he resorted to the only measure that was humanly possible to prevent the slaughter. ". . . having before me never-to-be forgotten instance and proof written in blood of the fatal consequence of reposing in such false security," he declared, "I was determined to do all that lay in my power to avert the blow, which I [was] convinced (and in which conviction I shall continue to my dying hour)[315] from the evidence [I] possessed, was impending over us." He further pleaded that an officer in his position was in an unenviable dilemma:

> . . . He is censured if he acts without the most positive proofs . . . and if he neglects the information conveyed to him and in the sequel it be found correct, he is equally liable to be called to account and is answerable for all the lives he might have saved by timely exertions. [316]

Welsh then went on to say that having taken the initial precautionary measures, he merely proceeded to ask for assistance and informed the officer in the neighbouring garrison of his own danger, for which he had substantial reason.

Grant defended himself by emphasizing the myth of Muslim conspiracy. The Vellore insurrection was not "a solitary instance," he observed.

> The infection had spread . . . a great part of the native army . . .
> contaminated . . . The timely discovery of the plots of the
> disaffected, prevented a repetition of massacre and bloodshed at
> Hydrabad, at Wallajabad, at Bangalore and at Nundydroog, and
> the conspiracy at the latter place was conducted with all the
> secrecy that distinguished the one at Vellore.

That being so, Grant argued, no importance could be attached to external appearance. ". . . treachery," he snapped, "does not walk openly and in the face of the day." Therefore, when a responsible officer warned him that his corps were meditating massacre, he took the only measure a prudent man would take. With the consent of all his senior officers, he declared, he disarmed the corps only to prevent them from doing mischief. Moreover, Grant argued that the disarmament did not humiliate the corps. Very blatantly, he flatly stated that the Indian soldiers had no feelings at all to be hurt.

> To those fine feelings, that regulate the conduct of the Gentlemen I
> am now addressing to that of pride of character. . . that nice and
> delicate sense of honor and that acuteness of sensibility, which
> make the disgrace of acting or of thinking ill more terrible than
> death, they are altogether strangers.

Therefore, he concluded very ingenuously, "Little mischief there was likely to arise from the measure of disarming the troops, whilst everything was to be apprehended from their enthusiasm."[317]

The court-martial found Welsh's and Grant's defences satisfactory and honourably acquitted them.[318] But the Government found the court's decision irksome. Bentinck, particularly, felt that the court acted injudiciously. He observed that "the only possible inference that can now be drawn from the marked and unqualified terms of acquittal is, that the sepoys were justly distrusted and disarmed." Such a conclusion Bentinck

172

argued was contrary to facts as well as "pregnant with the greatest political mischief." Though Bentinck found the decision mischievous, he yielded to it; however, he recommended that a general order must be issued to express Government's dissatisfaction at the officers' conduct.[319] The other members, including the Commander-in-Chief, approved the President's recommendation. Consequently, on March 20, a general order was published to that end.[320] In its dispatch to the Supreme Government too, the Madras Government expressed the same opinion. "An attentive view of the proceedings," it observed, "may justify a considerable degree of doubt respecting the accuracy of the grounds on which the decision of the court-martial has been founded."[321]

XIX

While the Palamcottah-Quilon agitations were still a fresh, intelligence of further disaffection arrived. It was stated that the corps in Wallajabhad were on the verge of mutiny. At this time Wallajabhad was garrisoned by the remainder of the first regiment and the first battalion of the sixth regiment. The latter had just come from Masulipatam, and it had a large number of low caste Hindus and Christians.[322]

It all began when a maid-servant informed Captain William Oliver that "something of a very serious nature" would occur after the pay day on December 1, and "that already some families have left the cantonment," a sure prelude to insurrection.[323] Consequently, Captain Robert Hughes, another officer, employed Muhammad Gullop Naique, whom he had befriended, with the promise of promotion, to procure "intelligence of what was going forward." After two days, Muhammad Gullop Naique returned with Sheikh Nutter, whom he alleged to have won over from the conspirators' camp of the sixth regiment. Sheikh Nutter told the officers that "the whole [the first of the sixth] were concerned and . . . an attempt to secure one would be a signal of revolt to the whole." However, he added

173

that the conspirators had not formalized any definite plans, but they were anxious about the forthcoming departure of the first regiment.[324]

This intelligence horrified the officers. They immediately deputed Major Joseph Hazlewood, commanding officer of the second battalion of the first regiment, to present their situation to the Commander-in-Chief and ask his advice. Hazlewood arrived at the Presidency on December 2.

After briefing the Commander-in-Chief, Hazlewood proceeded to air his views. The first battalion of the sixth regiment, he stated, has been induced to believe that it was brought down to Wallajabad in order to be made Christians as it was largely composed of low caste men. For that reason, he added it had become "entirely disaffected and ready to break out." Hazlewood attributed the agitation to what he described as "Mussalman principles and interests," and stated that the Hindus would join "the strongest party." On behalf of the Wallajabhad officers, he pleaded that at least four troops of cavalry should be brought down and stationed near Cavery Pauk, which is quite near Wallajabhad. That, he suggested, would facilitate the conspiracy to reach maturity and then allow the officers to trap the plotters without endangering their lives.[325]

During that afternoon, the Commander-in-Chief presented Hazlewood's report to the Board. The Board felt that the question was extremely delicate. An attempt to move in the cavalry to save the lives of British officers might endanger the *rapprochement* which the Government was strenuously striving to build, whereas holding off the cavalry might result in the sacrifice of their lives which in turn would annihilate all *rapprochements* once and for all. The choice was indeed painful. Quite naturally the Board found it impossible to arrive at a decision immediately. Consequently, the Board decided to adjourn until six o' clock in the same evening.[326]

At the appointed time, the Board reconvened and began its deliberation.

Strangely enough at this moment Bentinck lost his balance. He recommended that a detachment of British and Indian cavalry should be moved from Arcot to Wallajabhad, and that, he said, would at least "secure the lives of European officers."[327] Quite unexpectedly, Cradock now rose to the occasion. Such a measure, Cradock stated, would "inevitably overthrow the system of confidence," they were striving to achieve. He proceeded to state that the general interest of the army should be paramount. "I will overlook individual safety," he declared, "in the higher principle of avoiding the chance of mistake, and by this false step produce a general alienation of the native mind."[328] Petrie struck a similar note. "Lives, I fear," he declared, "must be risked," but probable partial evil must be met in order one, which may shake the firmest pillar of our Indian dominion." ". . . the assemblage of a coercive European force," Petrie argued, would give "complete confirmation" to the allegations "of our intentions to trample on their religion, to erect our churches on the ruins of their temples, and to make them converts by force to the Christian faith." Moreover, Petrie went a step further. He denied that the situation called for a coercive action. "From Wallajabhad," Petrie declared:

> I do not think the evidence before us, as to the disaffection of the native troops in that cantonment, will at this time justify the coercion, and direct interference of a European force. I may ask what are the overt acts of disobedience or mutiny which the Europeans are to coerce? There are none avowed, no direct mutiny or actual rebellion.

After observing that there was nothing more than reports of overheard conversations of hostile nature, he proceeded to state:

> The dread of the officers is natural, for what man will not dread the midnight assassin? But while under that apprehension his mind is not so capable of exerting its faculties and separating truth

from falsehood, reality from supposition and every object is then seen under a false and delusive medium. I am convinced that a vexatious search has often produced the disaffection which did not exist before.[329]

Oakes too opted for caution against coercion. He suggested that the present disorders could be better remedied by a public declaration of Government's policy of religious tolerance and protection of local usages and prejudices, rather than military coercion.[330]

Happily, in the multitude of councilors there was safety. The Board struck a compromise. It immediately sent Lieutenant-Colonel John Munro, the Quarter-Master General to Wallajabhad to investigate the alleged disaffection, empowering him to summon the cavalry at his discretion.[331] At the same time the Government decided to issue a general proclamation disavowing its intention to pollute the caste or convert Indians "by forcible means to Christianity," but pledging itself to show respect to and give protection "for their religion and for their customs."[332] The proclamation was issued on the following day, December 3.

Lieutenant-Colonel John Munro arrived at Wallajabhad in the same morning. By then some of the companies of the first regiment had already left the station on their march to Masulipatam. Munro spent that day and the next three days investigating the alleged disaffection.[333]

The investigation revealed that the alleged disaffection was "considerably exaggerated" and the troops were generally "well affected to the service." Munro secretly and separately interviewed several persons, including Sheikh Nutter and the two brothers of the maid-servant, who had given her intelligence.[334] Among all the evidences, Sheikh Nutter's and the two brothers' were the crucial ones. Sheikh Nutter stated that the disaffected ones were not more than seventy,[335] and they were all "the worst characters in the corps." They had not yet formulated any plans, and "their meetings and debates took place at night (in the mullah), and frequently after they had intoxicated themselves with arrack or bang." He further added that "the battalion was in general ignorant of it." The two brothers noted that they were informed of the intended mutiny by Subadar Muhammad Isuf, whom they described as much attached to the British service. But further investigation indicated that the two brothers' description of Muhammad Isuf was incorrect and that he was inimical to British interests.[336]

Munro's report came as a great relief to the anxious Government. It had every reason to be thankful that it did not succumb to Major Hazlewood's panic. By now the fuller reports, which had come from Palamcottah and Quilon, further indicated the obsessive and unfounded nature of the officers' apprehension. With much satisfaction, the Government concluded that the alarm in Wallajabhad too had "no material foundation."[337]

This second Wallajabhad incident was the last row to draw serious attention from responsible men. But the Vellore ghost did not immediately disappear into oblivion. It continued to linger and terrorize some obsessive characters.

XX

In December, 1806, Major Paul Bose, who was stationed at Sankerydrug at that time, suspected the fidelity of his battalion. Back in June, part of his battalion, the second of the fourteenth regiment, had resisted the turban. Ever since the Vellore insurrection, Bose followed his corps with a jaundiced eye, expecting nothing but treason and treachery.

On December 4, 1806, one of Bose's secret agents came to him with a report that a stranger had come from Seringapatam to Jemadar Permaul Naique, the Acting Adjutant, with the message that "the people of the battalions" in that station "were all one." In consequence, Permaul Naique invited many of the Indian officers and sepoys to his home, and the reporter insinuated Permaul Naique must have sworn them secretly into conspiracy.[338] From this report Bose inferred that his battalion was plotting to murder their officers in conjunction with their comrades in Seringapatam. The battalion's disposition appeared to confirm his apprehensive conclusion. ". . . there are a thousand appearances at present existing here," Bose wrote to Campbell on December 7, "which adds great weight to its truth, and which is better perceived than described."[339] He apprehended that the mutiny would not be "very distant from maturity."[340] "I have every reason to believe," he reported to Major-General Fuller a day later, "that migration of sepoys' families are daily taking place, a certain prelude to nefarious intention."[341]

Like James Welsh in Palamcottah, Bose wanted to act immediately and disarm the corps. But, fortunately perhaps, Bose did not possess Welsh's daring audacity. The small British man-power at his disposal, he feared was inadequate to make a bold front. He also considered the alternative of detaching the most suspected men and sending them off. But here again his courage failed him. He apprehended that the men had become more "cautious from the failure of their plots elsewhere and wiser from experience," and hence such a measure would arouse suspicion and accelerate "the mediated atrocities."[342] Therefore, Bose thought that the only alternative was to increase his strength, and then overawe the battalion. "To do this," he wrote to Campbell, "we require some assistance. A hundred European would suffice. Six or seven officers can never attempt it . . . if you can afford us that aid, I shall be thankful."[343]

Fortunately, Campbell received Bose's request just after he had received the Commander-in-Chief's circular letter urging the commanding officers to be cautious and manly. Furthermore, Campbell had limited resources.

Consequently, he did not respond to Bose's pleading favourably. "I feel myself unable to meet your wishes . . . both from my limited means and the sentiments conveyed to me from superior authority," stated Campbell.[344] The Government too did not respond to him favourably when he requested assistance. ". . . the intelligence furnished by Major Bose," the Board observed, "is not sufficient to warrant a belief of any serious disaffection in the corps, or to justify the adoption of any measures which would be calculated to manifest distrust in the loyalty and good conduct of the troops."[345] Therefore, no coercive measure was adopted; and the Vellore ghost disappeared the moment Bose regained his equilibrium. [346]

XXI

Major Joseph Hazlewood was continued to be harassed by the fear of conspiracy. As he marched towards Masulipatam with his battalion, he kept sending reports of "seditious" and "inflammatory" talks portending "a general mutiny" to the Commander-in-Chief and the Government.[347] But neither of them paid any serious attention. Consequently, upon his arrival in Masulipatam, he informed the Government in the strongest language that he possessed information regarding a conspiracy to drive the English into the sea and solicited that he might be permitted to appear and make his deposition before the Governor-in-Council.[348] Hazllewood hinted that "the conspiracy originated in Paris," and proposed that he would establish his allegation by positive evidences and witnesses.[349]

Hazlewood's intelligence however did not create any sensation. Those who had recovered from their obsession, with the Vellore phantom found Hazlewood's assertion merely amusing. Bentinck felt that Hazlewood might have been deranged.[350] Adjutant-General Agnew stated that Hazlewood was trying to make himself a messiah and stigmatized his information as "purchased."[351] T. V. Tod, the acting magistrate in Masulipatam, who had personal knowledge of Hazlewood's dealing with his men considered that he was "very credulous."[352] Nonetheless because of the forcible nature of his representation, the Government ordered him to come to the Presidency with "such evidences as he might require in order to substantiate" his allegation.[353]

Accordingly, Hazlewood, with his witnesses, Captain Robert Hughes, and few Indian officers and sepoys, embarked and arrived in Madras on February 15.[354] Upon his arrival, he submitted three papers for the Government's perusal. In those papers he tried to show that "the spirit of the present conspiracy was originally infused into the minds of the Natives by the emissaries of the French Government who came out with Mons Leger to Pondicherry on the *Bell Poul* frigate." They, he said, "selected pupils for their attachment to the fallen house of Tippu and Chaundah Sahib and instructed them in the mode secretly to promote and spread the conspiracy." It was the French intention, Hazlewood maintained, to cause a general alienation among the people to the British Government and seduce as many as possible to the French. Once that was done, the French would invade India, and with the support of the defected, they would overturn the present political order and re-establish Tipu Sultan's family in Mysore and Chanda Sahib's in the Carnatic under their hegemony. While such a seditious and conspiratorial campaign was in progress, Hazlewood pointed out, unfortunately the late innovations were introduced. Immediately the plotters used them as pretext to seduce those who would not otherwise have succumbed to their villainy. By the end of June and beginning of July, they had succeeded in infusing an alarming degree of defection, and a general rebellion was brewing. At that time, he said, fortunately the insurrection prematurally erupted in Vellore. This insurrection opened "the eyes of the Hindoos to the true cause and to the real extent of conspiracy," and the subsequent revocation of the orders removed the only grievance the Hindus were made to feel. Therefore, the Hindus withdrew from the combination.

This incensed the plotters, who "threw off all disguise" and since then, he observed, were openly preaching sedition against the British Government in the name of Islam. He further added that through his personal remonstrance alone he had won over many Hindus and some Muslims from the conspirators' rank. "These men," he declared, "will prove that my own individual exertions and discernment have prevented an insurrection against this government and against all British authority from breaking out in the Carnatic and probably raging at this hour."[355]

Having perused Hazlewood's sensational papers, the Government appointed a committee of three men—A. Scott, John Malcolm and John Munro—to examine the validity of his assertions.[356] The committee sat from March 3 to 18, listening patiently to what Hazlewood and his witnesses had to say. The information was voluminous, but it was almost wholly frivolous, ambiguous, disconnected, farfetched, and in many cases absurd, having no relevance to the points which Hazlewood purported to establish.[357]

At the end of many days of tedious and wearisome hearing, the committee submitted its report on March 19. The report stated that in all the proceedings, Major Hazlewood "brought no evidence in support of the opinion which he had stated to Government that the French were actually concerned in promoting and keeping up the spirit of discontent and disaffection recently exhibited in the Coast Army."[358] The report conceded that subsequent to the Vellore mutiny part of the battalion which Major Hazlewood commanded manifested "a serious spirit of disaffection and mutiny." But it proceeded to elucidate:

> The committee, however, does not think Major Hazelwood has
> established that this partial disaffection in his corps was the result
> of a general conspiracy or had any general object in its aim. On
> the contrary they think it is fully proved by the evidence brought
> forward by him to have been produced by the operation of the

dangerous influence and intrigues of some Native commissioned
and non-commissioned officers of the corps whose minds appear
to have been in a discontented and irritated state from the
occurrence of the mutiny at Vellore of which there are grounds to
believe some of them had knowledge and were even in some
degree concerned.

The circumstance of the majority of the discontented in Major
Hazlewood's corps being Mahomedans . . . appears to have made
a strong impression on that officer's mind . . . There does not
however appear to the committee the slightest evidence to
substantiate the existence of any regular plan or design on the part
of the disaffected in the corps Major Hazlewood commanded nor is
there any evidence to prove a combination with any other corps in
the service for the purpose of subverting the British authority . .
."359

Having commented on Hazlewood's evidences, the report concluded
with a diagnosis of the author himself:

The committee conceives that Major Hazlewood has been
actuated through this affair by a zealous and conscientious desire.
. . to avert a danger which he conceived threatened the British
interests in India, but they have observed with regret that he has
permitted the belief of a general Mahomedan conspiracy against
the British power to take such positive proofs of its existence
expressions and occurrences which under another temper of mind
would have made little or no impression and to this alone the
committee must ascribe the repeated and urgent representations
which Major Hazlewood had made to Government respecting the
existence of a general and dangerous conspiracy against the
British power which he certainly has not been able to substantiate
by any evidence whatever. . .

The committee . . . feel it a duty to state the opinion they have
formed from the evidence before them that the mode and nature of

their enquiries, the necessary encouragement given to informers and the avowed distrust shewn of the fidelity of the troops were calculated to destroy all confidence and indeed to generate the very danger which it was meant to avert, and they most earnestly hope no extreme will again occur to justify similar proceedings. [360]

The investigation cleared the fog and satisfied perhaps all except Major Hazlewood. As late as the 1830's, he stated that the cause of the agitation was a "real secret," and "up to this hour the Madras Government is in profound ignorance of it, unless Captain Hughes of the first (long dead) revealed it to them." [361]

XXII

During the early part of 1807, there were some rumours of minor political rebellions too. The Vencattegherry and the Calastry Rajahs were alleged to have been making "warlike preparation," but no serious attention was paid. The Governor merely ordered the collector to keep a closer check on them.[362] The *Shevaguna Zemindari* was reported to have been arming himself for rebellion, but an indirect investigation proved the allegation to be spurious.[363] The Resident in Tanjore, William Blackburne, picked up a man as an emissary of sedition carrying treasonable letter to the Rajah of Tanjore but the Government again did not lose its balance. It merely turned him over to the Zillah magistrate for trial.[364]

There were also some civil disturbances, obviously unconnected with the army. In February, a serious riot broke out at Negapatam against the Indian Christians. When the magistrate Elleston Sober went down with his peons to quell the riot, the crowd, of about five thousand, charged against him, intending "to make another Vellore business of it." Sober fled and took shelter in the *kachheri* with his men. However later on, a detachment which came from Tanjore quelled the riot and restored order to the town. It was alleged that the riot was incited by some who were hostile to British

Government.[365]

In April, a young Maratha Brahmin appeared near Pavanasaum in Tinnevelly district calling himself Ram Rajah, claiming to possess supernatural powers and purporting to crown himself in Tinnevelly. He had succeeded in mustering about three hundred followers. About a hundred of them were armed with muskets and others with bamboos. A detachment of sepoys was sent against his party. After a few days of hot pursuit in the hills of Pavanasaum, Ram Rajah was taken captive and his followers were either killed, captured or dispersed.[366] Later on, the captives were put on trial, and some of them, including Ram Rajah were transported to Penang for hard labour.[367] That was the end of Ram Rajah.

Once the agitation subsided, the Government turned its attention to the Vellore prisoners who were still languishing behind bars.[368] In April, the Government handed the civil prisoners, who numbered thirty-five, over to the magistrate of Arnee for trial; [369] and at the same time, it appointed two commissions, one in Vellore and another in Madras,[370] to specify the charge against the individual military prisoners.[371]

In July taking advantage of the new Governor-General Lord Minto's presence in Madras, the Government consulted him on the disposal of the prisoners.[372] Minto inclined to take Bentinck's moderate view. Consequently, with his concurrence, the Government decided to free the prisoners.[373]

Except the four who were implicated in murder the others were dismissed and sent home under guard.[374] A trifling allowance was given to each to meet his travel expence.[375] The commissioned officers, however, were given "a small pension" to save them from "beggary."[376] The four detained prisoners were handed over to the circuit court. They were subsequently tried and acquitted.[377]

Among the civil prisoners, Sied Hussain, son of Sied Guffar, alone was executed, another, Rustum, was transported, and three others were sent to labour on public works.[378] Remaining prisoners were released, including Jemmal-ud-din as he had been promised pardon since "he gave valuable information."[379]

Towards the end of 1807, sometime after the departure of William Bentinck and John Cradock from India, an attempt was made to revive the Vellore ghost. It occurred at Gooty, where the first battalion of the twenty-fifth regiment, formerly the first of the twenty-third, and His Majesty's 34th Regiment were stationed. On November 20, Ramaswamy naique reported to some British officers that about five months ago, on the first anniversary of the first Wallajalbhad alleged insurrection, Ram Singh and four other subadars solicited his assistance in a conspiracy to massacre British soldiers while they would be playing cricket in the nullah. He added that he refused to join the conspirators but made several unsuccessful attempts to report the matter to British officers. Ramaswamy naique also brought forward three witnesses to attest the veracity of his allegation.[380]

The commanding officer immediately put the alleged conspirators under arrest and informed the new Commander-in-Chief, Lieutenant-General Hay MacDowall, of the alleged plot. The Commander-in-Chief at once ordered a court-martial to try the five subadars. The trial disclosed astounding facts. The accuser Ramaswamy was discovered to have been basely motivated to incriminate the subadars, who were perfectly innocent, and he purchased his witnesses assuring them that they would be rewarded as Mustapha Beg had been in Vellore![381] With the Gooty affair the Vellore ghost disappeared from the Coast forever.

Southern Moat

186

CHAPTER SIX
REACTION IN ENGLAND

ON DECEMBER 23, 1806, *THE TIMES* ANNOUNCED, "Yesterday, letters were received at the India House from the East Indies . . . It appears that a very disagreeable affairs occurred at Vellore . . ."[1] All through January and February, *The Times* and several other newspapers carried accounts of the Vellore mutiny with gross exaggeration under the heading "Dreadful Occurrence in India" or similar titles.[2] Some of those accounts were highly inaccurate. In the first report, *The Times* stated that the insurrection was caused by "a quarrel about some women."[3] *The Morning Post* in one of its earliest accounts alleged that the fourteenth and sixteenth battalions were involved in the mutiny.[4] However, some accounts were nearly correct; particularly the extract from a private letter of an officer in India to his friend in Edinburgh, which appeared in many papers. The extract, after giving a detailed account, stated that the disaffection was caused by some disagreeable regulations lately introduced, and that they had been very "wisely" revoked by Lord William Bentinck.[5] Nonetheless rumours of a foreboding nature continued to persist. Some "partial insurrection," it was declared, had also occurred "among the poligars."[6]

These accounts quite naturally shocked all who had an interest in India. "The first account of the mutiny," Major Leith later reported, "occasioned, as I am informed, a sensation which it is difficult to describe."[7] The accounts too met with incredulity. "Nobody believes the accounts which have been received from India," wrote Arthur Wellesley to John Malcolm. He added that "the mind of every man is filled with suspicion and alarm."[8] Sweny Toone, a director, reported to Warren Hastings who was in retirement in his country house, and with whom he was in close contact, "Not [yet] any official account of the Vellore most infamous business. I cannot bring myself to believe it."[9] With the passage of time, as the directors and proprietors of the Company were better informed of the disagreeable orders, they became indignant "against the supposed authors of such an outrage on the prejudices of the Natives."[10]

The official reports of the Vellore insurrection arrived on February 17.[11] One report came from Fort William and another from Fort St. George. The covering letter from the former described the mutiny as "merely local," and stated that the disturbance happily ceased "with the recapture of the fort and the destruction of the perpetrators of this atrocious deed."[12] The latter alleged the mutiny to have "originated in plans of the deepest treachery," but stated that it would reserve its "conclusive judgement" till the Mixed Commission submitted its reports.[13] Both dispatches, which came overland, stated that the related papers would be transmitted by sea at the first opportunity.[14]

In the later part of September, 1806, the Supreme Government dispatched the *Sarah Christina* for the purpose of carrying all relevant papers on the Vellore insurrection to the home authorities. As scheduled, the *Sarah Christina* arrived in Madras on September 29, but due to some unforeseen reason it did not depart for England till October 15.[15] The Madras Government, along with the dispatches, sent Major James Leith,[16] the Judge Advocate-General, for the purpose of better explaining the conditions on the Coast to the interested parties at home.[17]

II

By the time the official reports arrived, the panic that swept through the Coast had already infiltrated England. The Vellore affair was declared to have "deep roots and extensive ramifications." All Muslims, it was suggested, had been alienated from the British Government. The Hindus too, it was insinuated, had become disaffected. Some suggested that the late conquests and annexations were the causes; others, added "too severe exaction of the revenue and the introduction of our courts of justice" were as much a cause as the former.[18] It appeared to many as if the whole of India was on the verge of revolt and the British Empire in the east was on the brink of disaster.

It particularly so appeared as disastrous intelligence had also come from the Continent. Napoleon Bonaparte had crushed Prussia at Jena and humbled Russia at Eylau. It seemed as if England alone was left to face her archenemy France. While her situation in Europe appeared grim, her Empire in the east was no better. It too appeared to be slipping from her grip. Such a loss even by an enemy's action would be grievous, but it would be intolerable if it was ever occasioned by the folly of her own administrators. The proprietors, the directors and the commissioners felt that the Madras Government must be entrusted to abler hands.[19]

On February 24, 1807, the Court of Directors met and deliberated on Vellore. A motion was immediately moved for the recall of the Governor, William Bentinck, and the Commander-in-Chief, John Cradock. However, the motion was not called to question but tabled to be taken up in the ensuing session.[20] The Board of Control indicated to the Court informally that it would approve the Court's recommendation without any hesitation.[21] On March 4, the Court met again, discussed the question of recall, but however deferred its execution until the arrival of the *Sarah Christina* which was then daily expected.[22] The recall, in all probability, was only a

189

matter of time. "I believe," Toone wrote on March 6, "the Court has or will instantly recal (sic) the Governor and [the] Commander-in-Chief of Madras."[23]

The *Sarah Christina*, after a voyage of five months, anchored at Cork on March 16. The dispatches were immediately taken to Chairman William Elphinstone's home. On Monday, March 23, the Court met "for the purpose of reading the dispatches." The Court appeared to have already made up its mind. "But alas," wrote Leith to Bentinck, "I was too late in getting here. I found the public mind preoccupied and fortified with prejudice against any further impression."[24]

On the very same day, perhaps most unfortunately for Bentinck, the *Brig Ariel*, carrying Major Welsh's panic-stricken letters and Maitland's covering letter, arrived. If the Directors needed any further causes for the recall of Bentinck and Cradock, these letters amply furnished them. If it were indeed true, as the letters purported, that there was a general conspiracy against His Majesty's Government in India and that the Vellore insurrection had been followed by one in Nundydrug and another now in Palamcottah, which had not yet been quelled, obviously there was substantial cause for alarm. Though the intelligence was groundless, it was the latest news from India, and it was the worst. The Directors became convinced that the situation on the Coast demanded the immediate recall of the Governor and the Commander-in-Chief.[25]

On April 7, the Court voted the recall of Lord William Bentinck and Sir John F. Cradock. Bentinck was removed from his office by a majority vote. The resolution that ordered the recall stated:

That altho the zeal and integrity of the present Governor of Madras, Lord Wm. Bentinck, are deserving of the Court's approbation, yet when they consider the unhappy events, which have lately taken place at Vellore and also other parts of his

Lordship's administration, which have come before them; the Court are of the opinion, that it is expedient for the restoration of confidence in the Company's Government that Lord Wm. Bentinck should be removed; and he is hereby removed accordingly.

But Cradock's recall was voted unanimously. The resolution unceremoniously stated:

That Lieutentant-General Sir John Francis Cradock, K. B. be removed from his situation as Commander-in-Chief, of the Company's forces on the Coast of Coromandel and second in Council at Fort St. George.[26]

Later on, the Court, in its second dispatch, specified its charges against John F. Cradock. It called his orders "injudicious," and described his investigation unsatisfactory. It pointed out that the inquiry ought not to have been whether the turban was offensive to the caste, rather what the sepoys thought of it. The Court also deplored his gross ignorance of the real state of the army at the time when he thought all was well.[27]

The Court did not find Bentinck equally culpable as he was not directly involved with the army. However, the Court felt that Bentinck exhibited "a want of that prudence and discernment so requisite in administrating the government of a numerous and peculiar people." It lamented that "instead of enquiring into the nature and extent of the objections made by the sepoys to the turban," Bentinck had most unwittingly ordered the same pattern of turban for his fencible corps.[28] It grieved that Bentinck's "zeal for the preservation of discipline had unfortunately failed to yield to the prejudices of the Native troops." Though Bentinck could not be held directly responsible for the insurrection, the Court felt that as head of the government he shared a great deal of the responsibility as he did not exercise adequate vigilance. Furthermore, the Court felt that "the restoration of confidence in the Company's Government" necessitated his dismissal.

"The reason generally assigned in common conversation," wrote Leith to
Bentinck:

> is that it was necessary to shew the Natives that the Legislature at
> home would not suffer the Government of the Country to remain
> longer in the hands of those in whose justice the Natives had no
> confidence.[29]

Charles Grant, the newly-elected deputy chairman, also expressed the same
sentiment. "The public sentiment especially in England seems to have called
for decisive steps," he added.[30]

However, it could be inferred from the very wording of the resolution,
"and also other parts of his Lordship's administration," that the Court had
been displeased with William Bentinck even prior to the arrival of Vellore
intelligence. It had found his financial policy unsatisfactory. The Court also
did not appreciate his too independent spirit and defiant attitude.[31] Perhaps
the Vellore insurrection merely furnished a pretext to get rid of an
unpleasant servant.

The Court desired to express its displeasure upon William Petrie too;
but only the impossibility of finding a suitable successor prevented it from
humiliating Petrie. The Court felt that he ought to have recorded the
sentiment which he claimed to have verbally expressed on July 4 that the
turban ought to have been regarded "as a question of political importance
than as one partially relating to the detail of discipline." As he did not
record, the Court observed that "a greater degree of responsibility for the
measure, then adopted rests with him." As there was no suitable successor,
Petrie was appointed temporarily to succeed Bentinck.[32]

The Court found the Adjutant-General Patrick A. Agnew and his deputy
Frederick Pierce highly culpable. No decision was taken on their conduct in
April. "I want to have the Adjutant General and his deputy moved from their

staff office," wrote Toone to Hastings on April 15, 1807. "They merit to be shot," he snapped, "yet I have not been able to prevail with the Court to come to prompt decision." He further added, ".... wait, wait, wait a little. They ought to be dismissed, but the ships are going and we have not time!! miserable."[33] A few days later, on May 4, he again wrote, "If no other man in Court will move it, I shall certainly bring it to a question, that they be removed from the offices of Adjutant-General and Deputy Adjutant General." Toone described Major Pierce as being "always adverse to the natives, and therefore a very improper man to be in the Adjutant General's office."[34] Two days later, on May 6, the Court unanimously voted out Agnew and Pierce from their offices and ordered them to return home immediately to answer for their conduct.[35]

The Court did not fail to notice Lieutenant-Colonel John Darley's attitude towards the corps. It condemned his behaviour "in terms of the strongest reprehension" and described the manner in which he enforced obedience as "so wanton and capricious an exertion of authority." The Court ordered that his command should be taken from him immediately and that he should never again be entrusted with Indian troops.[36]

III

On April 6, a few days after the formation of the Duke of Portland Administration, Robert Dundas succeeded George Tierney as president of the Board of Control.[37] Tierney, who was inimical to Portland's family, had already signaled the Court of the Board's approval of Bentinck's recall. After assuming the office, Robert Dundas made no attempt in favour of his chief's son. He wrote to the Duke of Portland on April 16 that the Board could not have done anything against the Court's decision without "committing government or the Board in a contest with the Directors in which the latter (from having the unquestionable power and right) must have been successful."[38]

The Board only altered and revised the draft of recall. It changed the communication draft to "a simple notification of recall, without giving any reason whatsoever for the measure."[39] The revised and final draft stated:

> Though the zeal and integrity of our present governor of Madras, Lord William Bentinck, are deserving our approbation, being of opinion that circumstances which have recently come under our considerations, render it expedient for the interest of our service that a new arrangement of our government of Fort St. George should take place without delay, we have felt ourselves under the necessity of determining that his Lordship should be removed, and we do hereby direct that Lord William Bentinck be removed accordingly.
>
> We also direct that Lieutenant-General Sir John Cradock, K.B. be removed from his situation of Commander-in-Chief of the Company's forces on the Coast of Coromandel and second in Council at St. George.
>
> We direct that agreeably to our former appointment William Petrie esq. do succeed to the Government until a permanent arrangement shall be adopted.[40]

After a long voyage, the ships carrying the order of recall arrived on the Madras road on September 9, and they were "anchored between three and four o' clock in the afternoon." But "the dispatches were not landed till late at night."[41] Bentinck and Cradock had no thought of the painful news awaiting them. Both of them felt that the Court of Directors would commend them for their respective measures. "I do not feel," Bentinck had often stated, "that any blame can attach to the Government. . . I confidently rely upon the approbation of the Court of Directors of what has been done."[42] Cradock was no less confident. He kept urging the Government to transmit all evidences and minutes to the Court of Directors in the hope of its full approbation.[43]

On the following day, the dispatches were brought, opened and examined. "Upon looking over the dispatches." Bentinck stated, "I found my recall . . . The words were to be removed 'without delay'."[44] The manner in which he was removed pained him grievously. "My removal was effected in a manner calculated to make it peculiarly mortifying and disgraceful," he later complained.[45] However, Bentinck felt a little better after a while. He recorded on October 4 while on his way home:

> For twelve hours after being acquainted with the news, I was a good deal knocked down. All unpleasant feeling immediately left me and from that time to this I have felt delight. I feel great delight at the thoughts of returning home.[46]

John Cradock too was greatly stunned. The abrupt dismissal, he later stated, caused "agitated feelings" and severely hurt him.[47]

On the following day, September 11, Bentinck formerly resigned his office and William Petrie was sworn in as Governor, and James Oakes and J. M. Casimayor as members of the Council.[48] Petrie's new Government asked Bentinck to continue to have the honours to which he was accustomed as governor till his departure, but he decidedly declined them as he felt that they would be incompatible with "the resolution of the Court of Directors."[49] With Petrie's consent, Bentinck however completed the business of his office, including the disposal of the prisoners.[50]

Unlike Bentinck, Cradock's reaction was very mean. He resigned his seat in the Council as well as the command of the Company's army, but he refused to surrender the command of His Majesty's troops in India, claiming that the Court's order could not and did not deprive him of His Majesty's command.[51] Bentinck and several senior officials remonstrated with him, but in vain.[52] As persuasion failed, Petrie's Government threatened to take disciplinary action against him. Consequently, Cradock most reluctantly submitted to the Government's pressure.[53]

In India the recall of Bentinck and Cradock produced a great outburst of sympathy for them, particularly in favour of the former. "No public event within the compass of my official career," wrote Alexander Falconer, a senior member of the Board of Revenue, "has given me more pain than the late orders for your Lordship's removal . . . I consider it a public misfortune . . . an unjust and indecorous prejudication of a case not understood."[54] A similar note of sympathy was struck by Sir Thomas Strange:

> Never can I forget that trying moment when after what had recently happened at Vellore, if there was confidence anywhere it was in you and in you only . . . To what individual influence but your own is it to be ascribed that we have got through another year . . . [55]

Letters of sympathy also came from numerous lesser civil and military officials as well. The British community proposed to give him an address, but he refused to accept it as he thought it would be discourteous to the Court[56] Even John Cradock expressed his sympathy for the dismissed governor. "Sir J. Cradock evidently made up to me," Bentinck recorded. "He frequently stated that the Court had acted most unjustly towards me. Policy might have required his removal. It was extraordinary that I should have been selected."[57] However, Bentinck was skeptical of Cradock's sincerity. For he added in the next strain:

> Sir John Cradock's professions describe no reliance. His wavering disposition is tossed about by every momentary feeling of irritation, reason taking no part whatever, deserves at the same time less reliance than less sincerity.[58]

Bentinck's chief encouragement came from his friend Sir Edward

Pellow. "In all my contentions," Bentinck observed, "he has been very much my friend." "Upon the present occasion," he stated, "he has offered us the best frigate to carry us home."[59] The *Pitt* was the proposed frigate.[60]

Bentinck also received a great deal of sympathy from local Indians. The day before his departure, they presented an address signed by about three thousand principal inhabitants. In the address, they expressed their gratitude for "the protection, security, and tranquility" which they had so long enjoyed, and especially thanked Bentinck for storing a large stock of grain to save the people "from the horror of a most grievous famine." Then they expressed their profound sorrow at his departure and wished him "all manner of happiness both in this and the world to come." Bentinck gladly accepted the address as an expression of loyalty to the British Government and thanked the Indians for their love and devotion and wished them "plenty and happiness.[61]" The next day, September 29, about four o' clock in the afternoon, as a dense crowd watched and guns boomed, Lord and Lady William Bentinck proceeded from the sea gate and boarded the frigate H.M.S *Pitt*, which at once set sail for England.[62]

The degree of sympathy the Commander-in-Chief might have received is unascertainable. Obviously some of his lieutenants expressed sorrow at his misfortune. But several, whom he had chastised during the days of power, took the opportunity to abuse him.[63] Also he was unfortunate, unlike Bentinck, in not having a friend to take him home immediately. Consequently, he was obliged to remain in Madras "without rank or salary" for about two months until the departure of the fleet when he and his family embarked for England at the cost of 3,500 pounds. Later, he complained that he was "degraded in the eyes of the civil and military world," and was exposed to "vexatious treatment and petty attack . . . from some worthless, low-minded characters."[64]

IV

After their return, Bentinck and Cradock filed their protest with the Court of Directors. Bentinck, immediately after his arrival in London, had an interview with William F. Elphinstone, who was the chairman of the Court when the recall was ordered. Bentinck was quite displeased with the interview. In his diary, on February 15, he recorded

> that the alarm and cry was so great that it could not be resisted. He talked much of the pain it had given him individually, and of the delay he had interposed. The conversation was very unsatisfactory and Mr. E. appeared to me to be nothing better than a canting rascal.[65]

Two months later, on April 16, Bentinck had another interview with the same "canting rascal." Apparently, Bentinck now found the interview quite satisfactory, although Elphinstone gave the same reasons for his recall. Three days later, Bentinck wrote to Edward Parry, Elphinstone's successor:

> Mr. Elphinstone made no difficulty in avowing to me, that with him the Vellore mutiny was the cause of my recall. He said that the argument at that time was, it is not necessary to consider nicely who was right or wrong, that a change in the government from whom the measures producing the dissatisfaction of the Native troops had proceeded was necessary and marking in the most pointed manner the disapprobation of the authorities at home.[66]

Bentinck added, "I felt that I had no reason to complain of the injustice of this act. I viewed it as a great misfortune only."[67] Injustice, he felt, could be done to him only if reparation were denied after a close examination of his "whole conduct" at a future convenient time.[68] Again Bentinck was not too mindful of the type of reparation. He primarily wanted the odium to be removed from his name. "My whole and sole object," he declared, "is to have expressed the favourable opinion of the Court, and to have removed, by an act as public as that which imposed it, the stigma from which my character suffers."[69]

The Court did not respond to Bentinck as speedily as he expected. Therefore, Bentinck prepared a memorial giving his account of the Vellore mutiny and refuting some of the charges commonly aired against his administration.[70]

In the *Memorial,* Bentinck claimed that the Vellore mutiny could not be attributed to him "directly or indirectly." He declared that he and his government were completely ignorant of the fatal paragraph in the code until sometime after the explosion and that the turban was thoroughly approved by many Indian officers. Bentinck made no reference to the recommendation made by the court of inquiry that the disturbances of May 6 and 7 were caused by the sepoys' belief that the turban was offensive to their caste. Bentinck admitted that the Commander-in-Chief expressed his misgivings on July 4, but he argued that at that time there was no reason to suspect either general or partial disaffection in the corps. He declared that the basis of the Commander-in-Chief's information, Lieutenant-Colonel Brunton, was quite unreliable as he had been very sick until lately. Furthermore, Bentinck stated that it was unsafe to revoke the turban order which had been once imposed with "the highest military tone." Yet, to allay the sepoys' fear, if they really had any, he said, his government proposed to issue a general order.

Further, Bentinck denied that the division of command in Vellore facilitated intrigue and conspiracy. "A division of command . . . does not necessarily imply a confusion of commands", he observed. There was nothing wrong with the system so long as each officer performed his functions judiciously and vigilantly. Bentinck contended that the indulgences given to the princes were neither extravagant nor injudicious. They were proper and necessary. Bentinck argued that a high reputation "for lenity and forbearance" had to be maintained, for in such a reputation, "no less than its reputation for vigour and military prowess," the ultimate safety of the Company rule in India depended. An offence against humanity would have been an offence both against our fame and our interests," he declared. He went on to say that Vellore too was not an improper place for the captive princes, if they had to remain south of the Narmada. Wherever the princes might have been, he observed they would have formed a "rallying point for the followers of their religion." Besides he contended that both in the selection of the place of their residence and the amount of their allowances, he had no part. They were determined by his predecessor, but he continued them, as he thought them to be unobjectionable. Bentinck claimed that he maintained "that happy medium . . . at once vigilant and humane, which the circumstances of the case enjoined."

Bentinck further refuted the rumour that he had introduced many innovations, particularly in the revenue and judicial departments and that these innovations had caused grave apprehensions amongst the people. He maintained that there had been no innovation except in the judiciary, and this particular innovation, he said, "was calculated to control rather the governors than the subjects." The creation of separate magistracy only rescued the people from tyranny and despotism, often times, of the government officials. He admitted that his judicial measures did curtail the military officials' unlicensed power and make the sepoy amenable to the civil and criminal courts. This, however, he argued, was a step in the right direction, and it would be nonsensical to complain that this measure was "a hardship upon the Army." He also admitted that his measures eliminated some of the laws which were prejudicial against the Hindus in favour of the Muslims. Nonetheless, by no means Bentinck declared that his judicial reforms formed the cause of the mutiny.

Bentinck also maintained that the measures he adopted in consequence of the mutiny were most effective. His diagnosis of the disease was correct and his remedy was appropriate. He said that having perceived the late orders as "the primary and essential cause of the insurrection," he revoked them; and having removed the virus, he followed the path of reconciliation and moderation to heal the wound, which eventually succeeded. He stated that the later agitations were primarily due to the officers' precipitate actions, and added that his measures had been completely vindicated by the peace and tranquility now reigning over the Coast.

The *Memorial* was well written. Its expression was lucid, and reasoning was basically sound. It was forcibly argued and well documented. It had a fifty-page body and a hundred-and-one-page appendix. Mark Wilks described it as "one of the ablest papers I ever persued."[71] The *Memorial* was submitted to the Court on February 7, 1809.

V

Even before Bentinck's submission of his *Memorial,* Cradock filed his protest with the Court. On June 1, 1808, he presented his first defence to the Court. It was entitled, *Detailed Letter Relative to the Insurrection at Vellore.* In ran thirty-seven pages and had no appendix. It was very poorly written, clumsy, much twisted and distorted. The presentation candidly betrayed the author's extreme anxiety to exculpate and extricate himself at all costs.

Cradock began his *Detailed Letter* lamenting that he had been "sacrificed without inquiry" and accorded "a severity of treatment hitherto unexampled in the British dominions" without a cause. The object of the *Detailed Letter,* Cradock declared, was the attainment of "truth", but he presented everything but the truth. He proceeded to state that he protested against the insertion of the invidious paragraph in the code but his lieutenants assured him that the regulations in question were the invariable practice in well-regulated corps, and therefore he yielded to the voice of "thirty years of experience" rather than obstinately stick to the "opinions formed by books." Further, Cradock stated that the proposed code was submitted "to the corrective eye of government," but he did not say that the paragraph in question was not included in the section which alone was to be scrutinized by the Government. He went on to say that if any of the late orders was to be construed as cause of the mutiny, it had to be the turban alone. But this too could not be, he contended, inasmuch as it was explicitly approved by the high caste officers. Like Bentinck, Cradock too made no reference to the penetrating observation of the court of inquiry. Moreover, Cradock stated that if the turban was truly offensive, the discontent would have been universal but he declared, quite incorrectly, that "the opposition . . . was local and confined to Vellore." Again, he observed that troops untainted with intrigue volunteered to wear the turban even after it had been revoked. Therefore, he concluded, that the turban was made only "a cloak . . . to veil the atrocious design of the rebels."

Having denied that his orders were obnoxious, Cradock proceeded to argue that if someone must be blamed for not detecting the brewing conspiracy, he was not the one. He had retired to Nundydrug in order to recuperate his health, leaving behind the whole staff at the Presidency for Government's assistance. He had given particular instruction to his staff to lay all matters before the Government. The Government, he said, was alone in the right situation to watch over the disposition of the army and people. Nonetheless, up in the hills, he added, he continued to maintain vigilance. The moment he heard from Lieutenant-Colonel Brunton, he sought the Government's advice. But the Government, he insinuated, made light of his information and failed to arrest the precipitous trend. He also stated that except for the division of command in Vellore, the conspiracy would have been detected and the insurrection would have been thwarted.[72]

About three months later, September 25, 1808, Cradock filed his second protest paper with the Court. It was entitled *Sketch of the Situation of*

Sir John Cradock, K. B. and K. C. Resulting from His Having Accepted the
Appointment of Commander in Chief of the East India Company Force at
Madras, in 1804. In the *Sketch,* Cradock primarily endeavoured to extricate
himself from the financial mess in which he was. He was in debt to the
Company to the extent of Rs.88,424.00 besides heavy interest on this
principal. Cradock got himself into this deep debt due to his own folly. In
1805, after he landed in Madras, he demanded and got his salary from the
Government, subject to the approval of Court of Directors, from the time he
was sworn into office in India House, in London. Unfortunately for Cradock,
the Court disapproved and ordered him to refund the sum which amounted
to Rs. 37,002.00 immediately. Cradock also cajoled the Madras Government
into paying him an extra salary as general officer in addition to his pay as
member of the Council and Commander-in-Chief. The Government again
granted it subject to the Court's approval. Unfortunately, again, the Court
disavowed it and ordered Cradock to refund the sum, which amounted to
Rs. 51,422.00. The Court also demanded that he ought to pay eight per cent
interest on these amounts commencing from January 1, 1807.[73]

In his *Sketch,* Cradock denied that the orders had any effect at all in
producing the mutiny. He again observed "that the regulations were
harmless." And that they had "subsisted for years coeval with their military
establishment in the Company's service." "Sir John Cradock defies
accusation of every kind," he thundered. "Let any person come forward
with a complaint," Cradock challenged, "and he is prepared to answer it
and assign his motive." Then he went on to say that "the true causes of the
Vellore insurrection, whether acknowledged or through policy denied or
disguised, are perfectly understood." He then asked the Court to admit "the
error of a hasty decision." Having observed thus, Cradock proceeded to state
the financial loss he had incurred, as he said, in consequence of his
acceptance of a position with the East India Company. He lamented that he

gave up a valuable appointment in Ireland, worth 2,500 pounds per annum and accepted the Company's service "in a remote and expensive country." In that country, through no mistake of his own, Cradock complained, he was "deprived of his station and all emolument, with no other support but that of his own character, till at length, at the charge of 3,500 pounds for himself and family, he embarked for Europe." The *Sketch* concluded with a note of disappointment and bitterness. "Perhaps," it observed, "Sir John Cradock exemplifies the singular instance of a commander-in-chief's return from India . . . without a fortune."

Lieutenant-Colonel Agnew and Major Pierce, who too had returned home as ordered, endeavoured to exculpate themselves. They brought a box full of letters from various commanding officers to show that the agitated regulations were by no means innovations. The letters indicated that at least in one battalion "the obnoxious orders" including the same pattern of turban had been in full force.[74] They also disclosed that the orders in question had been in practice in varying degrees.[75]

VI

The Court of Directors studied these representation and memorials in the light of the voluminous materials which had come from India, and it made its final judgement on Bentick, Cradock, Agnew and Pierce on July 25, 1809. The Court exculpated Bentick from any share "in originating the orders which for a time bore that character," but it still regretted that he failed to exercise "greater care and caution . . . in examining into the real sentiments and dispositions of the sepoys, before measures of severity were adopted to enforce that order." The Court felt satisfied with the measures which Bentinck had adopted in consequence of the insurrection, though it did not fully agree with his reasoning. It stated:

. . . in all the measures of moderation, clemency, and consideration, recommended by Lord William Bentinck after the mutiny, the Court, though not exactly agreeing with him in the data from which he reasoned, give him unqualified praise.[76]

Cradock too received a similar though not identical verdict. The Court acquitted him from "that wanton and imprudent violation of caste which was generally imputed to him," or "with any real violation or the intention of it." But it stated that the measures he had adopted to enforce obedience "though dictated. . . by a nice sense of the honour of military authority and the importance of subduing insubordination" were "nevertheless. . . unsuitable to the nature of the people with whom he had to deal." The Court maintained that Cradock ought to have consulted the common sepoys, the bulk of whom came to regard "the new turban with strong aversion, as incompatible with their caste." If such a "proper inquiry" had been instituted, the resolution stated, "the truth would have been ascertained," and the turban order could have been revoked "consistent with the honor of government, and of the commander-in-chief."[77]

The Court exonerated Agnew and Pierce from all culpability. They were declared right in maintaining that the orders "about marks of caste, whiskers and ear rings" had "the sanction of the practice of well regulated corps" over many years. However, Agnew was told that he was indiscreet for not advising the Commander-in-Chief to make a proper inquiry "into the real apprehensions of the common sepoys" after they had manifested "strong resistance," and Pierce was criticized for inserting into public enactment regulations "which had been formerly practised only through private influence." However, the Court quite naively added that, as in its observation, "the regulation had no effect in producing the mutiny" and the turban "had nothing in it contrary to caste". Agnew and Pierce were acquitted from the original charge under which they had been recalled. Consequently, the Court declared them eligible for reappointment to the office from which they were degraded, and ordered them to return to India.[78]

Quite naturally, Agnew and Pierce were pleased with the Court's verdict, but Cradock and Bentinck found them irksome. Bentinck found some of the Court's sentiments satisfactory, but he felt that they had not gone far enough. ". . . it did not, in my view," he declared, "render me that full measure of justice to which I thought myself entitled." Therefore, Bentinck decided "to make the *Memorial* public." Such a publication, he felt would enable all who might be interested in the Vellore affair to form "a correct judgement on the circumstances of that event," and also would vindicate his character and reputation.[79]

Understandably, Cradock was mortified with the Court's resolution. On October 31, 1809, he presented to the Court a letter expressing his "most solemn protest against a very considerable part of that resolution." He emphatically stated that he had resorted to all possible investigations that any human could possibly do. He was extremely angered at the Court's statement that he had failed to institute "a proper inquiry." "Will any member of your Court lay his hand upon his breast, and declare that he would or could have done more?" he asked.[80] Cradock threatened to appeal to His Majesty in order to demand a court-martial; however, he added that he preferred again to appeal to the Court's "liberality" and "every other consideration."[81]

Incidentally, Cradock was also infuriated with Bentinck's *Memorial,* as it was made public. He wrote to Bentinck, ". . . the perusal of your Lordship's Memorial and Appendix has given me real concerns." The *Memorial,* he declared, was "so directly and inveteratedly hostile to me." He lamented further that Bentinck's *Memorial* would nullify all his "statements and veracity." Then, in a hypocritical strain, he stated that unlike Bentinck's *Memorial*, his *Detailed Letter* and *Sketch* did not implicate or incriminate others.[82] Cradock was completely embittered with Bentinck. As late as June 18, 1810, Cradock wrote: "I shall always sincerely lament the unceasing indisposition of your Lordship's mind towards [me]."[83]

The Court of Directors did not retract its verdict despite Cradock's solemn protest. However, it condescended to grant Cradock some pecuniary concession. It recognized that Cradock did suffer considerable financial loss. Therefore, it decided to give him some monetary amelioration. His debt of 25,264 pagodas had now become 32,123 due to the eight per cent interest. The Court ordered him to pay only 12,000 pagodas and the remainder it stated would be relinquished.[84] Indeed, Cradock's constant pleading did not go without dividends.[85]

VII

The Vellore mutiny would not have caused further stir in England if the Christian missions, which were gaining momentum at that time, were not made a scapegoat. Immediately after the arrival of the Vellore intelligence, the anti-mission elements suggested that the mutiny could be traced partly at least to the activities of Christian missionaries. Charges produced counter charges. Before long a bitter controversy ensued. To understand aright this conflict, it is necessary to view it in its historical context.

While the East India Company remained a purely commercial institution, it paid at least lip-service to Christian missions.[86] But once it became a political power, the Company became nervous of the missions. Yet, it continued to tolerate missionaries like C. S. John, C. F. Schwartz and J. C. Kohlhoff as "they were so few in number and often proved useful in a secular capacity."[87] Many of the Company directors held the view that the Indian conservatism was impenetrable and that any attempt to invade it would only result in disaster to Company's rule. Therefore, they advocated the protection of all Indian religions and social organizations and resented anyone who tended to disturb the existing order. They regarded "the Company's government as a superstructure imposed upon Indian society by the requirements of trade."[88] It was for this reason that the Indian interest in the Parliament forced the defeat of William Wilberforce's resolutions in 1793, which aimed at the Indian advancement in useful knowledge and "religious and moral improvement."[89]

The last decade of the eighteenth century witnessed a tremendous surge in England for overseas missions. In 1792, the Baptist Missionary Society was founded, and in the following year its pioneer missionaries, William Carey and John Thomas, embarked for Bengal.[90] Two years later, in 1795, the London Missionary Society was organized.[91] In 1799, the Church Missionary Society was established.[92] Five years later, in 1804, came the British and Foreign Bible Society.[93]

This evangelical fervor was shared by some of the members of the East India Company too. They were both sympathetic and ardent advocates of overseas missions. Charles Grant and Edward Parry, in the Court of Directors, and Sir John Shore, later Lord Teignmouth, in the Board of Control, were strong champions of the cause of Christian missions. Grant and Parry assisted in the founding of the Church Missionary Society, and Teignmouth was the first president of the British and Foreign Bible Society.[94]

In India too some of the Company's servants were sympathetic towards evangelical endavours. In Bengal, George Udney, a member of the Government, William Chambers, master of chancery in the Supreme Court, and David Brown, the chief chaplain, were "friends of the missions."[95] On the Coast, Governor William Bentinck and Chief Chaplain R.H. Kerr were highly favourable to evangelism.[96]

These "friends of missions" were not too popular with their colleagues. Many in the Court as well as in India endeavoured to obstruct the mission activities. In 1793, Carey and Thomas had to be smuggled into India.[97] Jack Fountain, who joined them in 1795, had to enter Bengal as a factory official. William Ward, Joshua Marshman, William Grant, and Daniel Brunsdon, whom the Baptists sent in 1799, were forced to seek asylum in Serampore.[98] One of the directors was alleged to have said that he would rather see "a band of devils in India than a band of missionaries."[99] Sweny Toone used to mock Parry and Grant as the "pious chairs."[100] The following letter from a Resident in one of the Indian courts could be taken to represent the attitude of at least some Company servants:

> I most cordially assent to all the sentiments you express of the impolicy, or rather madness of attempting the conversion of the Natives of this country, or of giving them any more learning, or any other description of learning, than they at present possess. . . I can assure you that I do not feel so much anxiety and apprehension from the menaced designs of Buonaparte, as from the plans which have become so fashionable amongst the Puritans (sic) of the Indian House. This alarm has been chiefly excited by the pursual of some pamphlets, which have been issued from your Bible Societies, your Christian societies and other corporations of bigotry.[101]

The Resident was not without cause for alarm over Christian missions. At this time, some Indians did resent the type of materials which came out of the Baptist press in Serampore.[102] Some Indian lecturers in the College of Fort William too had been displeased with the nature of topics proposed for public dissertation in the College.[103] Some of the missionary inroads too had been attended with riots.[104] But far more than these, the disposition of Henry Martyn and particularly that of Claudius Buchanan had irritated many of the Company servants. Henry Martyn, that famous linguist, as Professor A. T. Embree puts it, was "tormented by the sins of the British community in

Calcutta as well as his own, and denounced his fellow Company servants no less vigorously than he did Hindus and Muslims."[105] If Henry Martyn was irritating, Claudius Buchanan was painfully unbearable. He was extremely harsh and arrogant and full of vanity. If Buchanan's character was upsetting, his schemes were particularly alarming.

In 1805, Buchanan came out with his grandiose scheme. In the topics he proposed for an essay competition in the universities of Oxford and Cambridge, he first sounded out his plans. Two of the topics he proposed were:

> The probable design of the divine providence in subjecting so large a portion of Asia to the British Dominion, and the duty, the means, and the consequences of translating the Scriptures into the Oriental tongues, and of promoting Christian knowledge in Asia.[106]

Buchanan came out openly in his *Memoir on the Expediency of an Ecclesiastical Establishment for British India,* which was published subsequently. In the *Memoir,* after presenting a lurid picture of Indian society, he argued that the only means of civilizing such a society was christianization. He declared that proselytism was "practicable" and British Government must undertake it, directly and indirectly. Then, he proceeded to point out that it was Britain's solemn duty to do so:

> Providence hath been pleased to grant to us this great empire, on a continent where, a few years ago, we had not a foot of land. From it we export annually an immense wealth to enrich our own country. What do we give in return? It is said that we give protection to the inhabitants and administer equal laws. This is necessary for obtaining our wealth. But what do we give in return? What acknowledgement to Providence for its goodness has our

nation ever made? What benefit hath the Englishman ever conferred on the Hindoo, as on a brother? . . .

Can anyone believe that our Indian subjects are to remain forever under our government involved in their present barbarism and subject to the same inhuman superstition? And if there be a hope that they will be civilized, when is it to begin, and by whom is it to be effected?

. . . shall a Christian people, acknowledging a Providence in the rise and fall of empires, regulate the policy of future times, and neglect a present duty; a solemn and imperious duty, exacted by their religion, and by their public principles, and by the opinion of the Christian nations around them! Or can it be gratifying to the English nation to reflect, that they receive the riches of the East on the terms of chartering immoral superstitions.

Having thus pointed out Britain's moral duty, Buchanan went on to argue that proselytism alone was politically sound policy:

We have consolidated our Indian empire by our power; and it is now impregnable; but will the Mahometan ever bend humbly to Christian dominion? Never, while he is a Mahometan. Is it then good policy to cherish a vindictive religion in the bosom of the empire forever? Would it not accord with the dictates of the soundest wisdom to allow Christian schools to be established, where the children of poor Mahometans might learn another temper. . .

A wise policy seems to demand that we should use every means of coercing the contemptuous spirit of our native subjects. Is there not more danger of losing this country, in the revolution of ages (for an empire without a religious establishment cannot stand forever), by leaving the dispositions and prejudices of the people in their present state, than by any change that Christian knowledge and an improved state of civil society would produce in them? And

211

would not Christianity, more effectually than anything else disunite and segregate our subjects from the neighboring states, who are now of the same religion with themselves; and between whom there must ever be, as there ever has been a constant disposition to confederacy and to the support of a common interest . . .[107]

Buchanan wanted an archbishopric for British India.

Its objectives, he stated, should be "the perpetuity of the Christian faith among Europeans in India and the civilization of the natives."[108]

If Buchanan's topics for the essay competition left any unalarmed, his *Memoir* left none.[109] Buchanan's grandiose scheme frightened even those who actively supported the missions. Lord Teignmouth wrote to Wilberforce:

But, I regret that the conversion of the Natives of India has been brought forward so conspicuously by the publication of Dr. Buchanan and his premiums for prize disputations, that Christianity may be introduced into India, and that the attempt may be safely made, I doubt not; but to tell the Natives we wish to convert them, is not the way to procced.[110]

If Buchanan's scheme frightened the friends of missions, it infuriated its enemies. "From the prizes he presumed to offer for certain exercises in the University of Cambridge," wrote a Company official in India, "I am convinced that he is a man of wretched and most unchristianlike vanity.[111]

VIII

It was while Buchanan's prize offers and *Memoir* were generating heat that the Vellore mutiny took place.[112] Those who had been already irritated with the evangelicals immediately stated that all that they had been forewarning were menacingly coming true. In Bengal, the reaction was quick and prompt. The Supreme Government closed down the chapel at Bow Bazar in Calcutta, which the Baptist missionaries in Serampore had recently opened, and restricted the missionaies' labours to confines of Serampore itself. The Government also ordered immediate deportation of the two Baptist missionaries, John Chater and William Robinson, who had just come from England to join their brethren in Bengal. However, after much persuasion the Government granted Chater and Robinson a temporary respite, and later on it relaxed its restrictions on missionaries.[113]

In England the uproar against Christian missions was violent. "The horrid business at Vellore," wrote Sweny Toone, "will I trust put a stop, at least for some time, to any attempts to disturb the religious opinion of the Natives."[114] Edward Parry and Charles Grant, "the pious chairs," were accused in the Court as being the indirect cause of the Vellore massacre since they had sent out evangelical chaplains and countenanced missionaries. ". . . certain individuals, myself among the number," Grant complained, "have been accused of abetting such measures, and so made indirectly parties to the mutiny of the Native troops."[115] Grant however rebuffed his enemies. ". . . we were gravely asked in Court," Sweny Toone wrote to Hastings, "if we were disposed to trample upon the cross. This will serve to shew you the temper and disposition of some men."[116] Buchanan's *Memoir* too incurred the Court's displeasure. "The opinion of the Court," Toone commented, "appears to be so decidedly against his views, that I can hardly suppose the possibility of the subject being introduced this year, in the shape of a question."[117]   E. Baber, a friend of Warren Hastings, added, "I cannot reflect on this subject [ecclesical establishment] and all its probable consequences without the most melancholy forebodings."[118] The Serampore missionaries too were not spared. Charles Grant reported,

213

I most of all suffer from the absurd, malevolent, and wicked stories which the weak, the prejudiced, and the enemies of Christianity have poured forth in this occasion to discredit, to bring into suspicion as dangerous, the few poor, and assuredly harmless efforts which have been made under the British Government to introduce the light of the Gospel into India.[119]

On June 17, 1807, a motion was tabled in the Court of Directors to order the missionaries home. Even those who held that the missionaries had nothing to do with the mutiny felt that the missionaries ought to be repatriated to make complete repatriation to the offended prejudices of the sepoys. The Board of Control too, with the exception of Lord Teignmouth, favoured the repatriation of missionaries.[120] However, prior to the session, the mission societies and evangelical-minded proprietors and directors maneouvred to calm the temper.[121] At the session, Parry used his privilege as chairman "to avoid a formal, perhaps acrimonious debate."[122] Sweny Toone, though anxious, hesitated to press the matter to a decision. The absence of Sir Francis Baring, an able anti-mission director, "left the opponents of Grant and Parry without a capable leader."[123] Charles Grant subsequently reported to David Brown:

The tide was so strong that if God had not been pleased to use two well-intentioned, though weak, instruments, in situations in which my colleague and I are, orders of a very different kind would in all probability, have been transmitted.[124]

In their anxiety to quieten the clamour against the Christian missions, Parry and Grant were prepared to trace the disaffection to numerous causes. In a letter to Robert Dundas, in May, 1807, they stated that the immediate cause of the mutiny was undoubtedly "the most imprudent regulations" which were artfully taken advantage of "by the Mahomedan adherents of the fallen families of Mysore and Arcot and by other enemies of the British Government," but added that there were many equally important predisposing causes. They went on to say that the Company Government during the late years had become extremely insensitive to Indians "excepting in respect to their religious prejudices." This, they explained, was largely due to the

> practice of sending men new to India to fill superior stations civil and military. . . Such men go with their opinions and habits formed solely upon European ideas and usages, utter strangers to the languages of India, to the people, their manners and customs, unable to hold any direct converse with the Natives . . . It has been the fashion too, with rulers of this description . . . to exclude all Natives from even the lowest degree of personal confidence.

Consequently, they said, the subjects were completely severed from their rulers. This gulf, they went on to point out, was further deepened in the army by the introduction of King's officers into the Company's army. "We have heard," they said, "that [these] officers . . .

> so far from admitting even the Native officers to an easy intercourse with them, do not allow them to sit down in their presence. This haughty demeanor . . . must have concurred, with other predisposing causes, to bring the minds of the sepoys into a state of alienation from their officers, which more easily fitted them for entering into the horrid scheme perpetrated at Vellore.

Then, they pointed out that the failure to associate the uprooted Indian nobility with British interest had also been a tremendous source of weakness. After portraying the condition of the upper class Indians, Parry and Grant stated:

In short, it is a general conception among them that they do not possess the rank and importance they ought to hold in the community of their own country . . . [125]

If they see a steady purpose of doing everything that can be done without them, they may be the more inclined, in return, to do without us, and to consider their interests and ours as opposed to each other.[126]

A few months later, Parry and Grant went so far as to say that there existed a general conspiracy in South India antecedent to the promulgation of the agitated orders. They observed:

The conspiracy in Vellore instead of being a sudden and insulated [isolated] thing, provoked by the orders respecting the turban, appears to have been a part, prematurely executed, of a design existing before the promulgation of those orders, for a combined insurrection in different garrisons at the same time, and the destruction of all the Europeans.

Tipu Sultan's adherents, now they declared, were not prime movers but only abetters of a general plot, in which even "French agents and emissaries" were active. They also lamented that disaffection had taken deep root among "certain of the poligars, zemindars and principal Hindoos in the Peninsula."[127] In fact, Parry and Grant were prepared to trace and attribute the alleged disaffection to anything and everybody except Christian missions and missionaries.[128]

As an immediate precautionary measure against further commotion, Parry and Grant suggested that an additional force of about 3,800 men ought to be at once dispatched to India.[129] They also recommended that a commission should be appointed to inquire into the general disposition and temper of the people, especially of Hindus, on the Coast, and to investigate the causes if disaffection was expressed. They proposed that the president of the commission should be the governor of Madras and the members either two or four in number should be sent from England. The proposed members should be "men of character, acquainted with India, but unconnected with the proceedings there during the last seven years, and excluded from the prospect employment there, at least on the Coast."[130] The chairs' diagnosis of the situation and their proposed solution gave Robert Dundas enough food for thought for several months;[131] however, the proposed commission never saw the light of day.[132]

When one of the proprietors, Thomas Twining[133] saw that the Directors had dropped the question of ordering missionaries home, at least temporarily, he decided to force the issue by bringing the matter before the public. In October, 1807, he published a pamphlet, *Letter to the Chairman on the Danger of Interfering in the Religious Opinions of the Natives of India,* and at the same time intimated that he would bring the matter before the General Court in December. "With infinite concern and alarm," he began, "I have lately heard of proceedings . . . in a quarter . . . to interfere in the religious opinions of the Native inhabitants of India." He then proceeded to state, having designated the quarter as the British and Foreign Bible Society,[134] that he had also heard that some of the trustees of the Bible Society were leading members of the Court of Directors as well as the Board of Control, and if that was true, he declared, "our possession in the East" was "already in a situation of most imminent and unprecedented peril." He then packed his thirty-one-page pamphlet with extracts from the reports of the Bible Society and Buchanan's *Memoir,*[135] indicating that a monstrous design had been devised to destroy the British Empire. "When religious innovation shall set her foot in that country," he solemnly warned, indignation will spread from one end of Hindostan to the other, and the arms of fifty millions of people will drive us from that portion of the of the globe, with as much ease as the sand of the desert is scattered by the wind, and recommended:

> that our native subjects . . . be permitted quietly to follow their own religious opinions, their own religious prejudices and absurdities, until it shall please the Omnipotent power of Heaven to lead them into the paths of Light and Truth.[136]

IX

Twining's outburst inaugurated a pamphlet war, lasting nearly two years, in which more than twenty-five writers took part. Some leading periodicals too took active roles in what was later described as "the battle of missions."[137] *The Evangelical Magazine, The Christian Observer,* the *Eclectic Review and The Quarterly Review* entered the campaign on the side of the missions whereas the *Edinburgh Review* championed the anti-missions cause.

Twining's pamphlet was almost immediately answered by Robert Owen, Secretary of the British and Foreign Bible Society, on behalf of his institution.[138] Twining's archenemy, "that fierce and fiery Calvinist, Andrew Fuller," was yet to come out with his answer.[139] Meanwhile Twining's cause found its greatest champion in Major John Scott Waring. If Twining's assault was a skirmish, Scott Waring's was a "heavy cannonade."[140]

Scott Waring's original pamphlet, *Observation on the Present State of the East India Company,* appeared in July 1807. At that time, it was published chiefly in reference to some financial matters. In it, Scott Waring stated that the mutiny had been caused by the intrigues of Tipu sultan's adherents. But in November, when he revised his pamphlet with the long preface, he exculpated Tipu Sultan's adherents from the accusations,[141] called the uprising "a religious mutiny" and demanded that the missionaries be brought home immediately. He alleged that there had been a "great increase of English missionaries of late years and the gratuitous distribution of our sacred scriptures throughout the whole country." But he still stated that missionaries were not "directly or indirectly concerned in the Vellore mutiny;' nonetheless, he added, the missionaries must be ordered home as the sepoys' fear remained unalloyed. "If therefore India is deemed worth preserving," he declared,

> we should endeavor to regain the confidence of the people, by the immediate recall of every English missionaries (sic) and by prohibiting every person in the Company's service from taking a part in circulating the translation of the Holy Scriptures in Hindostan.

Scott Waring then proceeded to lecture the evangelicals who were ardent and passionate about overseas evangelism. He told them that the command of Jesus Christ to go and preach to every creature was not applicable to them:

> . . . the command of our Saviour to his Apostles to preach the Gospel to all nations did not . . . apply to us. The gift of languages, and the power of working miracles were conferred on the Apostles. All extraordinary powers had long ceased, and the extraordinary commission . . . had ceased also.

Having thus given his exegesis, he added, that if the evangelicals were bent on intruding into other established religions, they should go "amongst the savages in America and in the islands of the South Seas," but never to India. The field which he proposed, he said, was "large enough for the employment of fifty thousand missionaries" and that they could have no reason to complain that they did not have room. In India, he declared, proselytism was simply impossible and impracticable and the missionaries would create only "mischief." Any attempt to proselytize in India, he warned, would simply multiply "Vellore" a thousand times over. "If there are any public men in England wild enough to conceive the conversion of the natives of India to be *probable,"* he cautioned, "let them consider what fatal consequences must ensue if their judgment should be erroneous." If responsible men were foolish enough to try such an arduous experiment, he said, "humanity requires that we should preserve the lives of our countrymen until we can send transport to bring them home."

Scott Waring also stated that to the very thing which the evangelicals were anxious to remove—the religious differences between Indians and Britons—Britain owed its political existence in India. He asked:

He [Buchanan] laments, as a great political evil, that there should be a difference of religion between us and our native subjects; but to that difference of religion more than to any other circumstance, do we owe the permanence of our empire in India. Does he suppose it possible that thirty thousand British subjects could retain an empire containing fifty millions of people if the Christian religion was universal in India?

Scott Waring then proceeded to attack the evangelical chaplains and the Baptist missionaries in Bengal. He described Buchanan's scheme as the wildest and most disastrous project the human mind has ever devised and R. H. Kerr's recommendation of free-English school system as "a deception of the basest kind," and "a scheme more repugnant to every principle of justice and true morality." His attacks on William Carey and his colleagues were extremely abusive, malicious and vicious.

Scott Waring's and Twining's pamphlets were industriously circulated in London in anticipation of the forthcoming General Court's session on December 23. The pamphlets did produce considerable effect, and a strong body of opinion favoured the recall of missionaries.[142] But the mission societies and evangelical clergymen launched their crusade with no less fervor than their enemies. The effect of their zeal outmatched their opponents.[143]

At the General Court, true to his promise, Thomas Twining introduced the question of missions. However, feeling that a considerable number of proprietors were unsympathetic towards his proposal, Twining offered to withdraw his motion if the chairman assured him that the attention of the Court of Directors "had been turned to the subject."[144] Parry was only too happy to assure him, knowing that the Court of Proprietors was much more hawkish than the Court of Directors.[145] Sir Francis Baring promised to champion the anti-missions cause in the Court of Directors and he did so when the Directors met on January 29, 1808. But the resolution went against Baring and his colleagues. On the following day, Toone reported to Warren Hastings:

> I think you will be anxious to hear the result of yesterday's debate. We were beat 13 against 7 upon the motions of Sir Francis. The saints are elevated—I never loved them, but now I detest them . . . Sir Hugh, Sir Wm Metcalfe, and myself fought side by side . . .[146]

An order to maintain *status quo* was subsequently transmitted to Calcutta. ". . . the adversaries are in despair . . . we shall be tolerated, and you may   go on as usual . . ." Joyfully reported Andrew Fuller to his brethren in Serampore.[147]

If the anti-missions cause received a defeat in the Court of Directors, it also got a series of rebuffs in the pamphlet war. In January, 1808, Andrew Fuller joined the fray on the side of the missions with his *An Apology for the Late Christian Missions to India.*[148] Scott Waring was the one to bear the full brunt. Fuller simply dismissed Scott Waring's information as out-of-date and his reasoning as illogical and injudicious. Scott Waring's recommendation to recall the missionaries, Andrew Fuller said, was a sheer folly. "It would be," he declared,

> a tacit acknowledgement on the part of Government, that, till
> instructed by the Vellore mutiny, they had entered 'the wild idea of
> compelling them to embrace Christianity,' but that now they had
> become sober, and relinguished![149]

Fuller was joined by an anonymous pamphleteer with a devastating
attack on Scott Waring's pamphlet. He reviewed Scott Waring's arguments
and stated that they were either inaccurate, self-contradictory or baseless,
and declared that the author was actuated by malicious baseness and
rancorous meanness.[150]

John Scott Waring, however, remained undaunted. In fact, he became
bolder. He brought out successively two other pamphlets appealing to the
Parliament to order the missionaries home.[151] Scott Waring was soon joined
by a Bengal officer with his *A Vindication of the Hindoos.* [152]

The Bengal officer stated that so long as the missionaries confined
themselves to "converting distressed orphans, or outcast Hindoos, who
sought refuge, in despair, for the loss of respectability, no material evil could
arise," but if and when the Indians suspected the Government to have
designs to convert them, he declared, the dreaded moment would have
arrived.[153] "In vain," he surmised,

> shall we seek security, in the shade of European force; the disparity
> of number is so great. . .the only alternative we should have left,
> that of timely quitting the country, ere the relentless storm of
> offended Religion burst on our devoted heads.

He then asked:

> Is it wise, is it politic, is it safe, to institute a war of sentiment
> against the only friends of any importance we seem to have yet left
> in India—our faithful subjects of the Ganges, by suffering

missionaries of our own clergy to preach among them the errors of idolatry and superstition . . . .

"It therefore behoves us," he recommended that

by every possible means, . . . [we] conciliate our native soldiers, and every man around us, by mild and rational demeanour, by every reasonable indulgence on the score of religious observance, and by a candour and a confidence that may obviate all distrust.[154]

A late Resident at Bhagulpore hastened to the assistance of the Bengal officer with his *The Dangers of British India from French Invasion and Missionary Establishments.* The late Resident declared that if the missionaries were allowed to continue their activities, they would "plunge Hindostan in rebellion and occasion the massacre of every Englishman." The Corsican Adventurer, he warned, would defeat England on the banks of the Ganges instead of the Thames if the missionaries were not ordered home at once. If the missionary was aided, he explained, "the whole country will be in arms;" if unaided, his means of subsistence would be investigated, and "some hidden motives" would be attributed to his supporters in England. Therefore, he appealed solemnly, "For God's sake, for the sake of all we hold dear in religion and in liberty. . . let us guard against any measure that can diminish the confidence of the people of Hindostan."[155]

The Bengal officer, the late Resident at Bhagulpore, as well as Scott Waring and Thomas Twining received a vigorous answer from John Lord Teignmouth. In his *Considerations on the Practicability, Policy and Obligation of Communicating to the Natives of India the Knowledge of Christianity,* Teignmouth stated, "If to convert the Hindoos to Christianity be indeed impossible, and if the attempt must end in our extermination, we must with whatever reluctance, relinguish it." "But," he added, "the advocates for the propagation of Christianity in India are not yet reduced to this desponding situation." He admitted that the caste barrier and local prejudices were strong but he asserted that they were overrated and proselytism was not "impracticable" and also politically "most desirable."

Teignmouth then went on to say that Vellore insurrection had no connection with the missionary activities at all. He observed that Scott Waring's allegation that there had been increase in the number of English missionaries and circulation of Scriptures was totally devoid of substance. Among the several missionaries sent out during the recent years, he said, only four resided on the Coast, though some others might have landed there *en route* to their different destinations. Among these four missionaries, he added, only one was English, Reverend Loveless, who resided in Madras. The other three Continental missionaries lived far apart, two in Vizagapatam and one in Palamcottah, and none near Vellore.[156] Furthermore, Teignmouth observed the Coast people were accustomed to missionaries since the beginning of the eighteenth century. He also added that lately there had been less circulation of the Scriptures and other religious literatures than usual. Then he claimed that there had been great demand for Tamil Bible, but it had not been met by the presses either in Tranquebar or Serampore.

Further Teignmouth asserted that "there is an argument, which to me is decisive against the opinions and suspicions of Major Scott Waring." That is, he said,

> in all the inquiries made at Fort St. George into the causes of mutiny at Vellore, in the course of which great number of the Native troops were examined, the increase of missionaries, and the circulation of the Scriptures, religious tracts, and pamphlets were never once mentioned by any of them. If these causes . . . had operated to produce them . . . would they not have been so stated by them?

Teignmouth also argued that the journeys of Doctors Buchanan and

Kerr to Malabar could not have produced any sensation. Such an allegation, he stated, would "appear perfectly ridiculous to any person acquainted with India." The intent of their mission might not have been known at all to the inhabitants of India. Furthermore, he added that Buchanan's much-agitated *Memoir* too could not have caused any apprehension among Indians as they might not have had any access to it. He admitted that missionaries had been in Bengal, and that they might have exhibited some imprudence in their publication, but he insisted that "the latter [Coast people] know no more of the missionaries in Bengal, nor of their proceedings than of those in Africa or Carass."

Finally, Teignmouth stated that "under the influence of panic and apprehension" Scott Waring and others had construed "ill-founded surmises and suspicions . . . into facts and proofs." Proselytism was practicable and also most desirable to strengthen the British dominion in India, he concluded.[157]

Among the reviews and periodicals that supported the missions cause, *The Christian Observer* and the *Eclectic Review* were most outspoken. The former described the proposed recall of missionaries "as highly unjust, inexpedient and shocking."[158] It also published a series of articles "On the probable designs of Providence in subjecting India to Great Britain." [159] The *Eclectic Review* condemned John Scott Waring's pamphlets as containing nothing but "naked self-evident absurdity," and accused the author of malignant hypocrisy in all his demeanour.[160] It had also no less severe condemnation for other anti-mission pamphleteers.[161]

In *The Edinburgh Review, The Christian Observer* and the *Eclectic Review* found their chief opponent. Its April issue (1808) seemed particularly unanswerable. After presenting a number of extracts from the missionary journals illustrating the assistance some of the missionaries had received from Government officials, disturbances incited by the Brahmins, and cases of ill-treatment some converts had suffered on the Coast, it observed:

It is hardly fair to contend, after these extracts, that no symptoms of jealousy upon the subject of religion had been evinced on the Coast.

It then turned its attention to Bengal. Here it cited extracts from the publication of the Baptist Missionary Society with arresting and sensation captions, such as "Feelings of the Natives upon Hearing Their Religion Attacked," "Hatred of the Natives to the Gospel," "Alarm of the Natives at the Preaching of the Gospel," "Hatred of the Natives," and "Hatred to the Gospel."[162] After presenting several unfavourable accounts, it remarked.[163]

Upon the whole, it appears to us hardly possible to push the business of proselytism in India to any length, without incurring the utmost risk of losing our Empire. The danger is more tremendous, because it may be so sudden; religious fears are a very probably cause of defection if the troops are generally defected, our Indian Empire may be lost to us as suddenly as [a] frigate or a fort.[164]

The Edinburgh Review's challenges were taken up by *The Quarterly Review*.[165] It began its observation by saying that the late controversy had been carried on "with more than the usual virulence and unfairness of polemical writings on both sides." Then it went on to say that the Vellore mutiny could be merely explained in the light of the obnoxious orders alone without bringing the missionaries into the picture. It stated that the orders in question were "as direct an outrage of their religious customs as it would be to prohibit baptism among Christians or circumcision among Mahomedans." The orders, it continued, were "a flagrant insult to their religion, an overt act of intolerance." Yet, it lamented, that the real cause had been covered up and missionaries were made scapegoats. "It is not to this day," it declared,

> made known whose folly provoked the massacre of so many
> British soldiers . . . lest the public voice in India and in England
> should call loudly for investigation; a tub is thrown out to the
> whale, the missionaries must serve as scape-goat, and Christianity
> and the Bible be called to account for what was occasioned solely
> by this unwise assault upon turbans and toupees!

However, *The Quarterly Review* stated that the missionaries were not
faultless. With all their cautions, it observed, their "journals contain
abundant proofs of daring and imprudent languages." Nonetheless, it added
that the manner the controversy had been conducted in England would
seem that "the missionaries and their advocates were persecuting the
Hindoos instead of preaching to them!" "Persecution may excite rebellion,"
it continued, but "preaching can only excite riots." Even this might not
happen in India, it added. Tipu Sultan, it clarified, coerced many Hindus to
become Muslims, but "no insurrection took place, and little other outcry
was heard than what the operation occasioned!" It refuted the allegation
that "the Portuguese lost their empire by their bigotry." They lost it, it
affirmed, "by neglect at home and misconduct abroad." "Bad governors and
weak ministers," it stated, "destroyed the Portuguese empire—not
missionaries, not intolerance."

The Quarterly Review then went on to say that Britain must seek
adherents in India. The Hindus and the Muslims, it noted, were Britain's
"subjects," and not "adherents," and as "subjects," they "would care little
for a change of masters." "It is adherents that we stand in need of," it
declared. Colonization, it observed, was impracticable. The tropical sun
forbade any English settlement; also the over jealous Company would not
permit it. It disapproved Alfonso de Albuquerque's concept of "mixed race"

as a violation of nature. The only alternative to secure the much-needed adherents, it stated, was proselytism.

> Only by Christianizing the natives, we can strengthen and secure ourselves . . . The interest and existence of the native Christians would be identified with those of the British Government and the Church in India be truly the bulwark of the State.

Even proselytism, however, it conceived, would not make a British Empire permanent in India. But it felt that "it would render it as permanent as it ought to be." Therefore, it remarked:

> India would be trained up in civilization and Christianity, like a child by its guardian, till such tutelage was no longer needed: our protection might be withdrawn when it ceased to be necessary, and the intercourse between the two countries would continue undiminished, just to that extent which would be most beneficial to both.[166]

With this article, the pamphlet war, which was inaugurated with Twining's outburst came to an end, but "the battle of missions" was prolonged till victory was won by the mission societies in 1813.[167] All along the opponents of the missions tried to use the Vellore mutiny to silence their enemies. Even in the parliamentary inquiry which preceded the renewal of the charter, several banked on the Vellore mutiny in their attempt to maintain the status quo.[168] However, the current of evangelism was too strong for the anti-evangelicals both in the public and Parliament. Consequently, the door to India was flung open for the evangelicals, although at one time they feared that the Vellore mutiny might lock it tightly forever.

CHAPTER SEVEN
THE CONSPIRACY THEORY

THE MOST POPULAR VIEW OF THE VELLORE MUTINY and disaffection was
that it was a Muslim conspiracy. It was first suggested in the heat of the
events and accepted by panic-stricken men. Ever since that tragic event, it
found a favourable hearing first among the interested contemporaries and
later among several historians of succeeding generations.[1] Despite its wide
acceptance, the conspiracy theory is not demonstrable.

The foundation of the Muslim conspiracy theory was the view that the
late military orders were in no degree disagreeable to the Indian troops.
According to this view, no innovation was introduced by the late military
orders. The shaving, trimming, no-ear ring, and no-sect marks orders were
"the invariable practice of the army." The regulations of the tenth
paragraph of the eleventh section could not have affected the two mutinied
battalions because the orders in question had been in practice more than a
year in the first battalion of the first regiment, and that had not been
communicated to the second of the twenty-third regiment. The new turban
too was inoffensive and harmless. A similar pattern of turban had been
worn in the army in the years past, and the drastic alteration in the turban
was made not in 1806 but in 1797. Furthermore, the new turban had been
earlier approved by three high caste sepoys, and later unanimously by

Indian officers. The turban was also left in the Adjutant-General's office several weeks for anyone's examination. If the turban had been offensive, the advocates of the Muslim conspiracy theory stated, surely someone would have expressed his disapproval. Having piled up similar arguments one after another, they concluded that the very fact that several battalions volunteered to wear the turban after its withdrawal surely nullifies all the allegations that the turban was offensive to the sepoys.

Having thus laid the foundation, the conspiracy theorists proceeded to build the superstructure of their view on the assumption that the spirit of intrigue and rebellion persisted unabatedly. They insisted that the incidents at Hyderabad, Wallajabhad, Nundydrug, Bangalore, Palamcottah, Quilon, again in Wallajabhad, and Sankerydrug were insurrections or attempted massacres. They also claimed that there was an increase in the number of wandering religious mendicants, whom they regarded as "emissaries of sedition." They further say that the majority of the participants and leaders of the real or alleged insurrections were Muslims, and asserted that the conspiracy aimed at the restoration of Muslim interest on the Coast.

Moreover, the Muslim conspiracy theorists stated that in Vellore the mutiny broke out solely due to the machination of the princes. Two of their chief spokesmen, Lieutenant-Colonel Forbes and Lieutenant Coombs, who spent several weeks investigating the cause of the mutiny, summed up their views:

> We firmly believe the conspiracy to have been originally projected by the princes, with the view of recovering their independence and the defection and revolt of the troops to have resulted from the intrigue and artifices of the princes' adherents.[2]

In Hyderabad too, the conspiracy theorists found intrigue as the cause of the meditated rebellion. John F. Cradock asserted, like many others, "that similar artifices" of "the chief sirdars" brought the Subsidiary troops to the verge of mutiny and bloodshed.[3]

The advocates of the Muslim conspiracy theory went on further to add that besides intrigue and seduction, which were the primary cause, there were other factors which facilitated the disaffection. They differed in their view as to what those contributing factors were, but they all agreed that there were such factors. John F. Cradock preferred to emphasize the civil and military arrangements, which he claimed to undermine the authority of the commanding officers and thus induced the ordinary sepoys to rebel against his officer. Cradock also hinted that the extension of Christianity might put "our existence in the country . . . at stake."[4] Similar warning was also sounded by John Scott Waring and his fellow anti-mission pamphleteers[5]. But Charles Grant and Edward Parry traced the indirect cause to everything except Christian missions. They found the predisposing causes especially in the poor *rapport* between Indians and their British rulers, and the Company's economic exploitation of India.[6] Thomas Maitland, the Governor of Ceylon, described the Subsidiary Alliance system the major indirect cause of the discontent. He denounced the alliance system as "tyrannical and oppressive, infinitely beyond anything that is known in any part of the world," and charged that it ate up the indigenous aristocracy and sapped Indian energy and vitality.[7]

A careful examination of the evidence indicates that the foundation of the Muslim conspiracy theory is not fool-proof. The assertion that the trimming, shaving, no-ear ring, and no-sect marks rules were "the invariable practice of the army" is only half truth. The practice of appearing on parade with shaven face, trimmed moustache and without sect mark and ear ring was not so prevalent as the conspiracy theorists purported it to be. In fact, this practice was fully followed in only one battalion. In several the practice was neither "usual" or "customary." Small sect marks and ear rings were permitted in all others; however, long beards and untrimmed moustaches were prohibited in nearly all.[8] The very fact that the tenth paragraph of the eleventh section caused consternation among several commanding officers surely betrays the insinuation that the practice in question was "the custom of well regulated corps" and "invariable practice of the army."[9]

Moreover, it is incorrect to say that the tenth paragraph of the eleventh section could not have had any material effect on the mutinied battalions. According to Major Joseph Hazlelwood, who commanded the first battalion of the first regiment in 1805, regulations to that effect were indeed transmitted to him from the Adjutant-General's office. But he refrained from implementing them as he considered they were injudicious; and yet, he did not inform the Adjutant-General or his deputy of his inaction "knowing their despotic power and their inclination to use it." Since the Adjutant-General's office was not informed of the true position, it took it for granted, but incorrectly, that the regulations in question had been carried out in the first battalion of the first regiment.[10] To the second battalion of the twenty-third regiment the regulations had not been communicated by the commanding officer; nonetheless, the men knew very well that such an order had come from the Adjutant-General's office.[11]

It could not be also stated that the turban was not displeasing to the army. It was true that a similar pattern of turban had been worn in the past, but it must be remembered that only one battalion, the second of the thirteenth regiment, wore such a turban. It was also true that the major alteration in the turban took place in 1797 and not in 1806, but it must be recognized that in 1806 a significant change did take place. The shape was altered, and two additional ornaments affixed. The shape of the turban was indeed quite offensive to the sepoys. They repeatedly declared that the new head dress was not a turban but "a European hat or drummer's cap." The

Mixed Commission admitted that the new turban resembled "the leather caps lately introduced into His Majesty's European regiments."[12] One of the ornaments, the leather cockade, might also have been offensive. It was said that these ornaments had been in use in the past; however, they were not commonly used. To be exact, the cotton tuft had been used by several battalions, but only one battalion wore the leather cockade.[13]

Moreover, it is true also that the high caste sepoys from Wallajabhad wore the turbans without objection, and they might have even expressed their approbation. However, in June, 1806, the very same battalion to which these sepoys belonged bitterly resented the turban. To understand this apparent paradox, one must keep in mind the time element. The sepoys had given their approval sometime prior to November 14, 1805, the date on which the turban order was promulgated. At this time, the sepoys could not have had any knowledge of the regulations as the code had not yet been published. Consequently, no suspicion could have risen at that time. Moreover, at first glance, the sepoys would not have noticed anything invidious in the turban; perhaps they did not see anything wrong until somebody else drew their attention to it. Misgivings arose in the army only after the publication of the military code. It is reasonable to assume that once suspicion arose, the turban which they once approved became detestable.

It is also true that the turban had been left in the Adjutant-General's office several weeks. But it does not mean that Indian officers went in and examined the turban. The exclusive nature of British officers would not have encouraged their Indian colleagues to visit the Adjutant-General's office. Even if they had done it and had found something indeed offensive, it is reasonable to conclude that instead of disclosing their true opinion to the British officers they would have merely stirred up the sepoys and common people against the turban.

It is further true that the Indian officers repeatedly expressed themselves favourable to the turban. But to accept their approbation at face value is to delude one-self. The lack of *rapport* between Indian officers and their British colleagues forbade any meaningful communication. John Cradock and William Bentinck had often acknowledged this sad fact.[14] Mir Ghalam Ali's advice to the twenty-one prisoners clearly indicates that the Indian officers had no faith in the possibility of redress. They knew that the turban originated in the Adjutant-General's office, and they also knew the obstinate character of these men from whom they had to expect consideration.[15] The Indian officers appeared to have felt that even if they protested, they would eventually be forced to wear the turban. Subsequent events only too soon confirmed their fear. All who declined to wear the turban were ruthlessly punished and in the highest military tone the commissioned officers were ordered to make up and wear the turban at once. Against such a threatening background, the officers were summoned to express their opinion. Surely, no one in his right mind, unless he was idealistic enough to risk his neck, would dare to express himself disagreeable to the military command. In this connection, Lieutenant-Colonel W. J. Wilson observes:

> As the defence of the turban rested chiefly on the evidence of the Native officers and soldiers . . . it may be well to consider what that evidence was worth. Bearing in mind the exceedingly summary, arbitrary, and severe manner in which the 2nd of the 4th had been dealt with. . . it ought not to have been a matter of surprise to anyone at all conversant with the disposition of the Native soldiery, that the Court [of Inquiry] should have failed to elicit any unfavourable opinion regarding the new turband. It was well known that the change had been recommended, either by the Adjutant-General or his Deputy, or both officers, who at that period . . . were supreme in respect to all matters connected with

native troops. With this knowledge, and with the punishment of
the 4th before their eyes, was it to be expected that the turband
would be condemned by the Native officers called upon for their
opinions? The extraordinary thing is, that opinions obtained under
such circumstances should have been gravely put forward as good
evidence in favor of the change . . . [16]

John Cradock, Nathaniel Forbes and others argued that the officers of
the very battalion which piloted the mutiny declared their unanimous and
full satisfaction with the turban. But it must be remembered that when they
made that solemn declaration Mustpha Beg had divulged the plot. The safety
of the conspirators lay only in cementing Forbes' naive notion that the
informant was insane. It would have been sheer folly, nay, suicidal at the
time, to reveal their abhorrence of the turban to their officers.

Undoubtedly, some battalions did volunteer to wear the new turban
after it had been recalled. The number of those battalions however was very
few indeed. It was no more than six.[17] The willingness of those battalions
could not however be taken to prove that others had been seduced, in the
absence of positive or corroborative evidence. It could only prove that they
had a greater proportion of less prejudiced men than others had.

That the turban was truly objectionable to the sepoys could be gleaned
from numerous other sources too. In Vellore, the ones who took the oath at
the mosque in April pledged themselves against the wearing of the new
turban. In the initial protest on May 6, the grenadiers stated that they would
not wear it, and if they did, their families would not live with them. Later, in
June, Muhammad Jaffer told his friend that he intended to sacrifice his life
on account of the hat. Sheikh Ramjuny observed that "all these people [he
mentioned seven] . . . consulted together that it was better for them to die
than to wear the topie, for nobody would give them water."[18] A month
before the mutiny, according to Thomas Marriott, "the mother of the Prince

Shukerulla was very earnest in recommending to him not to enforce the wearing of the new turban . . . and to do anything against their prejudices, would only make them disaffected, and do no good . . . that it would only disgrace them. . ."[19] Mustapha Beg himself told Lieutenant-Colonel Forbes that the sepoys were going to kill their officers "on account of the topees."

The same attitude towards the turban was expressed elsewhere also. Edward Locker stated that "the sentries at his own door mounted guard for some days with a shawl or handkerchief bound about the head, rather than wear the hateful turban."[20] The letter from Chicacole, Mysore, clearly indicates the apprehension of the troops at that station.[21] The letter addressed to the Nizam, whether real or fabricated, again illustrates the obnoxious nature of the turban.[22] Resident Sydenham was of the opinion, after his long investigation, that the late military orders were "the primary cause of the disturbance."[23] Aitwar Singh's warning to James Welsh further suggests that the turban was the cause of the alarm, conspiracy and planned massacre.[24] The hostile demonstration in Wallajabhad moreover unmistakably illustrates the resentment of the common people against the turban.[25]

That the turban was objectionable to the sepoys could also be seen from what they themselves said during the time of mutiny. They stated repeatedly that the orders and turban were the cause of their mutiny. Clarinda Rebero, the maid-servant to Mrs. Pritchard, observed that in response to her interrogation, the mutineers replied that "it was because their officers wanted them to wear (toppes) hats, and cut their whiskers."[26] Mrs. Potters testified, "When the sepoys were plundering me of my joys, they said, what can the Europeans do now, they cannot make us wear toppees. . ."[27] The sepoys who butchered Lieutenant-Colonel McKerras, Captain Willison, and Lieutenant Winchip abused them for ordering them to wear "the topie." Muhammad Moturbah, the Eunuch, stated that the mutineers told him in that morning:

> . . . the reason of the fight was. . .new turban, which made them look like Christians, and that they would lose their cast . . . that they themselves contrived and executed this business . . . they would have obeyed their European officers in everything else, but for this matter of the turbans they were made to lose their lives.[28]

One might question the reliability of Moturbah's assertion, but all others are undoubtedly above suspicion. It was also stated that the mutineers wanted to kill both John Jones and all his Indian workmen for manufacturing the leather cockade for the turban.[29]

John F. Cradock maintained that in the Military Court of Inquiry and not in the Mixed Commission the true cause of the mutiny was disclosed. As they were still under the shock of the collapse of their scheme, the witnesses plainly confessed what the real cause of the mutiny was—intrigue and conspiracy—in the Military Court. But by the time the Mixed Commission met, the witnesses had enough time for reflection, and consequently they came forward to screen the princes by alleging the turban as the cause of mutiny.

To anyone who has gone through the proceedings of the Military Court and the Mixed Commission, such insinuation is totally absurd. In the Military Court, among the nine witnesses who made reference to what they thought or what they heard to the cause of the mutiny, eight mentioned the turban, and only one, a Hindu, intrigue. This Hindu stated that Tipu Sultan's people urged him not to wear the turban. In the Commission, among the sixteen witnesses who referred to causes or related matters all of them mentioned the turban. Overall, in the Military Court, many witnesses went at length describing the horror of the night and the assistance given by the princes's people and Moiz-ud-din's role; in the Commission, except Forbes and Marriott, others largely dealt with what preceded the mutiny. Among the witnesses who were interrogated privately, one positively declared the princes to have instigated the mutiny, another asserted the turban as sole cause, and others referred to the turban also added that the Myssoreans did tell them not to wear it.

Unmistakably then neither the regulations nor the turban was wholly innocent or harmless. To some degree at least, they constituted innovations, and they were obnoxious to the troops. The Mixed Commission rightly observed, "that the turban was highly offensive to the prejudices of the sepoys, however much they may have concealed their feelings in that respect from their officers."[30] It is obvious then that the very assumption on which the conspiracy theory is built is spurious.

II

Like the foundation, the superstructure of the conspiracy theory also does not stand scrutiny. The assertion that the spirit of intrigue and rebellion remained unabated even after the revocation of the order is not demonstrable. In Hyderabad, the explosive situation petered away the moment Lieutenant-Colonel Montresor revoked the obnoxious orders. The so-called diabolical plot and attempted insurrections in other places were mere myths.

In Wallajabhad, in July, the only ostensible cause to suspect the loyalty of the troops was some "angry expressions of individuals." It must be remembered that those "angry expressions" proceeded from hungry men who had been kept without food from early morning drill till noon. Furthermore, the allegations came only from women and children, who claimed to have overheard them. However, the whole conduct of the troops negates all insinuations of disaffection. The corps, in full possession of arms and ammunition, marched out and into the cantonment with alacrity and in perfect obedience. Despite rigorous examination, the Commander-in-Chief could not find any symptoms of defection except for a few inflammatory declarations. The Indian officers insisted that the cause of the adverse expressions was the long detention in the barracks and disavowed any disaffection in the corps. The Commander-in-Chief despite his earlier determination to punish the corps was forced to conclude that there existed no evidence to support "the idea to anything like a concerted plan of disaffection and evil design" and attributed the officers' alarm to the "evident alteration of sentiment in their minds."[31]

In Nundydrug, suspicion and tension had risen to the boiling point. Solely on the report of an inflammatory conversation, and allusions of hostile remarks, two companies were marched off and their commissioned officers incarcerated. All appearances of quietness were interpreted as the calm before the storm. Secret agents were multiplied; and they were promised liberal rewards and promotions. In this climate of expectancy, it was reported to have been overheard: ". . . but wait and see what will happen in two hours." "The plot is discovered," the officers snapped. Another overheard report that "Something will happen tonight" confirmed fully their apprehension. Later, it was alleged that the sepoys had sent away their families—a sure prelude to insurrection.

Even if these reports were valid, they could form only presumptive evidence. But the manner in which the sepoys behaved during that eventful night and unforgettable morning nullifies in all reasonableness even such a conclusion. The irrefutable argument is that if the sepoys truly wanted to kill their officers that night, why did they not do so? If the sepoys had wished, they could have easily broken through the thin barricade and butchered their officers. The officers remained behind that thin barricade till two o' clock in the following afternoon. Perhaps, one might argue that sepoys were confounded by the discovery of their plot. This argument is not however convincing; for in all probability the sepoys were able to do what they were alleged to have intended—kill the officers, plunder their homes, flee into the hills and wait there till their comrades in other garrisons had risen. Even if one admits that the sepoys were cowards and were confounded by the officers' prompt measures, it would still be reasonable to assume that the sepoys would have fled from their barracks instead of waiting there for avenging swords.

Much has been construed on the allegation that the sepoys had sent away their families. However, the allegation is not fully demonstrable. It is true that three or four witnesses testified that they saw "a great number of sepoys' families go away" and one evidence maintained that the sepoys' camp was almost deserted. Nonetheless, it is unanimously agreed that all the families were in their huts at ten o' clock in the morning, the time when a few sepoys went down to visit them. If the families had been sent away as prelude to massacre, it is more than probable that they would have gone too far to return that morning. But the strongest reason to suspect the validity of the allegation is that the families themselves were never interrogated by the court of inquiry. Obviously the court, except the president, Lieutenant-Colonel Davis, had to justify their desperate action on the previous night. Perhaps they did not want to nullify the only evidence which could be construed as the strongest case for their action. To be sure, it is more than probable that some families were indeed seen going away. The question is why did they go? And where did they go? Did they go on usual business perhaps to neighbouring villages? Or did they flee on account of alarm? Whatever might have been the cause of the departure of the families, alarm or otherwise, and whatever might have been the validity of the overheard reports, the sepoys' behaviour nullifies the allegation that they had conspired to murder their officers on that night.[32]

In Palamcottah, the only evidence was James Welsh's butler's assertion that he overheard Subadar Sheikh Hyder to say that in ten days all British officers would be killed. As Dyce himself admitted there were strong reasons to suspect the veracity of the butler's evidence. Just a few days earlier the butler had had a violent quarrel with Sheikh Hyder and several Muslims and consequently he was inimical to them. Further, the butler alleged that the conversation took place in Tamil. The probability of Muslims discussing such grave matters in that language was indeed slim. As in Nundydrug, the sepoys' disposition gravely challenges the allegation. If the Muslim sepoys had been guilty, they would have immediately absconded, instead of loitering around the fort after they were expelled. William Petrie's argument is surely unanswerable: "If they were conscious of guilt, why return to Pallamcottah, and put themselves in the power of their officers?"[33]

The alleged plots in Bangalore, Quilon, Wallajabhad and Sankerydrug were pure fantasy. In Bangalore after a month's vexatious search, Lieutenant-Colonel Ogg confessed that he was gravely wrong in suspecting the fidelity of his corps. The Quilon affair was an insult, as John Cradock admitted, to the British officers' prowess. Lieutenant-Colonel Munro reported that the alarm in Wallajabhad was without foundation and grossly exaggerated. In Sankerydrug, the commanding officer was reprimanded, and the alleged conspiracy disappeared. William Bentinck was correct when he recorded, ". . . the conspiracies of Sankerrydroog, Palamcottah, and Quilon [for that matter Nundydrug, Bangalore and twice in Wallajabhad] have more the appearance of an insurrection of the officers against the sepoys, than of the latter against the former."[34]

This does not mean that no unrest or disaffection existed amongst the troops. No doubt rumours of disaffection continued to persist. This however could be reasonably attributed to the continued operation of the original cause. The Indian officers and soldiers' reaction in Palamcottah unmistakably indicates that the troops were still plagued with the fear of proselytism.[35] Obviously, the earlier rumours were still kept up by fakirs and others who were eager for gossip. However, this natural reaction would have submerged except for the officers' "unmanly panic."[36] The officers' extreme distrust of the troops, and the strong inducement they gave to the informants often generated alarming situations which otherwise would never have risen. It is safe to assert that except for the officers' precipitate vigilance, the Wallajabhad, Nundydrug, Bangalore, Palamcottah, and Quilon episodes would never have occurred.

The assertion that the overwhelming majority of the participants and leaders of the alleged conspiracies were Muslims, and therefore there must have been a Muslim conspiracy, is both incorrect and irrational. Among the twenty-one sepoys who refused to wear the turban in Vellore, eleven were Hindus, and one of the two sepoys who were ultimately so brutally punished, was a Hindu. The sepoy who led the demonstration to the commanding officer's home was a Hindu.[37] In the Wallajabhad resistance, the subadar who was alleged as the "secret cause" of insubordination was a Hindu.[38] In Nundydrug the alleged leader of conspiracy, Subadar Venkatachellum, was a Hindu. Out of the nine persons accused of mutinous conduct at that station two were Hindus, besides Subadar Venkatachellum.[39] The alleged leader of the plot at Sankerydrug was also a Hindu.[40] In fact, according to Major-General Dugald Campbell, in all the disturbances alleged or real "the sepoys of all caste appear to have entered with equal readiness."[41] In Vellore at least one Hindu subadar was in the inner circle of the plotters.[42] Some of the ferocious killers too were Hindus.[43] Purnia testified that the Hindus had been more alarmed than the Muslims.[44] In Hyderabad all the accused leaders were Muslims, however many Hindus had also sworn to mutiny.[45] The conspirators had in fact kept both Hindus as well as Muslims out of their circle if they suspected their reliability. It is well to remember that Mustapha Beg was a Muslim, and the chief informants in Wallajabad too were Muslims.[46] In fact, the panic-stricken officers suspected almost everyone. The criminal suspicion against Madava

Rao and Purniah is a monumental example.[47] Even if a majority of the agitators were Muslims, which might have been true, proportionately speaking, it could not be stated positively that they had ulterior motives. Because the Muslims occupied two thirds of all higher ranks, in any protest therefore they would appear to take the lead. However, their aggressive nature would also make them more active. Bentinck rightly pointed out:

> It is not surprising that the Mussalman should appear the foremost in every conspiracy. The character that makes them better soldiers also make them better conspirators than the Hindoos. They are more daring and desperate in character, more violent bigots in religion, filing two thirds of the commissions of Native officers and possessing in consequence the greatest share of influence. A conspiracy in which they were concerned would have the appearance of originating in Mussalman intrigue if the Hindoo native officer had not appeared in all instances to have united with equal ardor in the same cause.[48]

In the light of the above observation it is incorrect to say that the overwhelming majority of the agitators were Muslims and it is irrational to deduce the conclusion which the conspiracy theorists had drawn.

III

The allegation that hordes of emissaries were on the move seducing the troops demands closer examination. Despite the scrupulous measures adopted to track them, the Government failed to find any plan, connection or concert among the so-called "emissaries of sedition".[49] Though the alleged emissaries might have denigrated the British name and prophesied the speedy downfall of British Government, they appeared to have been chiefly interested in securing maximum alms.[50] It is also alleged that there was an explosion in the number of beggars, but since no statistic was taken, and no identity preserved, no one could have known even the near-exact number of the beggars. Perhaps, the alleged increase was only in the minds of the suspicious officers. The more the fakirs were sought after, the more ubiquitous they appeared. Even if there had been an increase in their number, there is an adequate explanation. The monsoon had failed; grains had become scare, and a devastating famine was stalking through the land.[51] Under such circumstances beggars would naturally multiply. Possibly the alleged emissaries of sedition were none other than mere victims of cruel nature.

If there indeed existed a conspiracy, contemporary Indians must have had some inkling of it. However, that was not the case. Mir Allum, the pro-English minister at Hyderabad, denied its existence.[52] Purnia, the Hindu prime minister at Mysore, disavowed such a supposition.[53] The leading citizens of Palamcottah and Tinnevelly did not believe it.[54] Except for a few anonymous letters and Subadar Secunder Cawn's deposition—the former was absurd and the latter was spurious—no evidence of the conspiracy was ever made by any contemporary Indians.[55] The weight of evidence positively repudiates the belief in conspiracy explanation.

IV

It is now appropriate to examine the charge that the princes in Vellore and the sirdars in Hyderabad intrigued with the troops in their respective neighbourhood and seduced them. Does the evidence support such a charge?

Nathaniel Forbes and John Coombs charged the princes of long plotting to regain their father's kingdom. Citing the third article of the oath of conspiracy, which enjoined the establishment of a Muslim kingdom, they stated that "an object of such magnitude . . . could not originate with the troops." "The conduct of the princes during the insurrection," they suggested, "strongly corrobates and supports this opinion." They went on to add that the princes worked through their adherents who through the tactics of insult and promise seduced the troops. Moiz-ud-din, they said, was the prime author, and Mohi-ud-din and Abdul Khalik were collaborators.[56]

If one could establish proof of intrigue prior to May, 1806, when the sepoys first articulated their abhorrence to the turban, one could conclude that the plot originated with the princes. Whereas if the evidence suggested that there was no intrigue prior to the May incident and that the initiative did not come from the princes, then one would have to look elsewhere for the origin of the conspiracy.

According to Sheikh Cassim, "The sepoys first shewed symptoms of discontent on the first arrival of the new-pattern turband (sic), and the people about the palace *then* began to tamper with the sentries. . ."[57] All evidences confirm Sheikh Cassim's deposition, and none contradicts it. The Forbes-Coombs report itself concedes that no evidence exists to indicate the existence of intrigue prior to the end of April or the beginning of May.[58] On the matter of initiative, Shekh Cassim hinted that it came from Moiz-ud-din. He stated that Jemmal-ud-din intrigued with the sepoys and made offers in Moiz-ud-di's name. Jemmal-ud-din while admitting the charge, explained that the initiative came from some Muslim sepoys, and that he encouraged other sepoys in Moiz-ud-din's name but without his concurrence. Jemmal-ud-din asserted that Moiz-ud-din was not informed of the conspiracy till about June 23. Forbes and Coombs dismissed Jemmal-ud-din's statement as an attempt to exculpate Moiz-ud-din. Since one is here faced with one man's word against another, one has to take into consideration related matters in one's attempt to arrive at the truth.[59]

The charge that Jemmal-ud-din tried to exculpate Moiz-ud-din is not wholly warranted. At this time Moiz-ud-din, along with other princes, had been shipped off to Bengal and there he had been already given severe punishment on the assumption of his complicity in the massacre. It was Jemmmal-ud-din and not Moiz-ud-din who was in need of exculpation at this time. Therefore, Jemmal-ud-din could have easily fixed the responsibility on Moiz-ud-din without any qualm. Nonetheless, one should point out that Jemmal-ud-din had been promised complete pardon, and therefore he could have assumed all the responsibility upon himself making Moiz-ud-din appear as least culapable as possible. This explanation however does not answer the question of prime responsibility.

However, there is substantial reason to conclude that neither Moiz-ud-din nor any of his adherents could have seduced the troops.

First, the troops could not have been bribed. Moiz-ud-din was totally bankrupt. For almost a year prior to the mutiny he was under voluntary cut of Rs. 1,000 a month to clear his arrears.[60] None of his adherents had independent resources to bribe the troops. Therefore, all suggestions that the corps had been bribed are without any foundation. It is appropriate to cite the torrent which came from Usman Cawn, the senior subadar of the first battalion of the first regiment, when Major Hazlewood stated that the battalions must have been bribed:

> What! Those poor boys confined in a prison? If the wealth of the Padsha of the great Nabob his father was never able to corrupt any of us, how could these boys corrupt two battalions! [61]

Secondly, the two mutinied battalions were in no sense attached to Moiz-ud-din or any other princes. The first battalion of the first regiment had been ever since its inception an enemy of Hyder Ali's family. Its members came largely from Tanjore; and in addition to taking active part in all the Mysore wars, they had also obstinately refused all the tempting offers of Tipu Sultan.[62] The second battalion of the twenty-third regiment, which was constituted largely of poligar elements, had just come from Madura. It had been less than fifty-five days in Vellore when the rebellion broke out. It is most unlikely that Moiz-ud-din or his adherents won the battalion over in such a short period.[63]

Forbes and Coombs charged Moiz-ud-din's adherents with having seduced the troops through insult and promise. As observed earlier there is no evidence to suggest that any Mysorean incited the troops prior to the May incident. After that incident undoubtedly the princes' adherents incited the troops. However, their incitement could not be interpreted as seduction unless it could be proved that they were the only ones who did so. But the facts are different. The Wallajabhad incident forcibly demonstrates that common people in general resented the military orders and incited the troops against acquiescence.[64]

These evidences indicate that the plot did not originate with Moiz-ud-din or his adherents. Moiz-ud-din could only be accused of collaboration and not with initiation. Therefore, the origin of the conspiracy must be traced elsewhere.

Mohi-ud-din and Abdul Khalik were accused of collaboration in the conspiracy. To arrive at the truth, it is essential to examine the evidence against each of them minutely.

The allegation against Mohi-ud-din was based on the depositions of Sheikh Cassim and several others. Sheikh Cassim often referred to "the princes" in plural, and he even mentioned Mohi-ud-din by name. In fact, he went so far as to infer that Mohi-ud-din was anxious about the forthcoming mutiny. "Five or six days before the night of the conspiracy," he stated:

Ramdeen sepoy of the light company, 1st of 1st, was sentry at Mahuddeen's palace; he was posted at two o' clock and between that time and four, Mohuddeen came out three times, and enquired of him 'if the insurrection had not yet been'. . . Sultan

Mohuddeen told him, 'I am ready with 500 men in my own pay, outside to assist . . . [65]

Sheikh Cassim also alleged that on that fateful morning "the princes" could have come out if the mutineers had not dispersed.[66] Ramawamy, Murti, Cawsy Singh sepoys and Cassim Ali, a former sepoy, stated Mohi-ud-din to have taken active part in that morning. The evidence against Mohi-ud-din appears considerable.[67]

It would seem that Mohi-ud-din must have been at least a collaporator. However, a closer scrutiny casts serious doubt on the validity of the evidence. It is true that Sheikh Cassim particularly mentioned Mohi-ud-din by name. Nonetheless, it must be remembered that Sheikh Cassim's evidence was based on the report of another, Ramdeen. It is not impossible as N. B. Edmonstone, the Secretary to the Supreme Government, pointed out that due to the similarity of the two names, "the sepoy may have mistaken one name for the other or Sheikh Cassim himself may have committed the same error in delivering his deposition."[68] Sheikh Nutter's sepoy's remarks strongly suggests the above observation. He alleged that Moiz-ud-din, not Mohi-ud-din, had four to five hundred men in the *pettah*.[69] There is strong reason to assume that Mohi-ud-din's name had been often mistakenly used for Moiz-ud-din's. For instance, Ramaswamy's charge against Mohi-ud-din with some variations had been attributed to Moiz-ud-din by several other witnesses.[70] It is likely that Murti and Cawsy Singh were not sure of Mohi-ud-din's identity. Cassim Ali acknowledged his ignorance of the physical appearance of the prince, but stated that he was told that it was Mohi-ud-din.[71] Unfortunately, the Military Court of Inquiry and the Mixed Commission made no attempt to clarify this confusion. Besides these probable confusions, there is a stronger presumptive reason against Mohi-ud-din's gullibility. Mohi-ud-din was older than Moiz-ud-din. He was also the only legitimate son of Tipu Sultan. In recognition of his pre-eminence among the brothers, he alone was addressed with the title of "Sultan." It is most improbable that a person of such pre-eminence would join a conspiracy which aimed at the enthronement of his younger brother. If one argued that Mohi-ud-din consented to the plot because of his amiable and deferential disposition, one could counter-argue that his non-aggressive and "contented" attitude would not have permitted him to enter into scheme of rebellion against a powerful government. The manner in which Mohi-ud-din continued with the marriage ceremonies of his sister again seriously challenges his knowledge of the plot.[72] It is reasonable to conclude, as N. B. Edmonstone did, that:

> From such confusion of persons it seems unjust to decide upon his guilt. A suspicion may perhaps be entertained, but the whole tenor of Moizooden's conduct . . . appears to implicate him and him only in whole guilt of first fomenting and subsequently assisting in the insurrection.[73]

The allegation against Abdul Khalik is based on one single deposition alone. Before the Mixed Commission, Murti sepoy declared:

> . . . I went first to the palace of Khalick Sahib. Khalick Padshaw was standing at the door appareled with a red handkerchief about his head, and a silk and cotton quilt wrapped round him. There were four or five sepoys standing at his door. The door was half open, and he came to the door and said to the sepoys what is going on? They replied, The coffers wanted them to wear hats, leather stocks, and to cut whiskers. Therefore, they were going to kill all the coffers, and set the princes up. Khalick Padshaw replied very well, and went in immediately and shut the door. This was about six in the morning.[74]

In the appendix to the Forbes-cum-Coombs report, a slightly varied version of Muri's deposition is given:

> I then went near the house of Khalick Badshaw. He came out and
> stood at the door. . . Meer Husain sepoy was near the door and
> made salam. Khalick Badshaw said, 'What is the matter, sepoy.'
> Meer Hussain replied, 'In the time of the Sultaun, I eat (sic) much
> of your provisions. Now your country is gone. The coffers have
> deprived you of it. My family is now come here and I have taken
> service with these coffers. Now they are going to make us cut our
> whiskers, wear leather stocks and the topees are ready. Hereafter
> we shall be ordered to wear shoes and mits together. All the
> Mussalmen have therefore united for our religion and our faith.
> We have killed all the coffers. This is the time for the flag of the
> faith to fly and the drum of the faith to sound. We will soon place
> a Mussalman prince on the throne and we will protect him.'
> Khalick Badshaw replied, 'May victory attend you'.[75]

Whether the former or the latter and enlarged account is true, it is
quite unjustifiable to incriminate Abdul Khalik just on the basis of one
evidence alone. The Supreme Government was quite right when it dismissed
the charge stating, "It is superfluous to remark that the whole of the
proceeding evidence scarcely affords the slightest ground of suspicion
against Abdool Khaulick."[76]

In Hyderabad too there was no evidence of conspiracy. No formal
inquiry was conducted there, but Resident Sydenham did carry out some
secret investigation. He concluded that first came discontent, and then the
enemies of the British perhaps exploited it. However, Sydenham pointed out
that the disaffection was not due to intrigue but something else.[77]

V

A study of the persons who articulated the Muslim conspiracy theory
casts grave doubts upon the validity of their view. Nearly all the conspiracy
theorists had vested interests in their explanation. To men like Cradock,

250

Agnew, and Pierce, the Muslim conspiracy theory provided a safe escape from the responsibility for the disaffection and mutiny. To men like Gillespie and Hazlewood, such an explanation made them saviours of the British Empire in the east. To Grant and Parry, it served another purpose: it became a scapegoat to protect the Christian missions.

However, the Muslim conspiracy theorists should not be accused of hypocrisy, particularly the military men. Once they got the idea, it became an obsession with them, and they truly believed in a conspiracy. Assuming that the Indian sepoys were incapable of mediating rebellion without incitement the military men concluded that a conspiracy alone could explain the discontent, disaffection and mutiny.

As regards to the causes which were alleged to have facilitated the disaffection and mutiny, evidence suggests that some of them were valid and others were not. The allegation that Bentinck's revenue and judicial measures had alienated the people is not demonstrable. As Maya Gupta points out in her dissertation, *Lord William Bentinck in Madras, 1803-1807*, there was no major land settlement in South India at this period which could have caused sufferings to the indigenous people.[78] In the judiciary, some innovation did take place. Zillah courts were established, and the collector was deprived of his magisterial functions. The criminal code was modified to give the Hindus parity with the Muslims. In addition, the military officers were strictly prohibited from interfering with the affairs of the civil population. Perhaps, some Muslims were hurt at the loss of their preferred status and some officers feared that they could no longer harass the civilians as they liked. Bentinck's regulations by and large only protected the inhabitants from their oppressors, who were often, as Bentinck noted, government servants.[79] There is no conceivable reason to suggest that these were unfavourable to Indians. If they had been, they would have been complained of. In all the proceedings of the revenue departments and the various courts of inquiry, which were held in different parts of the country in 1806, not a trace to that effect is found.[80]

VI

The charge against the Christian mission too is not demonstrable. The Protestant missions had been on the Coast since the beginning of the eighteenth century. The first missionaries, Bartholomew Ziegenbalg and Heinrich Plutchau, landed in Tranquebar in 1706, and the Bible was first published in the Tamil language in 1724. Throughout that century, Christian missions gradually expanded; and by the beginning of the nineteenth century, there were mission stations in Madras, Tranquebar, Tinnevelly, Tanjore, Trichinopoly, Vellore, Vizagapatam and several other places. The Indian reaction to the Christian missions was lukewarm and at times cool. Though the Indians held some missionaries like Christian F. Schwartz in high esteem, they did not refrain from molesting their converts. However, no large scale resentment was ever manifested against either the missionary or his converts. Generally speaking, the missionary was treated with indifference and his converts with pity.[81]

There is no reason to suppose that at the beginning of the nineteenth century, the Indians, on the basis of mission activities alone, regarded the missionaries in any way different from the past century. Contrary to John Scott Waring's allegation there had been no dramatic increase in the number of missionaries.[82] The increase in the volume of Christian literature is uncertain.[83] No Indian might have known the object of Buchanan's travels in South India, or of Kerr's investigation in Malabar, or of the former's *Memoir.* If Indians had been alarmed at the mission activities, they would have said so. But not even an allusion is found in any of the proceedings of the courts of inquiry or in other documents. Likely, the alarm existed only in the minds of the government officials. However, the "alarmists" were not without excuse. Buchanan's pomposity and the evangelicals' zeal furnished more than adequate cause for apprehension.

The other alleged predisposing causes such as the poor *rapport* between Indians and their rulers, the failure to associate the Indian aristocracy with the ruling power and the consequent dismay on its part, and the economic exploitation of India are valid in different degrees. The aloofness in which the Government stood was deeply deplored. The wretched condition of the aristocrats kept them simmering. The exclusive spirit of the military officers and the insolent attitude of many of them tended to alienate the Indian troops from them. The poor pay which the Indian troops received, compared to the British, was deeply resented. Repeated allusions to these factors are found in the proceedings of the courts of inquiry: "The coffers treat us like dogs;" "They are holding all the positions . . . They have riches in plenty, but give us only trifling allowances. . ." There is enough evidence to suggest that the Indian officers and their men felt humiliated, insulted and exploited. Undoubtedly, this feeling of estrangement facilitated disaffection and mutiny.

Thus, the foregoing analysis, which shows that there was a degree of alienation between the governors and the governed, demonstrates that the Muslim conspiracy theory is wrong. The truth is that the Indian troops did object to the new regulations and the use of the turban, but that once these orders were rescinded, the basis of unrest became eliminated. The evidence clearly demonstrates that the conspiracy theory was first proposed in the heated aftermath of the mutiny. There was no concrete evidence produced to support the theory; but under the circumstances, it is understandable why panic-stricken British officers suggested it, and why certain persons and parties both in India and England were interested in popularizing the theory. Therefore, the commonly held theory that there was a widespread Muslim conspiracy in South India is unfounded.

Jalakandeswarar Temple inside Vellore Fort

CONCLUSION

TO APPRECIATE THE NATURE AND CAUSE of the Vellore mutiny, one must understand the psyche of the people in a vertical relationship. In such a situation, especially between people of different races and cultures, there always exists a degree of latent hostility. The stronger has an air of condescension toward the weaker; the latter has a simmering though often disguised resentment toward the former. As the stronger becomes confident of his strength, he is less considerate of the weaker; while the weaker's sense of helplessness merely accentuates his resentment. The stronger's disposition is also marked by overbearing conduct and the weaker's by timidity.

Furthermore, if the stronger has established his supremacy without any or substantial resistance from the weaker, the former concludes that the weaker is incapable of effective response. But if the stronger has achieved his pre-eminence due to the active or passive co-operation of the weaker, the former's attitude towards the latter is not one of gratitude but of contempt. On the other hand, if the weaker had been once the stronger, in most cases he attributes to the present conqueror that attitude and those motives which he had when he was the master. But if the weaker had been also subjected in the past, he often reads in the present a repetition of his former experience. The knowledge of these human reactions is the key to the right understanding of the prelude and aftermath of the Vellore mutiny.

Undoubtedly, the military orders—the shaving, trimming, no-sect marks, and no-ear rings regulations and turban orders—had the effect of approximating the Indian sepoy's dress and appearance to that of his British colleagues, who was of another faith and whom the sepoy considered infidel and outcaste. In this innovation both the Muslim and the Hindu saw a prelude to forced proselytism. The Muslim attributed to the British what he himself did when he was a conqueror—the intention of converting the conquered people to his religion. The Hindu saw in the late orders a prelude to what he had previously suffered from Muslim hands. They both truly believed that the British were about to destroy their respective religions and social institutions and absorb them all into Christianity.[1]

The basic reason for the Indians to assume such a view was that the East India Company had just emerged supreme in South India. If such military orders had been enacted twenty or thirty years earlier, they might not have attached any importance to them. But now the Company had become paramount, and the orders it instituted, taken as a whole, gave the impression that it was following in the footsteps of the Arab and Afghan conquerors.

Obviously the Indians misconstrued the British intention. A dialogue would have dispelled the misconception under which the Indians labored. But theirs was a vertical relationship wherein no meaningful dialogue was possible. At best only a timid monologue would be attempted. That is what happened on May 6. But the reaction of the stronger was wholly inconsiderate. John Darley at once silenced the grenadiers and later the battalion. John Cradock's response was a typical reflection of the psyche of the governors toward the governed. He suppressed the resistance with an iron hand; and though he instituted a court of inquiry, his insolence led him to dismiss the court's valuable findings. He was prepared for full coercion so long as the Government was behind him. William Bentinck too reflected the psyche of the ruling. To him "the passiveness and mildness of the Indian character" was a guarantee against the possibility of "an explosion."[2] He observed, "I deem it essential to insist on implicit obedience; and I am certain the worst consequence would result from any concession on this point."[3]

Repression often silences the repressed but not always without danger to the repressor. For in every repressive act, a seed is potentially sown to the ultimate destruction of the repressor. Years may fly, decades may pass, but sooner or later the time of reckoning comes. The simmering relationship which is hardly felt by the stronger explodes when he least expects it. That is what happened in Vellore.

The authorities felt all was well. To them there was not a symptom of discontent after the Wallajabhad incident. The very measure which secured the sepoys' ostensible acquiescence sealed the point of no return. The troops now fully believed that the authorities were "inflexibly bent upon the abolition of the distinctions of tribe and caste and the compulsory introduction of an outward conformity at least to the practices of Christians."[4] Initiative for the mutiny came from some desperate sepoys. The second battalion of the first regiment gave its blessing. The presence of the princes perhaps acted as a catalyst. And then came the explosion.

The panic in the aftermath of the mutiny was solely due to the British officers' unwillingness to admit that the troops did have initiative and stamina. Since the officers concluded that the sepoys could not have risen without incitement, they came out with the conspiracy explanation which became an obsession with them. If they had faced up to the reality that the mutiny was an extreme act of desperate men whose quivering voice had been silenced by their ruthlessness, they would have saved themselves from numerous sleepless nights.

That the direct cause of the mutiny was the military orders could not be doubted. But the orders in themselves did not produce the explosion. It was the ill-effect of that vertical relationship which made the sepoys misconstrue the intentions of the orders and also made the authorities insensitive to the apprehension of the sepoys. Given these factors a mutiny was inevitable in 1806.

If the mutiny had not broken out in Vellore it would have in Hyderabad. But for the Vellore insurrection, the authorities in Hyderabad would not have revoked the orders on their own, and the brewing rebellion would have run its full course. A more devastating carnage would have then resulted. If not in Hyderabad, mutiny would have taken place somewhere else. The alarm was mounting in various garrisons in different degrees. It was only the prompt suppression of the rebellion and the revocation of the obnoxious orders that deterred the erupting conflagration.

A REFLECTION

HERE ARE SOME THOUGHTS THAT FLASHED through my mind as I typed and revised the manuscript which I wrote more than 45 years ago.

First, I was impressed by the sense of accountability the British had. Each time they did something they wrote a report on it: what they did and why they did it. They kept one copy, and sent another to their superior. This was done by practically everyone, starting from the lieutentant incharge of a small detachment to the governor in Fort St. George (Madras). Everyone was accountable to the higher authority, the final authority being the Parliament in Westminster, England (the impeachment of Warren Hastings was a proof of that).

Secondly, among the British, there were two types of people. One type had the "I am my brother's keeper" attitude, and the other type had that of "me first and foremost". Some examples of the former were men like Charles Grant, Edward Parry and Thomas Munro and of the latter were John Scott Waring, Thomas Twining and Sweny Toone. These two types of people are found in every age, culture and country. The former are the light of the world and salt of the earth. On the other hand, the latter constitute the darkness that covers our planet and poison our private and public life. The details may differ but the attitudes are one and the same.

Interestingly, often the latter considered themselves as people of tolerance and prided themselves having respect for others "to do their thing". They condemned the former as people of bigotry who tried to impose their beliefs on others. On the other hand, the former denounced the latter as people of indifference and called on them to care – to have "I am my brother's keeper attitude".

Thirdly, cursed is the society when its members find their primary identity in their caste, race, religion or tribe and give their loyalty to it. Sadly, that is how the Indian society of the early nineteenth century was. Jawharlal Nehru tried to get the Indians to think of themselves as Indians first and foremost, and any and everything else second. Blessed are we if we identify ourselves as humans first and give our loyalty to the common humanity that we all share.

Fourthly, the Vellore mutiny and its prelude and postlude provided several examples of humanity at its best as well as at its worst. Empathy and arrogance, caring and retribution, compassion and revenge were all displayed. No group had monopoly on goodness or evil. Good and bad people were in both groups.

Fifthy, I am surprised at the march of history. The scientific revolution and European expansion resulted in our modern world. The late 18th and 19th century Europeans were supremely confident of their culture, military, politics, religion and above all in themselves. They took for granted that the march of Europe, especially of Britain would continue for centurie to come. Some reflective people of the Vellore Mutiny generation were aware that the old order was being replaced by a new one, European and global. But, hardly anyone foresaw the transformation of Europe itself in the twentieth century.

One evening in the summer of 1969, after spending the day in the archives of the Baptist Missionary Society, I came out of the Piccadally underground Station. I heard the chanting of "Hare Rama, Hare Krishna" by

British youngsters in their saffron robes. At that scene, I spontaneously found myself uttering, "This is revenge!" At that time and for several weeks, I was pouring over the debates on "christianizing India" which were taking place at about the time of Vellore Mutiny. Here, in the very heart of London, once the very centre of Christian Missions, I was listening to "the prayers and hymns of heathenism!" The champions of the Missions of the early 19th centuary could never have imagined that so many of their descendants would abandon the Christian Faith in favour of those religions which they denounced pagan or heathen. They also could not have imagined the triumph of Big Bang Cosmology (Secularism) in their country. This is indeed amazing! This is truly incredulous! I am fascinated by the march of history!

ABBREVIATIONS

ABR	INSTITUTION
BFBS	British and Foreign Bible Society
BLO	Bodleian Library, Oxford
BM	British Museum
BMS	Baptist Missionary Society
IOL	India Office Library
PRO	Public Records Office
UE	University of Edinburgh
UN	University of Nottingham

ABR	INDIA OFFICE RECORDS
BSPP	Bengal Secret and Political Proceedings
HMS	Home Miscellaneous Series
MJP	Madras Judicial Proceedings
MMP	Madras Military Proceedings
MMPP	Madras Military and Political Proceedings
MPP	Madras Political Proceedings
MPUP	Madras Public Proceedings
MSP	Madras Secret Proceedings

ENDNOTES

INTRODUCTION

1. Tipu Sultan was slain on May 4, 1799, in the Fourth Anglo-Mysore War.
2. As the result of Subsidiary Alliances, the princes came to lean on the British for their protection from their enemies.
3. Henri Prentiout, *L'ilse de France sous Decaen*, 1803-1810 (Paris : Librairie Hatchette et Cie, 1901), pp. 374-377; MSP, Volume 17, pp. 292-7, 309-14
4. MSP, Volume 17, pp. 292-297
5. MSP, Volume 17, pp. 309-314
6. H. H. Dodwell (Editor), *The Cambridge History of India, V, British India,* 1497-1858 (Delhi: S. Chand and Co., 1963), pp. 467-75
7. *Ibid*

CHAPTER I: VELLORE

1. James Welsh, *Military Reminiscences* (London: Smith, Elder and Co., 1830), I, 7-8; Charles F. Kirby, *The Adventures of an Arcot Rupee* ((London: Saunders, Otley, and Co., 1867), II, 152-153
2. James Welsh, *Loc. Cit.*
3. Charles F. Kirby, *The Adventures of an Arcot Rupee,* II, 159-160
4. George Valentia, *Voyages and Travels to India, Ceylon, the Red Sea, Abyssinia, and Egypt in the Years, 1802, 1803, 1804, 1805 and 1806* (London: William Miller, 1809, I, 399
5. *Ibid.*, pp.399-400; James Welsh, *loc. Cit.*; Robert Orme, *A History of the Military Transactions of the British Nation in Hindustan* (London: F. Wingrave, 1861), I, 45; A Keene, "The Mutiny at Vellore, July 10th, 1806." *United Service Magazine* (October to March, 1907), XXXIV, 95
6. *M.* Martin (Editor), *The Despatches, Minutes and Correspondence of the Marquess Welleslley (*London: W. H. Allen, 1837), II, 80-81
7. H. E. A. Cotton, "Thomas Hickey: Portrait Painter. . .", *Bengal: Past and Present* (October to December, 1924), p. 159
8. HMS, Volume 508, pp. 258, pp.252-253 Thomas Marriott's paper
9. M. Martin, *op. cit.,* pp. 27-29
10. *Ibid.,* p. 62
11. George Valentia, *op., cit.,* p.400; Sydney C. Grier, "The Mutiny at Vellore in 1806." *Bengal: Past and Present* (October to December, 1924), pp. 166-167
12. MPP, Range 122, pp. 898-904
13. M. Martin (Editor), *op. cit.,* p. 21
14. MPP, Range 316, Volume 117, pp. 1298-1305; Range 317, Volume 10, pp. 950-951.Thomas Marriott to Chief Secretary, 11-6-1806
15. MPP, Range 317, Volume 5, pp. 94-102, Thomas Marriott to George Strachey, 15-1-185; HMS, volume 508, p. 253, Thomas Marriott's deposition

16   HMS, Volume 508, pp. 280-281, Thomas Marriott's paper
17   MPP, Range 317, Volume 9, pp. 207-210, William Bentinck's minute, 7-3-1806; HMS, volume 508, pp. 282-283
18   *Ibid*
19   MPP, Range 316, Volume 117, pp. 1298-1305
20   George Valentia, *op. cit.*, p. 402
21   MPP, Range 317, Volume 3, pp. 1276-79, 1334-35
22   MPP, Range 317, Volume 10, pp. 559-561
23   Tipu Sultan's mahal had 420 women, and Hyder Ali's had 380
24   George Valentia, *op. cit., p.* 401
25   MPP, Range 316, Volume 117, pp. 1298-1305; Range 317, Volume 5, pp. 94-102; Volume 10, p. 895
26   HMS, Volume 508, p. 268
27   MSP, Volume 22, pp. 2839-40, Doveton to Wilks, 20-3-1800
28   *Ibid.*, pp. 2816-17, Thomas Marriott's deposition
29   HMS, Volume 508, p. 245, Thomas Marriott's deposition
30   MSP, Volume 22, pp. 2840-41, Doveton to Wilks, 20-3-1800
31   *Ibid.*, pp. 2817-21
32   HMS, Volume 508, pp. 317-320, Garrison standing orders
33   *Ibid.*, p. 244, Thomas Marriott's deposition; p. 320; Garrison standing orders
34   *Ibid.*, pp. 320, Garrison standing orders
35   MSP, Volume 22, pp. 2833-34, Wilks to Doveton, 27-2-1800
36   MPP, Range 317, Volume 5, p. 88
37   Women went to visit their relations who lived in the *pettah* by covered *doolies*.
38   MSP, Volume 22, pp. 2843-44, Doveton to Wilks, 20-3-1800
39   HMS, Volume 459, pp. 152-154, Wilks to Doveton, 10-4-1800
40   MSP, Volume 22, pp. 2830-31. Wilks to Doveton, 27-2-1800
41   HMS, Volume 459, p. 186, Reports
42   HMS, Volume 460, pp. 115-116, Reports
43   HMS, volume 459, p. 185. Reports
44   HMS, Volume 460, pp. 113-117, Reports
45   HMS, Volume 464, pp. 73-81, 105-114, 221-268; Volume 465, pp.4a-5a, Reports
46   MSP, volume 19, pp. 1039-40
47   HMS, Volume 508, p. 238, Thomas Marriott's deposition
48   HMS, Volume 508, pp. 341-350, Thomas Marriott's memorandum
49   Sheikh Par was kept in prison. As Abdul Khalik did nothing to get him released, Par disclosed the true story.
50   HMS, Volume 508, pp. 350-357, Thomas Marriott's memorandum
51   Deceit
52   HMS, Volume 508, pp. 357-362, Thomas Marriott's memorandum
53   MPP, Range, Volume 5, p. 95
54   This was said to have happened after the death of his uncle Moyen-ud-din on January 3, 1805.
55   According to Mark Wilks, Hyder Ali's "avowed and public opinion" was "that all religions proceed from God, and are all equal in the sight of God; and it is certain, that the mediatory power represented by Runga Sawmey, the great idol in the temple of Seringapatam, had as much, if not more of his respect, than all the Imam, with Mohammed at their head." *Historical Sketches of the South of India* (Madras: Higginbotham and Co., 1869), II, 378
56   HMS, Volume 508, pp. 362-368, Thomas Marriott's memorandum
57   MMPP, Range 254, Volume 41, p. 6048; HMS, volume 508, pp. 249-251, Thomas Marriott's paper

58   HMS, Volume 508, pp. 249-251
59   MMPP, Range 254, Volume 41, p. 6048
60   HMS, Volume 508, p. 251
61   He was a second generation Company servant. His father Randolph was a Resident in Balasore when Warren Hastings was in Murshidabad in 1759. Mrs. Hastings appeared to have been Thomas' brother Charles' godmother. Sydney C. Grier, *op. cit.*, p. 167
62   IOL, MSS, Eur. C. 133, Volume 2, pp. 77-78, Randolph Marriott to Warren Hastings, 17-2-1806
63   MMPP, Range 254, Volume 39, pp. 4226-27, A. Wellesley to Lt. Col. Doveton, 18-6-1799
64   MPP, Range 316, Volume 115, pp. 517-518, J. Webbe to Thomas Marriott, 7-4-1801
65   MPP, Range 317, Volume 5, pp. 86-89
66   HMS, Volume 508, pp. 325-326
67   IOL, MSS, Eur. C. 133, Volume 2, pp. 79-80, Randolph Marriott to Warren Hastings, 8-5-1806
68   *Ibid.* pp. 81-83
69   *Ibid.*, pp. 83-84
70   *Ibid.*, p. 84
71   IOL, MSS, Eur. C. 133, Volume 2, pp. 74-76, Randolph Marriott to Warren Hastings, 9-7-1798; Sydney C. Grier, *op. cit.*, p. 167
72   MPP, Range 317, Volume 5, pp. 86-89
73   George Valentia, *op. cit.*, p. 401
74   MSP, Volume 22, pp. 2813-16
75   HMS, Volume 508, pp.326-328
76   *Ibid.*, pp.332, 339-340
77   UN, Pw Jb, 25, pp. 348-353, Thomas Marritt to Wm. Bentinck, 11-7-1806
78   MMP, Range 255, Volume 50, pp. 2773-74
79   MPP, Range 317, Volume 9, pp. 154-155
80   MPP, Range 317, Volume 10, pp. 485-489, Wm, Wm. Bentinck's minute.
81   BLO, MSS, English Misc. b. 30, f. 33, Amelia Fancourt's account
82   MPP, Range 317, Volume 10, pp. 485-489
83   MPP, Range 317, Volume 6, pp. 633-39, Fancourt to Bentinck, 4-5-1806
84   MPP, Range 317, Volume 9, pp. 152-154, Ross to Fancourt, 17-12-1806
85   *Ibid.*, pp. 39-41, Thomas Marriott to the Chief Secretary, 9-1-1806
86   Finally, Marriott was asked to draft a plan for the effective policing of the *pettah*. When that paper was in transit to the Supreme Government the mutiny broke out. MJP, Range 322, volume 13, pp. 2298-2317
87   MPP, Range 317, Volume 10, pp. 634-636, T. Marriott to G. Buchan, 2-5-1806; MRP, Range 276, Volume 6, pp. 1048-78, Wm. Petrie to Wm. Bentinck, 27-3-1806
88   MPP, Range 317, Volume 10, pp. 485-489
89   John Cradock was upset because John Fancourt was an officer of the King's service, not the Company's
90   MPP, Range 317, Volume 10, pp. 489-492, John Cradock's minute
91   *Ibid.*, 492-495, Wm. Bentinck's minute, 9-5-1806
92   *Ibid.*, p. 495, Wm. Petrie and James Strange's minutes, 9-5-1806
93   MSP, Volume 22, pp. 2811-12, Thomas Marriott's deposition
94   HMS, Volume 508, pp.150-151, Thomas Marriot's deposition
95   MMP, Range 255, Volume 67, pp. 1842-55, The proceedings of a court of inquiry, 3-3-1806

CHAPTER II: THE COAST ARMY

1   This chapter deals only with the Indian branch of the Coast Army, later known as the Madras Army and not with the British part of it.

2   Grenadier was the first or head company in a battalion. Grenadiers were supposed to be the choicest men of the battalion.

3   Sepoys boys were prospective sepoys.

4   William J. Wilson, *History of the Madras Army* (Madras: Government Press, 1883), I, 1-21; II. 122-149, 288-291; III, 154-166; MSP, volume 18, pp. 46-73

5   The comparative strength of the Indian and British establishments of the Coast Army in 1806:

	Indian	British
Infantry	46,000	6,000
Calvary	3,500	900
Foot Artillery	170	900
Horse Artillery	80	100
Fencibles	1,000	---
Gun Lascars	2,600	---
Pioneers	1,700	---
Totals	55,050	7,900

Invalids are excluded.

6   HMS,Volume 507, pp. 441, 478

7   MMP, Range 255, Volume 72, pp. 4077-82

8   MMP, Range 255, Volume 75, pp. 5869-79

9   Charles F. Kirby, *op. cit.,* I, 296; Count Bjornstjerna, *The British Empire in the East* (London: John Murray, 1840), p. 154

10   W. J. Wilson, *op. cit.,* II, 176, 182; III, 91. The sepoy-boy establishment was only for the infantry.

11   W. J. Wilson, op. cit., I, 227

12   H. H. Dodwell, *Sepoy Recruitment in the Old Madras Army* (Calcutta: Government of India, 1922), pp. 29-30, 40

13   MMP, Range 256, Volume 24, pp. 808-830; Range 253, Volume 77, pp.1157-67; W.Y. Carman, *Indian Army Uniform. . . Cavalry* (London : Leonard Hill Ltd., 1961), p. 133; Patrick Cadell, "The Uniforms of the Madras Army," *Journal of Society for Army Historical Research*, XXVII,171-173; W.J. Wilson, *op. cit.,* II, 99. The real change in the turban took place, according to Deputy Adjutant-General Major Frederick Pierce, in 1797, when the former, which was nothing more than winding of cloth around a piece of iron frame was abandoned in favour of that which is described above. While reporting this change to the Court of Directors, the Board wrote that it had given it "every consideration which a subject of that delicate and important nature required." Quoted in W. J. Wilson, *op. cit.,* II, 348

14   MMP, Range 256, Volume 25, pp. 1831-35, 1854-60. A painting by a Tanjore artist, 1797. Add, India Office Art and Picture Library

15   Patrick Cadell, *op. cit.,* pp. 171-173; W. J. Carman, *op.cit.,* p. 131; Charles Gold, *Oriental Drawings* (London: Bunney and Co., 1806). There is no pagination in Gold's *Oriental Drawings.*

16   W. Y. Carman, *op.cit.,* p. 132; *Indian Army Uniforms . . Artillery, Engineers and Infantry* (London: Morgan-Grampion, 1969), p. 27; W. J. Wilson, *op. cit.,* II, 122; III, 155; Charles Gold, *Oriental Drawings.*

17   MMP, Range 256, Volume 25, pp. 1831-60

18 MMP, Range 256, Volume 25, pp. 1840-42
19 Since there has been much misconception regarding the dress and appearance of the sepoy, I have given the basis of my statement in Appendix C.
20 Charles F. Kirby, *op. cit.*, I, 291; HMS, Volume 510, pp. 276-278
21 *The General Order, 1806*, p. 164; W. J. Wilson, *op. cit.*, II, 173, 331
22 W. J. Wilson, *op. cit.*, I, 229-230
23 W. J. Wilson, *op. cit.*, I, 148., 148, 271; Count Bjornstjerna, *op. cit.*, p. 154
24 *The General Order, 1806*, p. 159
25 W. J. Wilson, *op. cit.*, I, 230-232. There were also lance-naique, kot-havildar, havildar-writer, havildar-major, jamadar-adjutant.
26 S. C. Hill, *Yusuf Khan* (London: Longmans, Green and Co., 1914), p. 241
27 W. J. Wilson, *op. cit.*, II, 173-174
28 Quoted in *Ibid.*, p. 174
29 S. C. Hill, "The Old Sepoy Officer." *The English Historical Review* (1913), XXVIII, 265
30 S. C. Hill, "The Old Sepoy Officer." *Op. cit.*, p. 262
31 MSP, Volume 24, pp. 3810-13
32 Alexander J. Arbuthnot, *Major-General Sir Thomas Munro* (London: C. Kegan Paul and Co., 1881), II, 378
33 W. J. Wilson, *op. cit.*, III, 69, 93-94. To reach the maximum, one had to remain at least ten years in a given position. There was no office of subadar or its equivalent in the foot artillery, gun lascars and pioneers.
34 W. J. Wilson, *op. cit.*, III, 69, 93-94
35 Quoted in *Ibid.*, p. 89
36 *Ibid.*, II, 181
37 *W.* J. Wilson, *op. cit.*, III, 93
38 Thomas Munro, *Disaffection in the Native Army, p.* 12
39 Henry T. Prinsep, *History of the Political and Military Transactions in India, 1813-1823* (London: Kingsbury, Parbury and Allen, 1825), II, 160; Herbert Compton, *A Particular Account of European Adventurers of Hindustan, 1784-1803* (London: T. Fisher Unwin, 1892), p. 64
40 Until 1837, all the Presidencies' troops were paid alike. Amiya Barat, *The Bengal Native Infantry: Its Organisation and Discipline, 1796-1852* (Calcutta: Firma K. L. Mukhopadhya, 1962), p. 132
41 W. J. Wilson, *op. cit.*, III, 88-89. A seer is nearly about two pounds.
42 A British private was paid Rs. 12.00 a month. MMP. Range 255, Volume 74, pp. 5676-85
43 W. J. Wilson, *op. cit.*, III, 90-150
44 *Ibid.*, pp. 92-93
45 MMP, Range 255, Volume 75, pp. 5869-79
46 MJP, Range 322, Volume 15, p. 3389; W. J. Wilson, *op. cit.*, I, 153; II, 290; III, 98
47 James Welsh, *op. cit.*, p. 14; H. H. Dodwel,, *op. cit.*, pp. 31, 37. Recruits raised in the same areas and members and relatives of same families were as far as possible kept together. That was considered to have fostered co-operation and attachment. H. H. Dodwell, *op. cit.*, p. 32. That might have been fine, but such groupings carried the inherent possibility of extreme secrecy if ever disaffection occurred.
48 H. H. Dodwell, *op. cit.*, p. 41
49 *Ibid.*, pp.31-37
50 W. J. Wilson, *Op. cit.*, II, 290
51 President's Secret Correspondence (109), pp. 10-12
52 Bazar allowance is that allowance which came to the commanding officer (usually one-fifth) from the duties imposed on spirituous liquor, tobacco, and other drugs sold

within the cantonment. Table allowance is that amount given to the commanding officer to assist him to maintain his standard of living, usually about Rs. 1,200.

53   A special allowance given for drilling the sepoys.

54   Amiya Barat, *op. cit.*, p. 64

55   *Ibid.*, pp. 64-65

56   Quoted in *Ibid.*, p. 66

57   HMS, Volume 510, pp. 349-351

58   In 1806, four-fifths of the commands were filled by the King's officers, although the Company's officers were in the majority. President's Secret Correspondence (109), pp. 3-5, 9-13; Amiya Barat, *op. cit.*, pp. 54-60

59   HMS, Volume 510, pp. 349-351

60   MMP, Range 255, Volume 72, pp. 4242-4245

61   President's Secret Correspondence (109), p. 12

62   G. B. Malleson (Editor), *Kaye's and Malleson's History of the Indian Mutiny of 1857-58* (London: W. H. Allen and Co., 1891), I, 159-160

63   Amiya Barat, *op. cit.*, pp. 76-77

64   Charles Gold, *Oriental Drawings*

65   Count Bjornstjerna, *op. cit.*, pp. 154-156

66   B. N. Majumdar, *A Study of Indian Military History* (New Delhi: Army Educational Stores, 1963), pp. 49-64

67   W. J. Wilson, *op. cit.*, II, 100-103. Wilson's statement in this connection is worth citing: "It is worthy of remark that while the British soldiers were always paid up to date, or nearly so, the native army, serving alien masters, was kept constantly in arrears for several consecutive years, notwithstanding which, and the extreme severity of the service, it steadily resisted, with few exceptions, the numerous offers conveyed by emissaries of Hyder and Tippoo. Such fidelity, under similar circumstances, is without parallel in the military history of any nation." p. 103

68   W. J. Wilson, *op. cit.*, II, 300-302

69   *Ibid.*, pp. 138-141

70   The mutineers took over the fort, confined their officers, and stated that they would execute all the officers if they were attacked. During the period of rebellion, which lasted for about two weeks, they tortured some of the officers by making them sit on hot stones with heads bared against the blazing sun. One of them, Captain John Macalister, succumbed to this treatment. A compromise was reached, and then the troops surrendered. Two leading mutineers were subsequently blown from a gun, several others flogged, and the regiments reduced. This occurred in 1784. W. J. Wilson, *op. cit.* II, 151-154

71   W. J. Wilson, *op. cit.*, II, 18-19

CHAPTER III: THE OBNOXIOUS ORDERS

1   HMS, Volume 510, pp. 241-242, J. F. Cradock's minute, 2-10-1806

2   HMS, Volume 510, pp. 275-277, J. F. Cradock's minute, 2-10-1806

3   MMP, Range 255, Volume 48, pp. 1246-48, J. F. Cradock's minute, 12-3-1805. Major Pierce had been in India about twenty-five years, out of which he had been Deputy Adjutant-General for eight years.

4   MMP, Range 256, Volume 24, p. 818, Pierce to G. Barlow, 8-1-1808

5   HMS, Volume 507, pp. 463-465, Pierce to Cradock, 26-7-1806

6   After the mutiny Cradock wrote to Pierce: "It must be in perfect recollection that my instructions to you were 'to mark in red ink' every deviation from the last Book of Regulations." HMS, Volume 507, p. 462. To which Pierce replied: "I regret that I

cannot call to my remembrance your Excellency's particular injunction to note every direction, and addition, in red ink, but merely in general terms that they should be brought to the notice of Government and such as were not founded upon existing orders and appeared to me to require the confirmation of Government." HMS, Volume 507, pp. 463-465

7 *A Code of Regulations* (March, 1806), Section 11, Paragraph 10

8 HMS, Volume 507, pp. 459-460, 464-465, Pierce to Cradock, 26-7-1806

9 Major Pierce; Lieutenant-Colonel Patrick A. Agnew, the Adjutant-General; Lieutenant-Colonel-Alexander Orr, the Quarter-Master General

10 HMS, Volume 507, pp. 450-461, Pierce to Cradock, 26-7-1806

11 HMS, Volume 510, pp. 274-275, J. F. Cradock's minute, 2-10-1806

12 HMS, Volume 507, pp. 419-422, Cradock to Pierce, 21-7-1806

13 MMP, Range 256, Volume 24, pp. 818-819, Pierce to Barlow, 8-1-1808

14 Quoted in William Bentinck, *Memorial* (London: John Booth, 1810), p. 7

15 Quoted in William Bentinck, *op. cit.*, p. 60; W. Bentinck's minute, 15-7-1806; HMS, Volume 507, pp.508-515, W. Petrie's minute, 29-7-1806

16 HMS, Volume 507, pp. 345-350, Agnew to Cradock, 18-7-1806; pp. 450-461, Pierce to Cradock, 26-7-1806

17 All of these ornaments had been already introduced in the turbans of some battalions.

18 MMP, Range 256, Volume 24, pp. 813-814, Pierce to Barlow, 8-1-1808

19 HMS, Volume 508, p. 105, Report of the Mixed Commission

20 W. J. Wilson, *op. cit.*, III, 169

21 *A Code of Regulations* (March, 1806), p. 2

22 HMS, Volume 508, p. 279, Lt. Coombs' deposition

23 Based on general observation of the proceedings of the various courts of inquiry

24 W. J. Wilson, *op. cit.*, III, 179-171

25 Some Muslim rulers had propagated their religion by the sword. As late as late eighteenth century, Tipu Sultan had followed this inglorious practice.

26 HMS, Volume 507, pp. 278-279, Allegarry's testimony

27 HMS, Volume 507, pp. 382-383, Sheikh Ahmed's testimony

28 HMS, Volume 508, pp. 188-189. The exact time of the introduction of waistcoat and stock is uncertain. However, it was done prior to John Cradock's arrival. These items were nonetheless not introduced into the whole army.

29 MSP, Volume 25, pp. 4267-68, Jemmal-ud-din's testimony

30 MSP, Volume 25, pp. 4257-58, Sheikh Ramjuny's testimony

31 HMS, Volume 507, pp. 383-384, Sheikh Ahmed's testimony

32 The narration of the events of May 6 and 7 is constructed from the evidence given at the court of inquiry, May 17 to 24, 1806. HMS, Volume 507, pp. 17-101. Where other sources are used, they are cited in proper places.

33 HMS, Volume 508, p. 148, Thomas Marriott's testimony

34 That is, he reduced them from their ranks.

35 The subadar and the kot havildar had the same name.

36 The Indian commissioned officers merely went and complained to the British officers that the men were not obeying their orders.

37 The other reason given earlier, that of their objection to the imprisonment of the twenty-one sepoys, was not given at this time.

38 It was translated by Sheikh Nair, kot havildar of the 50th company, who spoke "very good English."

39 After the roll-call, Fancourt told Darley "that the men appeared to him perfectly obedient and orderly." Darley was much frustrated with his battalion's irregularities. He wrote to John Cradock on May 10 asking that he might be transferred from the command of the second battalion of the fourth regiment. He stated that in his twenty-

six years of service, he "never knew an instance. . . of sepoys refusing to obey any order of their superiors which was not encouraged underhandly by the commissioned officers." He felt much humiliated by Fancourt's order to restore the swords to the Indian officers. He said, "I do sincerely regret that their swords were restored to them." Darley felt "a severe example was necessary," and he recommended dismissal of "a proportion of the commissioned ranks from the service," "and reduction from the ranks a portion of the non-commissioned." (HMS, Volume 507, pp. 10-14

40 Men on the parade were mostly not the same men who were on the roll-call previous day. These men were on garrison duties on the 6th. "Dhoot" is alleged to mean "get out," or a kind of noise made in calling dogs, or a kind of noise sepoys made when they saw the new moon.

41 Quoted in William Bentinck, *op. cit.*, pp.92-93, Cradock to Fancourt, 7-5-1806. After the mutiny, an alleged copy of this letter was circulated with the insertion "whether to eat pork or wear a hat" after the clause, "who hesitates a moment to obey an order," in paragraph 3. MSP, Volume 30, pp. 2146-48

42 MSP, Volume 30, pp. 2163-66, Agnew to H. MacDowall, 5-12-1807

43 Commenting on Cradock's determination to enforce obedience, E. Baber wrote to his friend, Warren Hastings: "The punishment of the sepoy is a melancholy proof how the heart may be hardened by prejudice; for the mistaken notion of discipline in this instance is as much prejudice as the zeal of a Catholic when he condemns a heretic to the flames and calmly beholds in the midst of them." BM, MSS, Add 29182, I, 177-178

44 Quoted in W. J. Wilson, *op. cit.,* III, 172

45 MMP, Range 255, Volume 69, p. 3005

46 J. F. Cradock, *Detailed Letter* (London: 1808), pp. 19-20

47 It sat from May 17 to 24

48 MMP, Range 255, Volume 72, pp. 4199-4204, The rport

49 HMS, Volume 509, pp. 16-19, The private opinion of the court

50 HMS, Volume 507, pp. 16-17, McKerras to Cradock, 25-5-1806

51 MMP, Range 255, Volume 72, pp. 4091-93

52 Eleven were Hindus and ten were Muslims.

53 HMS, Volume 507, pp. 106-107

54 HMS, Volume 507, pp. 137-139

55 Quoted in W. J. Wilson, *op. cit.,* III, 172

56 MMP, Range 255, Volume 72, pp. 4100-11. The six non-commissioned officers complained when they were reduced that they were instigated by the kot havildar and the subadar of their company.

57 HMS, volume 507, p. 167, Darley to Agnew, 3-7-1806

58 MSP, Volume 20, pp. 1225-1245, Sheikh Cassim's deposition. Kot havildar of the eighth company advised the men not to do so, and they obliged.

59 HMS, Volume 508, pp. 207-8

60 Some of these voices were Muhammad Jaffer, Imam Khan, Sied Modin, Sheikh Nutter, Sheikh Secunder, Havildar Dowd Cawn.

61 HMS, Volume 507, pp. 278-280, Allegarry's testimony

62 Based on general evidences

63 HMS, Volume 508, pp. 175-178, Major Trotter's and Lt. Coombs' testimonies

64 MSP, Volume 25, pp. 4275-76, Based on the testimonies of several sepoys

65 MSP, Volume 20, pp. 1225-45, Sheikh Cassim's deposition

66 MMP, Range 255, Volume 72, pp. 4249-53, Bose to G. Harcourt, 10-6-1806

67 He was transferred from the Nawab's service in 1799 directly as an officer.

68 MMP, Range 255, Volume 72, pp. 4249-53

69   MMP, Range 255, Volume 72, pp. 4245-49, Harcourt to Agnew, 11-6-1806
70   MMP, Range 255, Volume 72, pp. 4086-88
71   HMS, Volume 507, pp. 146-148
72   Now "the 1st of the 1st" and "the last of the last" of the Coast Army were in Vellore.
73   The exact date of the arrival of the second battalion of the first regiment is uncertain. The battalion left Seringapatam on May 14 and reached Wallajabhad on June 12. MSP, volume 22, pp. 2320-25. It is reasonable to assume that the battalion could not have been in Vellore prior to the last week in May.
74   MSP, Volume 20, pp. 1225-45, Sheikh Cassim's deposition
75   The conspiracy could not have been formed while the second battalion of the first regiment was in Vellore. Because after its arrival in Wallajabhad, it sent a message that other battalions were making their turbans, and "the sepoys of the 2nd of the 1st. . would wear them if the 1st of the 1st did, and they looked to the 1st of the 1st for an example, being. . . the right wing of their brigade." *Ibid.*
76   The exact date is uncertain. The conspiracy must have been formed between June 5 to 10.
77   MSP, Volume 20, pp. 1225-45
78   MSP, Volume 25, pp. 4258-66
79   MSP, Volume 25, p. 4225, Forbes-Coombs to Harcourt, 15-10-1806
80   Havildar Esoph Cawn of the second battalion of the twenty-third regiment stated: "At first Lt. and Adjutant Coombs was to be the only victim but latterly (sic) it was resolved to kill all Europeans." HMS, Volume 508, p. 457
81   HMS, Volume 508, pp. 204-205; MSP, Volume 20, pp. 1225-45; Volume 25, pp. 4279-81. Sheikh Nutter's Sheikh Cassim's and Jemmal-ud-din's depositions
82   MSP, Volume 20, pp. 1225-45, Sheikh Cassim's depostion
83   Subadars Sheikh Adam and Sheikh Homed; Jemadar Sheikh Hussain; Havildar Fakir Muhammad
84   Subadar Sheikh Imam; Jemadars Rungapah and Ramaswamy; Havildars Sheikh Modin, Gopallao, Mostelligao, Appeeras, and Pickagerrao
85   Subadars Mur Muhammad, Sheikh Imam and Sheikh Ahmed; Sepoy Cawder and Mohuddin Khan
86   Subadar Sied Nully and Ramlingam Naique
87   MSP, Volume 20, pp. 1225-45
88   MSP, Volume 25, pp. 4279-81, Jemmal-ud-din's testimony
89   HMS, Volume 508, pp. 142-144, Muhammad Ashruf, the horse keeper's testimony
90   HMS, Volume 508, pp. 165-166, Marriott's testimony
91   MSP, Volume 25, p. 4284, Jemmal-ud-din's deposition
92   HMS, Volume 508, pp. 137-138, Mirza Sied Churudmud Ali's deposition. Moiz-ud-din told Ali this eleven days before the mutiny.
93   MSP, Volume 25, p. 4272, Jemmal-ud-din's deposition
94   He wanted his cousin Hyder Hussain Cawn also to spend the night with him.
95   Marriott did not grant permission.
96   HMS, Volume 508, pp. 148-166, Marriott's deposition
97   MSP, Volume 20, pp. 1225-45; Volume 25, pp. 4272-73, Sheikh Cassim's and Jemmal-ud-din's testimonies
98   MSP, Volume 25, pp. 4277-79, Jemmal-ud-din's deposition
99   HMS, Volume 508, p. 458
100   MSP, Volume 25, pp. 4245-51
101   MSP, Volume 20, pp. 1225-45, Sheikh Cassim's deposition
102   He reminded Forbes of one previous occasion when he himself put Mustapha Beg under arrest for irregular behaviour.

103   According to the account, while Mustapha Beg was going home about 8.00 p.m. to take his supper, Dowd Cawn and Muhammad Jaffer called him and disclosed the plan to him.

104   The narration is based on the depositions given by Forbes and Mustapha Beg. MSP, Volume 25, pp. 4245-51; HMS, Volume 508, pp. 123-135, 182-185

105   MSP, Volume 25, pp. 4311-18, Ruston Ali Shah's deposition. One English widow, Mrs. Burke told the Mixed Commission that she came to report to Lt. Col. Fancourt "what she heard, as well as to apply for her husband's prize money," but as she told him that she was a widow, he refused to hear her. Marriott asserts that she was an extremely fussy woman and had made allegations without any substance. HMS, Volume 508, pp. 254-58, 277-78. However, she did not know anything about the conspiracy. Some writers like Erick Wakeham and I. H. Thornton incorrectly say that she fully corroborated Mustapha Beg's evidence. Wakeham, *The Bravest Soldier* (Edinburgh: William Blackwood and Sons Ltd., 1937), pp. 91-123; Thornton, *Campaigners Grave and Gray* (Cambridge: The University Press, 1925), pp. 87-109

106   The second battalion of the twenty-third regiment was perhaps informed of the plot on June 16, 1806

107   MSP, Volume 20, pp. 1225-45, Sheikh Cassim's evidence

108   Quoted in W. Bentinck, *op. cit.*, p. 92, Cradock to Bentinck, 29-6-1806

109   John F. Cradock, *op. cit.*, p. 31

110   W. Bentinck, *op. cit.*, pp. 9-10. Lt. Col. Brunton had been seriously ill just before that time.

111   HMS, Volume 507, pp. 149-151

112   HMS, Volume 507, pp. 249-251, W. Petrie's minute, 14-7-1806

113   One might say, "prejudice" is by definition that which is "unfounded;" perhaps the Council meant something that had been believed for a long, or considered for a long time, to be offensive.

114   HMS, Volume 507, pp. 149-151, Bentinck to Cradock, 4-7-1806

115   HMS, Volume 507, pp. 151-153

116   *Ibid.*, pp. 149-151. On the same day in a private letter to Cradock, Bentinck wrote: "We conceive that it is now too late to recede, and that if marks of discontent and insubordination should still continue, no time should be lost in imposing the authority of the Government." But he added that if the sepoys' apprehension was real, it must be removed by the publication of the order. UN, Pw jb 727, 192-193

117   *Quoted in J.* F. Cradock, *op. cit.*, pp. 30-31

118   William Bentinck, *op. cit.*, p. 11

119   Quoted in *Ibid.*, pp. 95-96, Cradock to Bentinck, 9-7-1806

120   MSP, Volume 25, pp. 41229-31, Forbes-Coombs to Harcourt, 15-10-1806

121   MSP, Volume 20, pp. 1225-45, Sheikh Cassim's deposition

122   Imam Khan informed Jemmal-ud-din and then Memmal-ud-din took the message to Moiz-ud-din.

123   MSP, volume 25, pp. 4287-88, Jemmal-ud-din's deposition

124   Apparently, there were some disturbances. For three or four sepoys went to the Tailor Amoran's house, "plundered all his clothes, abused him, threatening to shoot him for having made up the new turbans." HMS, Volume 507, pp. 271-273. Rangapah stated that on July 9, there were many horsemen "in a disorderly manner sham fighting with each other." Perhaps it was due to the wedding. HMS, Volume 507, pp. 208-209

125   UN, Pw Jb, pp. 354-357, Marriott to Bentinck, 17-7-1806; MMP, Range 255, volume 75, pp. 6172-74, Harcourt to Reynel, 16-9-1806

126   A. Keene, "The Mutiny at Vellore," *United Service Magazine* (October, 1906 to March, 1907), XXXIV, 96-104. Details were: 44 British privates, 2 drummers, 4

corporals, 3 serjeants under Lieutenants Ely and Popham, 251 Indian privates and naigues, 4 havildars, 9 jemidars, and subadars, and under Lieutenant O'Reilly. W. J. Wilson, *op. cit.*, III, 176-177

127   HMS, Volume 508, "State of the Garrison of Vellore on the 9th July, 1806." The figures include all who lived in the *pettah* too, but excludes children, women and visitors.

128   HMS, Volume 507, pp. 303-305; Volume 508, pp. 212-213. Jemadar Rungapah's and Subadar Sied Hussain's depositions

CHAPTER IV: THE MUTINY

1   HMS, Volume 507, pp. 341-342. The narration is reconstructed largely from the depositions given either in the Military Court of Inquiry or the Mixed Commission or both. For the sake of convenience, the names of the witnesses will not be given unless they are extremely essential.

2   Subadar Sied Nubby of the 23rd regiment, who later lost his life in the mot while making his escape, told the grenadiers of his battalion not to get up, but to seize Sheikh Cassim if he came again.

3   HMS, Volume 507, pp. 208-9, 281-2, 306-7, 355-7; Volume 508, p. 205; MSP, volume 24, pp. 4253-57

4   The barrack guards consisted of 1 serjeant, 2 corporals, and 12 privates. MMP, Range 255, volume 75, pp. 6169-72

5   MMP, Range 255, Volume 6169-72, Cosgrave's testimony. Cosgrave was severely wounded but survived.

6   HMS, Volume 508, pp. 190-191, 265-266

7   According to W. J. Wilson's estimation, the British part of the main guard "consisted of about 20 rank and file, with one or two serjeants and a subaltern." *Op. cit.*, III, 176

8   MMP, Range 255, Volume 75, pp. 6169-72, Piercy's testimony

9   " Down with White man "

10   " Kill the bastard "

11   UE, MSS, 913; HMS, Volume 507, p. 314; Volume 508, pp. 260-66

12   BLO, MSS, Eng. Misc. b. 30. f. 32

13   The guard was there because Lt. Ewing kept the battalion's books.

14   MMP, Range 255, Volume 74, pp. 5383, Jones and Dean's Report; HMS, Volume 508, pp. 156-158, 258-9

15   MMP, Range 255, Volume 80, pp. 8764-68; HMS, Volume 507, pp. 343-4; Volume 508, p. 156; MSP, Volume 25, pp. 4253-56, 4318

16   HMS, Volume 507, pp. 210-11; MMP, Range 255, Volume 80, pp. 8887-93. Abdul also shot Lts. Popham and O'Reilly.

17   HMS, Volume 508, pp. 186-188; MMP, Range 255, Volume 80, pp. 8887-93

18   Marriott says that he met Coombs near his home and told him that "he had better run upstairs." As he had just gone, the sepoys came, but they did not molest Marriott. HMS, Volume 508, pp. 155-7. Coombs escaped the sepoys' fury in 1806, but he was shot accidentally by a sepoy in 1833 at Pallavaram. W. J. Wilson, *op. cit.*, III, 183

19   William Hickey calls him "Chaund," and alleges him to be the foster-brother of Smart. Alfred Spencer (Editor), *Memoirs of William Hickey* (London: Hurst and Blackett, Ltd., 1925), IV, 335-337. But from Ramji's deposition, it would seem that Shwash Khan was more like servant rather than anything else. HMS, Volume 507, pp. 329-332

20   HMS, Volume 507, pp. 329-332; John Blakistan, *Twelve Years' Military Adventure* (London: Henry Colburn, 1829), I, 297-298

21 HMS, Volume 508, pp. 208-210. Conductor Samuel Gill left behind 3 children as orphans. The mother had died on August 20, 1805. The children were: John, 6; Elizabeth, 2; Amelia, less than a year old. MMP, Range 255, Volume 79, pp. 8337-8; Range 256, Volume 2, pp. 562-5

22 The account of Mann's death is nowhere found, but he was certainly killed. HMS, Volume 508, pp. 322-323

23 HMS, Volume 508, pp. 239-40; MMP, Range 255, Volume 74, pp. 5597-96

24 UE, MSS, 913

25 UE, MSS, 913

26 BLO, MSS, Eng. Misc. B. 30. F. 32

27 HMS, Volume 508, pp. 156-158

28 Accounts differ. Sheikh Ebraham is alleged to have shot Armstrong from behind while he was talking to the men on the wall. MMP, Range 256, Volume 9, pp. 4898-4900. But Sheikh Nutter tells that Allegarry sepoy made a salaam and then shot him from the wall. HMS, Volume 508, pp. 205-6. Other evidences substantiate the second statement. Muhammad Ali, a servant of Prince Shak'r Ulah, dispatched Armstrong with sticks. HMS, Volume 507, pp. 384-5; Volume 508, pp. 172, 273-4

29 Ones who lived outside the fort were: Lt. Col. Nathaniel Forbes, Major Charles Trotter, Captains E. P. Stevenson, Joseph Greenstill, Lt. J. W. Oliver, B. Blake, and Major J. E. Cootes

30 MMP, Range 255, Volume 78, pp. 6167-6174

31 HMS, Volume 508, pp. 184-186. HMS, Volume 508, pp. 70-72

32 HMS, Volume 508, pp. 213-214

33 *Ibid.*, p. 504

34 Fatteh Hyder told Muhammad Moturbah, the Eunuch, "I am not such a fool to come out." HMS, volume 508, pp. 269-270

35 *Ibid.*, pp. 219-220

36 HMS, Volume 508, p. 200

37 *Ibid.*, p. 199

38 Accounts differ. Moiz-ud-din insisted that sepoys came to plunder, and while plundering they found the flag and took it away. Others stated that they saw Moiz-ud-din deliver the flag with his own hand. The flag had the insignia of the sun in the centre, with stripes against the background of red and green field.

39 MSP, Volume 25, pp. 2494-95; HMS, volume 508, pp. 159, 266

40 Special arrangement was made for the Hindus. Murti sepoy says: ". . . a great many sepoys came into the palace to get water as they were tired, and out of Sultan Modeen's house were brought new pots full of water for them and some Pariahs and Moormen drank out of them. A havildar of the 23rd battalion told Sheikh Adam the Gentoos would not drink out of those pots and that he must get puckaulas for the Gentoos. A puckaully was accordingly brought out for them. . ." HMS, volume 508, pp. 221-2

41 HMS, Volume 508, pp. 200, 222, 266; Volume 507, p. 305. Perhaps most of the food-stuffs were leftovers from the previous evening entertainments and brought from Mohi-ud-din's house.

42 The horse was the same that had been hired for trial. Moiz-ud-din did not ask his servant to saddle, but the mutineers ordered him twice, "terrified him and made him saddle the horse." (HMS, volume 507, pp. 286-7; Volume 508, pp. 223-4

43 HMS, Volume 508, pp. 191-192, 195-196, 285-286, 324-332

44 HMS, Volume 507, pp. 324-332

45 HMS, Volume 507, p. 354. It is stated that Willison had made a cap very similar or exactly of the same pattern as the new turban. The sepoys thought that "he was not

satisfied with obliging them to wear a hat, but to show them that it was a hat, he wore one himself of the same fashion." HMS, Volume 508, p. 151

46 HMS, Volume 507, p. 213; Volume 508, p. 259

47 HMS, Volume 507, p. 212; volume 508, pp. 258-259

48 BLO, MSS, Eng. Misc. B. 30, f. 22

49 HMS, Volume 508, pp. 210-11

50 *Ibid.*, pp. 187-188

51 HMS, Volume 508, pp. 179-180

52 *Ibid.*, p. 503. 529, BLO, MSS, Eng. Misc. b. 30. F. 21-22

53 HMS, Volume 509, pp. 129-142, Coombs-Forbes to Harcourt, 6-9-1806

54 One of the slain *hirkarhs* belonged to Moiz-ud-din's apartment; the other was unknown. HMS, Volume 508, p. 162

55 Permaul naique and Venkatachellum sepoy. Both of them belonged to the first battalion of the first regiment. MSP, Volume 25, p. 4318

56 HMS, Volume 508, p. 265

57 *Ibid.*, pp. 151-2

58 HMS, Volume 507, pp. 358-9; MMP, Range 255, Volume 80, p. 8773

59 HMS, Volume 507, pp. 325-6, 329

60 *Ibid.*, p. 329. John Read was being protected by some sepoys, but suddenly a larger group came and overwhelmed them and was about to kill Read. At that time, Sam Rao stepped forward and stopped the murderous strike.

61 Another sepoy, finding that there was life in Fancourt, went to kill him; but he was stopped by Ramu. HMS, Volume 508, pp. 222-3. Fancourt expired about 4:30 p.m.

62 BLO, MSS, Eng. Misc. b. 30. F. 32

63 MMP, Range 225, Volume 80, pp. 8774-7

64 HMS, Volume 507, pp. 212-4; MMP, Range 256, Volume 27, pp. 2784-87

65 HMS, Volume 508, pp. 181-2

66 Ely's daughter. Potter's child was shot in the leg accidentally.

67 HMS, Volume 508, p. 156

68 See pages 114-115 (in the original; check in the final)

69 HMS, Volume 508, p. 187

70 *Ibid.*, p. 504; Volume 507, pp. 271-2

71 BLO, MSS, Eng. Misc. b. 30. f. 20

72 MSP, Volume 20, pp. 1225-45

73 HMS, Volume 508, p. 476

74 *Ibid.*, Volume 507, pp. 172-73

75 MMP, Range 255, Volume 74, pp. 5587-96

76 MMP, Range 255, Volume 75, pp. 5587-96

77 John Blakistan, *op. cit.*, p. 291; A. Keene, "The Mutiny at Vellore, July, July 10th, 1806" *op. cit.*

78 L. H. Thornton, *op. cit.*, p. 96

79 Gillespie was born in 1766 of Irish and Scottish parents. He came to India in 1805 and took charge of the H. M. 19th dragoons. His first military act in India was the suppression of the Vellore mutiny. He was killed at Kalunga in 1814 in the Nepalese war and was buried at Meerut. E. Wakeham, *op. cit.*, pp. 91-123

80 BLO, MSS, Eng. Misc. b. 30. F. 32

81 HMS, Volume 507, pp. 157-161, Gillespie to Bentinck, 10-7-1806, 11:00 a.m.

82 The time of Gillespie's arrival and the reduction of the fort is not clear. Accounts have to be harmonized. Gillespie says that he got the message at 6:00 a.m. At one place, he says the guns arrived about 10:00 (HMS, volume 507, pp. 157-161), but in another that the fort was in his hand by 10:00 a.m. He also states he sent a letter to George Harcourt just before 8:00 a.m. (HMS, volume 507, pp. 187-190) His letter to

Bentinck stating that he had taken the fort was written at 11:00 a.m. Dean and Jones say that the sepoys attacked them at about 8:00 a.m. and they also say that the cavalry came a little after they had returned from the magazine. Between the occurrences of these two events, they went to the barracks, sallied out, went all the way to the magazine and returned to the gateway. This would take at least 45 minutes. One must also remember that it would take 1 ½ hours to travel from Arcot to Vellore.

Since there is discrepancy in the reporting of timings, I propose the following:

a.	Gillespie receives the message	6:00 a.m
b.	Attack on the house	7:00
c.	Returned from magazine	8:00
d.	Arrival of Gillespie	8:15
e.	Arrival of guns	9:15
f.	Reduction of fort	10:00
g.	Letter to Bentinck	11:00

83   HMS, Volume 507, pp. 157-161, Gillespie to Bentinck, 10-7-1806

84   *Ibid.*, pp. 168-169, Gillespie to Bentinck, 11-7-1806; E. Wakeham, *op. cit.*, pp. 107-108

85   John Blakistan, *op. cit.*, p. 293

86   Gillespie's biographer says that Gillespie ascended by "a chain formed of the soldiers' belts." *A Memoir of Major-General Sir Robert Rollo Gillespie* (London: T. Egerton, 1816), p. 102. But Gillespie stated that he ascended by a rope. HMS, volume 507, pp. 157-161, Gillespie to Bentinck, 10-7-1806

87   MSP, Volume 22, p. 2851

88   HMS, Volume 507, pp. 168-174, Gillespie to Bentinck, 11-7-1806

89   John Blakistan, *op. cit.*, p. 295

90   *Ibid.*, p. 294

91   *Ibid.* p. 295

92   R. R. Gillespie, *A Memoir,* pp. 103-104. However, Gillespie stated before the reassembled Mixed Commission that Marriott hesitated to take him to the palace; but upon assuring him that he intended only to guard the princes, he did. MSP, Volume 22, pp. 2852-53. A contemporary Indian was perhaps right when he said, "The providence seems to have spared the life of Lt. Col. Marriott for the protection of the late Sultan's family; otherwise, not a soul would have remained alive." HMS, volume 507, pp. 360-2

93   HMS, Volume 507, pp. 155-57, Marriott to Bentinck, 10-7-1806

94   *Ibid.*, pp. 157-161, Gillespie to Bentinck, 10-7-1806

95   HMS, Volume 507, p. 154

96   *Ibid.*, pp. 174-6

97   *Ibid.*, pp. 168-176

98   *Ibid.*, pp. 200-207, Harcourt to Bentinck, 13-7-1806

99   MPP, Range 317, volume 11, pp. 1210-11; MMP, Range 255, Volume 75, pp. 5988-98; Volume 76, pp. 6640-45; Volume 79, pp. 8156-57

CHAPTER V: AFTERMATH—PANIC

1   UN, Pw Jb 25, pp. 152-6, J. Leith to Bentinck, 16-7-1806

2   HMS, Volume 507, pp. 196-200, Gillespie to Bentinck, 12-7-1806. Earlier Gillespie had asked for 3 battalions from Wallajabhad. But as he now felt that they might have

been also intrigued with, he ordered them to halt at Arcot. HMS, Volume 507, pp. 187-190

3   HMS, Volume 507, pp. 168-174, Gillespie to Bentinck, 11-7-1806
4   HMS, Volume 507, pp. 187-190, Gillespie to Harcourt, 12-7-1806. Gillespie was incorrect. Moiz-ud-din was fourth and not third son.
5   HMS, Volume 507, pp. 201-107, Harcourt to Bentinck, 13-7-1806. Gillespie and Harcourt recommended the removal of the princes to Madras.
6   HMS, Volume 507, pp. 163-4
7   *Ibid.*, pp. 161-3, Bentinck to Harcourt, 11-7-1806
8   The members were: Lt. Col. Dodsworth and Major Dowse from the military department and Nathaniel Webb and I. H. D. Ogilvie from the civil department. HMS, Volume 507, pp. 181-2
9   HMS, volume 507, pp. 214-6, G. Buchan to Harcourt, 15-7-1806
10   William Bentinck, *op. cit.*, p. 34
11   Quoted in W. Bentinck, *op. cit.*, p. 60, Bentinck's minute, 15-7-1806
12   William Petrie in a long minute stated that "the dissatisfaction" had been "general" but "very respectable authorities" denied it, and not having the means to gain accurate information he yielded on July 4 to the Council's decision. He also warned against alienating the sepoys: "With India on our side we may set our European foes at defiance, but if we lose the affection of our native subjects, and sovereignty in the East will vanish like a dream." HMS, volume 507, pp. 248-57
13   W. Bentinck, *op. cit.*, pp. 61-62
14   HMS, Volume 507, pp. 223-4, Cradock to Bentinck, 14-7-1806
15   UN, Pw Jb 25, pp. 367-72, Marriott to Bentinck, 15-7-1806. Cradock particularly stated, ". . . in the wrong measures of allowing them the indulgences that have been granted, and in the division of authority between the commandant of the garrison, and the paymaster of stipends and the consequent degradation of the former."
16   HMS, Volume 507, pp. 225-28, The Proclamation
17   William Bentinck, *op. cit.*, pp. 61-62
18   HMS, Volume 507, pp. 233-6, Cradock to Agnew, 15-7-1806
19   HMS, Volume 507, pp. 243-6, A Statement, 15-7-1806
20   *Ibid.*, pp. 292-5, Cradock to Hay MacDowall, 17-7-1806
21   *Ibid.*, pp. 371-2, Agnew to commanding officers, 17-7-1806
22   HMS, Volume 507, pp. 239-243, Cradock to Bentinck, 15-7-1806
23   UN, Pw Jb 25, pp. 158-165, Leith to Bentinck, 17-7-1806
24   HMS, Volume 507, pp. 322-323, Cradock to Bentinck, 18-7-1806
25   *Ibid.*, pp. 369-371, Bentinck's minuites, 22-7-1806
26   *Ibid.*, pp. 373-4, 374, 374-5, Petrie's and Strange's minutes, 22-7-1806
27   Cradock reluctantly yielded to the pressures. He stated: "I confess, I think the Order, as expressed, ought to gratify their feelings. . . However, I can never quit this subject, brought forward in any shape, without expressing my persuasion that the turban, unconnected with artifice or machination, weighs not a straw in the scale of present agitation." HMS, Volume 507, pp. 375-6, 23-7-1806
28   HMS, Volume 507, pp. 431, 441
29   *Ibid.*, pp. 389-393
30   William Bentinck, *op. cit.*, p. 35
31   *Ibid.*
32   Most of these 161 sepoys were new recruits.
33   HMS, Volume 507, pp. 600-610
34   HMS, Volume 508, p. 2, Buchan to Dyce, 1-8-1806
35   The second battalion of the first regiment was commanded by Major Joseph Hazlewood, the second battalion of the fourteenth regiment by Major Paul Bose, and

the first battalion of the twenty-third regiment by Lt. Col. Bowness. MMP, Range 255, Volume 73, pp. 4708-9

36   MSP, Volume 19, pp. 1101-2. The narrative is reconstructed from the depositions given in the court of inquiry.
37   HMS, Volume 507, pp. 587-8, Bose to Lang, 25-7-1806
38   *Ibid.*
39   *Ibid.*, pp. 431-33, Lang to Cradock, 25-7-1806
40   HMS, Volume 507, p. 571
41   Ibid., pp. 436-38, Lang to Cradock, 26-7-1806
42   *Ibid.*, pp. 561-2
43   *Ibid.*, pp. 438-9, Lang to Gillespie, 26-7-1806
44   *Ibid.*, pp. 433-6, 436-436-8, Lang to Cradock, 26-7-1806
45   *Ibid.*, pp. Captain Smith's account
46   *Ibid.*, pp. 433-6, Lang to Cradock, 2607-1806
47   *Ibid.*, p. 579. Gillespie wrote to Cradock, "My poor willing fellows as well as horses are much knocked up." *Ibid.*, pp. 439-40
48   *Ibid.*, pp. 439-40
49   *Ibid.*, pp. 579-82
50   *Ibid.*, pp. 492-3, Gillespie's address
51   HMS, Volume 507, pp. 487-91, Gillespie to Cradock, 28-7-1807
52   MSP, Volume 19, pp. 1100-1104, 1110-19; Volume 20, pp. 1275-94
53   HMS, Volume 507, pp. 426-31, Cradock's minute, 27-7-1806
54   Secret Letters from Madras, Series 1, Volume 3, 30-9-1806, paragraph # 116
55   Against the opinion of the authorities, it was discovered that out of 853 men, only 64 came from Tinnevelly, 671 from Carnatic and Tanjore, 72 from Guntur and Circar, 31 Madura and Dindigul, and the remainder from outside of the Presidency of Madras. HMS, Volume 507, pp. 591-93
56   HMS, volume 507, pp. 515-16, Petrie's minute, 29-7-1806
57   *Ibid.*, p. 431, Cradock's minute, 27-7-1806
58   *Ibid.*, p. 481
59   *Ibid.*, p. 441
60   *Ibid.*, pp. 553-60, Cradock to Bentinck, 31-7-1806
61   *Ibid.*, pp. 475-79, Bentinck to Barlow, 29-7-1806
62   *Ibid.*, pp. 587-88, Cradock's report
63   *Ibid.*, pp. 553-60, Cradock to Bentinck, 31-7-1806
64   The Subsidiary force in Hyderabad consisted of two regiments of Indian cavalry, six battalions of Indian infantry, a few companies of Indian artillery and pioneers, His Majesty's 33rd Regiment and a detachment of British artillery. The garrison was commanded by Lt. Col. Thomas Montresor.
65   MSP, Volume 21, pp. 2280-87. A sepoy Mir Abbas "got a letter from a friend in Col. Irton's battalion at Chicacole, which contained an exact drawing of the new turban," and asked what the sepoys plan to do a bout it.
66   HMS, Volume 509, pp. 259-280, Sydenham to Edmonstone, 22-8-1806. Besides the late orders, the sepoys in Hyderabad complained of the loss on exchange when in the field, and also of the prohibition of drum beating in the cantonment and being made to muster hourly when on guard. These two regulations were introduced by Lt. Col. Elliott when holding temporary command of the troops.
67   HMS, Volume 509, pp. 259-280
68   HMS, Volume 509, pp. 259-280, Sydenham to Edmonstone, 22-8-1806, paragraph #10
69   *Ibid.*, #28; pp. 281-96, paragraph # 5
70   Some referred to the loss in the exchange too.

71 HMS, volume 507, pp. 538-45, Montresor to Thomas Sydenham, 21-7-1806. In September, a letter was brought to Montresor. It was addressed to the Nizam, allegedly by Subadar Gholam Sied Hussain, stating that the English were "taking steps to convert" the Indian troops, but the Muslims were determined not to apostatize, but to rebel, and requesting the Nizam to assist them in their rebellion. It was said to have been written some time in mid-July, although no date was found on it. The letter was picked up by a sweeper with a bundle of other papers in the palace, given to a sepoy, who transmitted it to the Commandant. George Barlow stated that the letter must have been a fabrication. The circumstances suggested that it could not have been genuine. Besides the fact that one might question the probability of a sweeper having access to such a document. Subadar Gholam Sied Hussain could not have intrigued with the Nizam as well as Rao Rumbha because their "interests were contradictory." HMS, Volume 509, pp. 355-6; MSP, Volume 22, pp. 2509-18

72 UN, Pw Jb, 25, pp. 390-393, Montresor to Bentinck, 18-7-1806

73 HMS, Volume 507, pp. 538-45, Montresor to Sydenham, 21-7-1806. Montresor wrote to Sydenham: ". . . is it not better in this critical state of affairs, when the troops at Vellore have already mutinied, and reports of a disaffection throughout the army prevalent, I say, is it not better at once to do away everything that may be deemed a just, or at least a general cause of complaint."

Sydenham replied: ". . . every consideration must yield to the imperious necessity of guarding against the unfortunate extremity, which whatever be its termination, would threaten the most imminent danger, not only to our political interest in this court, but to the general peace of India." HMS, volume 507, pp. 537-38

74 HMS, Volume 507, pp. 525-6, Sydenham to Bentinck, 24-7-1806; pp. 526-35, Sydenham to Edmonstone, 23-7-1806, paragraph # 16

75 HMS, Volume 508, pp. 5-6. Later on Cawn's statement was found to be incorrect.

76 MSP, Volume 20, 1225-45, Sheikh Cassim's deposition

77 Quoted in W. Bentinck, *op. cit.*, 101-2, Cradock's minute, 2-8-1806

78 Secret Letters from Madras, Series 1, Volume 3, 30-9-1806, paragraph #203-220

79 Secret Letters from Madras, Series 1, Volume 3, 30-9-1806, paragraph # 203-220

80 HMS, Volume 508, pp. 21-26, Bentinck to Barlow, 3-8-1806

81 *Ibid.*, pp. 27-31, Bentinck to Maitland, 3-8-1806

82 HMS, Volume 508, pp. 36-40, Bentinck to Harcourt, 4-8-1806; pp. 98-100, Buchan to Harcourt, 12-8-1806

83 HMS, Volume 508, pp. 31-33, Buchan to Wilks, 3-8-1806

84 *Ibid.*, pp. 21-26, Bentinck to Barlow, 3-8-1806

85 HMS, Volume 510, pp. 77-84, Bentinck to Maitland, 3-8-1806

86 Quoted in G. R. Gleig, *The Life of Major-General Sir Thomas Munro* (London: Henry Colburn and Richard Bentley, 1830), p. 362

87 UN, Pw Jb 726, pp. 41-54, Bentinck to Minto, 20-10-1806

88 HMS, Volume 508, pp. 40-42, Circular letter, 3-8-1806

89 *Ibid.*, pp. 36-40, Buchan to Harcourt, 4-8-1806

90 *Ibid.*, pp. 495-99, Oakes' minute, 18-8-1806. About 30,000 Muslims lived in and around Madras.

91 HMS, Volume 508, pp. 499-500, 507-08, 524, Cradock's Bentinck's and Petrie's minutes

92 HMS, Volume 508, pp. 87-92, Harcourt to Bentinck, 9-8-1806

93 UN, Pw Jb 25, pp. 416-428, Marriott to Bentinck, 17-8-1806

94 HMS, Volume 508, pp. 93-98

95 HMS, Volume 508, pp. 525-28, Harcourt to Buchan, 20-8-1806

96 UN, Pw Jb 25, pp. 430-34, Marriott to Bentinck, 21-8-1806

About the remaining families Charles Marriott stated on September 3, "the families of the princes are quite composed, apparently much happier than one could reasonably have expected. As long as the princes were on the road to Madras, they constantly expected that after having visited your Lordship, some of them, if not all could be allowed to return. Since their departure, they are now anxious about their own removal to Bengal." Pw Jb 25, pp. 561-63

97   Secret Letters from Madras, Series 1, Volume 3, 30-9-1806, paragraph # 236-245. Arrangements were made to move all Tipu Sultan's adherents to Mysore except the ones in confinement. HMS, volume 508, pp. 490-95

98   HMS, Volume 508, pp. 77-78, Cradock's minute, 5-8-1806

99   *Ibid.*, pp. 79-81, Bentinck's minute, 9-8-1806

100   *Ibid.*

101   Ibid., pp. 81-84

102   MSP, Volume 19, pp. 1014-15, Campbell to Cradock, 17-7-1806

103   HMS, Volume 508, p. 65, Harcourt to Cradock, 4-8-1806

104   *Ibid.*, pp. 101-02, Blackburne to Buchan, 4-8-1806

105   *Ibid.*, pp. 486-87, Wilks to Bentinck, 8-8-1806

106   *Ibid.*

107   Ibid., pp. 103-121, The Report

108   Quoted in G. R. Gleig, *op. cit.*, pp. 363-65

In a letter to his father, Thomas Munro, after citing the tenth paragraph of the eleventh section, stated: "This trifling regulation, and a turban, with something in its shape or decorations to which the sepoys are extremely averse, were thought to be so essential to the stability of our power in this country, that it was resolved to introduce them, at the hazard of throwing our native army into rebellion. One battalion had already in Vellore rejected the turban, and been marched to Madras, with handkerchiefs tied about their heads; but the projectors were not discouraged. They pushed on their grand design, until they were suddenly stopped short by the dreadful massacre of the 10th of July. They were then filled with alarm: they imagined that there was nothing but disaffection and conspiracy in all quarters, and that there would be a general explosion throughout all our military stations. There was unfortunately, however, no ground for such apprehensions. . . nothing but an attempt to force the disagreeable regulation upon them would tempt them to commit any outrage, and that whenever this design was abandoned, every danger of commotion would be at an end, and the sepoys would be as tractable and faithful as ever. Their discontent had nothing in it of treason or disaffection. It was of the same kind as that which would have been excited in any nation, by a violent attack upon its prejudices." Quoted in *Ibid.*, pp. 366-67

109   MSP, Volume 21, pp. 1847-50, Barlow to Bentinck, 11-8-1806

110   MSP, Volume 21, pp. 1850-60, Barlow's minutes, 11-8-1806. Governor Maitland very promptly dispatched a detachment of six hundred men to the Coast. The first batch landed in Nagapatnam on August 15 and the last batch in Madras on August 20. They were all re-embarked within a few weeks. HMS, Volume 509, pp. 78-84, 91-95

111   HMS, Volume 509, pp. 33-34, Bentinck's minute, 26-8-1806

112   *Ibid.*, pp. 35, 47-48, 143-48, Cradock's Petrie's and Oakes' minutes

113   *Ibid.*, pp. 509, pp. 149-154, Bentinck's minute, 8-9-1806

114   *Ibid.*, pp. 339-342

115   UN, Pw Jb 727, pp. 247-251, 2-10-1806

116   UN, Pw F 1203, 17-9-1806

117   HMS, Volume 509, pp. 333-39, Bentinck's minute, 23-9-1806

118   *Ibid.*, pp. 104-06
119   *Ibid.*, 99-108
120   *Ibid.*
121   *Ibid.*, pp. 113-119, Bentinck's minute, 3-9-1806
122   *Ibid.*, pp. 143-148, 185-192, Oakes' and Petrie's minutes
123   *Ibid.*, pp. 385-6, Harcourt to Agnew, 23-9-1806
124   *Ibid.*, pp. 227-237, Bentinck's minute, 13-9-1806
125   *Ibid.*
126   *Ibid.*
127   *Ibid.*, pp. 240-243, Petrie's and Oakes' minutes, 16-9-1806
128   Ibid., pp. 237-240, Cradock's minute, 14-9-1806
129   Ibid., p. 243
130   Ibid., pp. 185-92, Petrie's minute, 10-9-1806
131   *Ibid.*, pp. 148-49, Oake's minute, 6-9-1806
132   *Ibid.*, pp. 192-95, Bentinck's minute, 11-9-1806
133   MSP, Volume 24, pp. 3744-62, Barlow to Bentinck, 29-11-1806
134   William Bentinck, *op. cit.*, pp. 31-35
135   MMP, Range 256, Volume 2, pp. 454-460
136   *Ibid.*
137   MSP, Volume 28, pp. 897-99, Dyce to Welsh, 6-8-1806
138   Quoterd in J. W. Kaye, *The Life and Correspondence of Major-General Sir John Malcolm* (London: Smith, Elder and Co., 1856), I, 372-73
139   MSP, Volume 28, pp. 899-900. Bentinck had also exaggerated. Writing to Maitland, he said, "Three battalions formed for exercise at Wallajabhad have been all implicated." HMS, Volume 5 10, p. 78
140   He did not let them go because he felt that an "improper conversation. . . would. . . take place a meeting of . . . (this] kind." MSP, Volume 22, pp. 2463-66, Ogg to MacDowalll, 21-8-1806
141   Sheikh Hussain was sentenced to death, but Cradock commuted it for permanent banishment. MMP, Range 255, Volume 78, pp. 7775-77
142   Captain MacPherson, who saw the alleged "tricolour flag" stated that it consisted of "three pieces, from two to three feet square each, of *cumbly*, of *chinz* (apparently the end of a woman's cloth) and of white cloth, perhaps a piece of the same. They were not sewed together. . . nor was there any appearance of their having been united." The colours were black, red, and white. When they were tied together and hoisted, it was "a symbol of wretchedness and rags." UN, Pw Jb 49, pp. 337-348
143   The fakirs taught materialistic philosophy, and advocated incest and sodomy. MSP, Volume 23, pp. 3342-72
144   William Petrie did not go. He assigned some other reason, not the dread of massacre. UN, Pw Jb 38, pp. 104-05
145   Edward Hawke Locker, "Vellore," *Plain Englishman* (1821), II, 487-490
146   HMS, Volume 508, pp. 279-280, Govind Rao, deposition
147   Rev. Claudius Buchanan wrote to Henry Thornton from Seringham on September 4, 1806: "I have been just conversing with the Brahmins of this celebrated pagoda. . . and they have been enquiring about Bounaparte (sic). They have heard that on his arrival, they were all to be made Christians.

"A rumour has for some months pervaded India, that all castes are to be made Christians . . . The strange rumours of conversion is (sic) perhaps auspicious to the event itself; as the shaking of an old building announces its approaching fall . . ." Hugh Pearson, *Memoirs of the Life and Writings of the Rev. Claudius Buchanan* (Oxford: The University Press, 1817), II, 42-44

148   HMS, Volume 28, p. 760. This was so generally believed around Palamcottah that Lt. Col Alexander Dyce published a district order to refute the rumour.

149   HMS, Volume 509, pp. 343-359, Sydeham to Buchan, 14-9-1806

150   MSP, Volume 23, pp. 3174-75; 3210-14; 3450-56

151   MSP, Volume 28, pp. 839-41. This line of reasoning is apparent among almost all the battalions where courts of inquiry were instituted.

152   MSP, Volume 22, pp. 2469-77, Custory Subadar's statement, translated from Tamil

153   MSP, Volume 22, pp. 2477-78

154   *Ibid.*, pp. 2785-87

155   *Ibid.*

156   Ibid., pp. 2480-81, 2656-58

157   Ibid., pp. 2485-86

158   Ibid., 2660-61

159   Ibid., pp. 2661-63

160   *Ibid., pp. 2674-77*

161   Arnasum was a naique of the first battalion of the 12th regiment. He was on leave in Nundydrug. Custory employed him as one of his agents. *Ibid.*, pp. 2666-69

162   *Ibid.* The letter to Bangalore stated: "In consequence of information which cannot be doubted, indeed almost certain, that a rising amongst our men was to take place this night for the purpose of massacring all the Europeans. . . without immediate assistance of a strong party of your detachment, the most serious consequences to us, will most probably ensue." *Ibid.* pp. 2491-92, Cuppage to Davies, 18-10-1806

163   *Ibid.*, 2669-70

164   Davis left Bangalore about 8:00 a.m.

165   In the same letter, he wrote: "I am excessively fatigued. The road was covered with water, and the march was lengthened several miles by tanks, nulllahs, and deep ground. We came upwards of 40 miles in less than 6 hours." *Ibid.*,2492-94, Davis to Reynell, 19-10-1806. He came with 2 troops and one gun. *Ibid.*,pp.2495-96, Cuppage to Reynel, 19-101806

166   At the arrival of intelligence from Nundydrug, the Commander-in-Chief ordered Hay MacDowall to proceed to Nundydrug and Bangalore and institute courts of inquiry. In Nundydrug, the court began to function long before the Commander-in-Chief's orders arrived. In Bangalore it began on October 29, subsequent to the arrival of the order. Cradock also empowered MacDowall "to adopt such prompt and decisive measures . . . for arresting the progress of disaffection." He also dispatched the remainder of H. M. 22nd Light Dragoons from Arcot to Bangalore. *Ibid.*, pp. 2496-98

167   *Ibid.*, pp. 264-65

168   *Ibid.*, p. 2763

169   *Ibid.*, pp. 2676-78

170   *Ibid.* In this connection Mark Wilks rightly pointed out that two subadars had been arrested and two companies had been sent off, and "these were matters of notoriety," and they would spread the rumour that there was trouble in Nundydrug. MSP, Volume 25, pp. 3881-88, Wilks to Bentinck, 28-11-1806

171   MSP, Volume 22, pp. 2671-2

172   *Ibid.*, pp. 2673-74, 2681-82, 2686-87

173   *Ibid.*, pp. 2672-73. It was also stated that there was "much disaffection" at the time of Vellore mutiny. *Ibid.*, pp. 2670-71 Similar risings were meditated in Nundydrug and Chittledrug at that time. *Ibid.*, p. 2681. The sepoys had often stated, "We conquered the country for Europeans. . . They are not such great people, and the English power could not force us to wear the turban." *Ibid.*, pp. 2762-63

174   *Ibid.*, pp. 2752-61

175   *Ibid.*, p. 2780

176   *Ibid.,* pp. 2752-64, 2774-84
177   *Ibid.,* pp. 2766-73, MacDowall to Agnew, 31-10-1806
178   MSP, Volume 23, pp. 2930-36, Davis to Cradock, 4-11-1806
179   *Ibid.*
180   *Ibid.*
181   *Ibid.,* pp. 2892-95, MacDowall to Agnew, 1-11-1806. During the inquiry, seven
       others were picked up and imprisoned. The charges against them all were "making
       use of seditious and mutinuous language." HSP, Volume 25, pp. 4378-81. Custory
       and Abdul Cawder subadars were richly rewarded. The former received land at
       Collicaud, near Palamcottah, and latter in Trichinopoly. MMP, Range 256, Volume 4,
       pp. 1234-35, 1232-34
182   MSP, Volume 22, pp. 2482-85, Ogg to Cradock, 15-10-1806
183   MSP, Volume 23, pp. 2898-99
184   MSP, Volume 22, pp. 2482-85
185   *Ibid.,* p. 2663, Ogg to Reynell, 20-10-1806
186   *Ibid.,* pp. 2482-85
187   *Ibid.*
188   *Ibid.,* p. 2665, Ogg to Reynell, 21-10-1806
189   *Ibid.,* pp. 2693-95, Ogg to Reynell, 25-10-1806. Here is the above referred letter:
       "The following is a translation of a treaty of peace between the English and French
       lately received from Madras. From friendship to you I have taken great trouble to
       procure this, that you may communicate it to the presence (sic). I only give you the
       heads, but there is sufficient to form an opinion that the star of the Mahomedans is
       becoming propitious. . . Until the arrival of valourous gentlemen [the French] the
       business will not be perfectly understood. . . the enemies of the faith imagine that the
       Shah Zadas will not return to their country. This is a very foolish conceit. By the
       blessing of the Almighty there is a prospect of my princes soon being at liberty. . ."
       Ibid. The letter was translated from Persian. According to Cazy, the Munshi's friend,
       in whose bundle the letter was found, the parcel belonged to a relation of his, who
       died just ten days earlier. He said that he had no idea about the letter, as it was not
       customary to open the deceased's belongs until forty days elapsed. MSP, Volume 23,
       pp. 2917-18
190   MSP, Volume 22, pp. 2689-91. The relevant passage runs: "I have a full month of
       business still at Bangalore. Certain gentlemen who serve in this battalion are
       faithfully devoted to Hazerat Duste Guir. After satisfying the wishes of those
       gentlemen and firmly fixing them as the true servants of Mahuboob Soobhany, I will
       proceed to Seringapatnam." *Ibid.* Cawdry came from Sera, where he had been a
       school teacher. He was there to raise some funds for his family. He had been in
       Bangalore for about two months. MSP, Volume 23, pp. 2913-15; Volume 25, pp.
       4020-21

       Mark Wilks, who read the letter, remarked that "it was the letter of Soofee
       giving to his Peer an account of his religious labours." UN, Pw Jb 49, pp. 355-
       360
191   MSP, Volume 22, pp. 2688-89
192   *Ibid.,* Volume 23, pp. 2697-2901
193   MSP, Volume 23, pp. 2937-39, MacDowall to Ogg, 28-10-1806
194   UN, Pw Jb 49, pp. 365-90, Letters, November, 1806
195   MSP, Volume 23, pp. 2895-2919
196   *Ibid.,* p. 2991. The witness was Ramaswamy. He said that he heard it from Sied
       Hussain, who claimed to have heard it from Cassim Cawn. A few others too said that
       they heard similar things from Cawn. But Cassim Cawn completely denied it saying
       that the accusers were all his enemies. *Ibid.,* pp. 2993-99

197   *Ibid.*, pp. 3084-85. Barry Sahib was the sepoy. But he denied it.

198   *Ibid.*, p. 3083. Muhammad Moraod was the sepoy, but he too denied it.

199   MSP, Volume 25, pp. 4083-84

200   MSP, Volume 23, pp. 3152-53. According to Mark Wilks such expressions were part of the commonly spoken in the markets to secure alms. He states: "this is a part of one of the most common forms of begging: there are orators of this description who will trace the decline of all the empires from the days of Rama. The whole substance is this: 'Empires pass away; life is uncertain; riches fleeting; give while you have the power to give.' I venture to affirm that one thousand such speeches are repeated every morning under the noses of the Madras police." UN, Pw Jb 49, pp. 442-461

201   MSP, Volume 23, pp. 3141-46; Volume 25, pp. 5104-06. The song was a eulogy on Tipu Sultan. It abounded with abuses of the English as well as Purnia.

202   *Ibid.*, pp. 3157-68

203   *Ibid.*, pp. 3217-19. There was also a rumour that Purnia kept a person to spy on Ogg, MSP, Volume 25, pp. 3982-83

204   *Ibid.*, pp. 3861-67, 3896-98

205   *Ibid.*, pp. 3944-48

206   *Ibid.*, pp. 3963-81

207   UN, Pw Jb 49, pp. 462-65

208   *Ibid.*

209   MSP, Volume 25, pp. 3893-94

210   *Ibid.*, pp. 4174-77, OGG to MacDowall, 23-11-1806

211   *Ibid.*, pp. 3985-94, Bentinck's minute, 24-12-1806

212   *Ibid.*, pp. 3994-98, Bentinck to Purnia, 24-12-1806

213   *Ibid.*, pp. 4179-81, Bentinck to Ogg, 24-12-1806; UN, Pw Jb 727, pp. 308-09, Bentinck to Ogg, 11-12-1806 (private letter)

214   While Cradock wrote this minute on November 9, the court of inquiry was still sitting in Bangalore, and yet without any evidence Cradock stated that the Bangalore detachment would have risen but for the presence of His Majesty's 22nd dragoons.

215   MSP, Volume 23, pp. 3006-14, Cradock's minute, 9-11-1806

216   William Bentinck, *op. cit.*, p. 36

217   *Ibid.*

218   UN, Pw Jb 49, pp. 377-78, Wilks to Bentinck, 23-10-1806

219   *Ibid.*, pp. 427-37, Wilks to Bentinck, 25-11-1806

220   MSP, Volume 24, pp. 3764-71, Barlow to Bentinck, 4-12-1806

221   MSP, Volume 28, pp. 903-904

222   There were only four companies, and in the whole detachment only nine persons were accused of even expressing mutinous words.

223   MSP, Volume 28, pp. 903-907

224   MSP, Volume 25, pp. 4181-83

225   MSP, Volume 23, pp. 3019-20

226   *Ibid.*, pp. 3443-50

227   *Ibid.*, pp. 3458-60

228   See pages 153-154

229   MSP, Volume 28, p. 766

230   MSP, Volume 27, p. 20

231   The ghost was said to be that of acting commandant of the 9th battalion, Muctum, who had been blown away from gun in 1785 for inciting the corps to mutiny.

232   MSP, Volume 24, pp. 3537-38, Welsh to Dyce, 25-11-1806

233   MSP, Volume 27, pp. 60-61, Aitwar Singh's deposition. Welsh's version runs as follows: "He told me. . . he wished to remain and watch over my safety, adding in an elevated voice, 'I have no friends, no relations here but you. . . If it were possible that

the men of this corps could so far forget themselves as to attempt your life, my only wish is to defend it and die at your feet.' I asked him if he had heard any news. He replied, 'No Sir, who will tell me any.'" MSP, Volume 24, p. 3539

234 MSP, Volume 24, pp. 3540-41, Welsh to Dyce, 25-11-1806
235 MSP, Volume 28, pp. 816-817
236 MSP, Volume 24, pp. 3541-42, Welsh to Dyce, 25-11-1806
237 *Ibid.*, pp. 3542-43
238 MSP, Volume 28, p. 770
239 MSP, Volume 24, p. 3542, Welsh to Dyce, 25-11-1806
240 *Ibid.*
241 *Ibid.*, p. 3543
242 MSP, Volume 28, pp. 859-61, Hepburn's deposition
243 Sheikh Hyder is described by Dyce: "a man of distinguished merit as a soldier and other ways possessing considerable ability and talent" and exercising "predominating influence." MSP, Volume 24, pp. 3526-36, Dyce to Buchan, 25-11-1806
244 MSP, Volume 24, pp. 3544-45, Welsh to Dyce, 25-11-1806
245 *Ibid.*
246 MSP, Volume 28, p. 733, Dyce's deposition
247 MSP, Volume 24, pp. 544-48, Welsh to Dyce, 25-11-1806
248 *Ibid.*, p. 3527, Dyce to Buchan, 25-11-1806
249 *Ibid.*, p. 3547
250 MSP, Volume 23, pp. 3261-62, Welsh to Campbell, 19-11-1806
251 UN, Pw Jb 667, Welsh to Lindsay, 19-11-1806
252 MSP, Volume 28, pp. 735-36
253 MSP, Volume 24, pp. 3553-54, Welsh to Dyce, 25-11-1806
254 *Ibid.*, pp. 3633-34, Dyce to Buchan, 25-11-1806
255 MSP, Volume 28, pp. 754-55
256 MSP, Volume 24, p. 3549
257 *Ibid.*, pp. 3510-11
258 MSP, Volume 27, pp. 18-65
259 MSP, Volume 27, pp. 18-19
260 Nobody knew where the fakir came from. Permaul used to refer to him as the Vellore fakir because once his mistress stated that that fakir appeared to have come from Vellore. MSP, volume 27, pp. 37-38
261 MSP, volume 27, pp. 20-21. Permaul stated that he went on the night of the 18th because he heard on the 15th that they were to meet on the 18th.
262 MSP, Volume 27, pp. 39-41
263 *Ibid.*, pp. 26-29, 33-41, 48-55
264 *Ibid.*, p. 36
265 *Ibid., pp. 305-07*
266 MSP, Volume 24, pp. 3570-72, Dyce to Campbell, 25-11-1806
267 *Ibid.*, pp. 3526-27, Dyce to Buchan, 25-11-1806
268 MSP, Volume 28, p. 741, Dyce's deposition
269 MSP, Volume 23, pp. 3411-14, Dyce to Campbell, 21-11-1806; Volume 24, pp. 3526-36. Dyce to Buchan, 25-11-1806
270 MSP, Volume 23, pp. 3416-18, Dyce to Campbell, 22-11-1806
271 *Ibid.*
272 MSP, Volume 28, pp. 793-97
273 MSP, Volume 24, p. 3532. "The direct evidence given by Major Welsh's butler," Dyce observed later, "appears to be so greatly invalidated by the known existence of jealousy and of a quarrel between him and Soubadar Shaik Hyder." (MSP, Volume 27, p. 3 20

274   MSP, Volume 23, pp. 3416-18
275   MSP, Volume 24, pp. 3697-98, Dyce to Campbell, 2-12-1806
276   MSP, Volume 28, pp. 745-46
277   *Ibid.*, pp. 930-36
278   *Ibid.*, pp. 968-69
279   *Ibid.*, pp. 964-67
280   *Ibid.*, pp. 930-36
281   MSP, Volume 24, pp. 3569-70. McDowall to Welsh, 22-11-1806
282   *Ibid.*
283   MSP, Volume 27, pp. 93036
284   MSP, Volume 24, pp. 3520-21, Grant to Macaulay, 23-11-1806
285   MSP, Volume 28, pp. 930-36
286   MSP, Volume 23, p. 3415. Lindsay later admitted that his apprehension was "ill
        founded." *Ibid.*
287   MSP, Volume 23, pp. 3258-59, Campbell to Buchan, 21-11-1806
288   *Ibid.*, 3260-61, Campbell to Buchan, 21-11-1806
289   *Ibid.*, 3400-03, Campbell to Buchan, 22-11-1806
290   *Ibid.*, pp. 3403-07, Campbell to Dyce, 22-11-1806
291   *Ibid.*, pp. 3260-61, Campbell to Buchan, 21-11-1806
292   *Ibid.*, pp. 3403-07, Campbell to Dyce, 22-11-1806
293   MSP, Volume 24, pp. 3627-33, Maitland to Bentinck, 24-11-1806
294   The exact number was 337, including Mercer. MSP, Volume 24, pp. 3654-55
295   About 150 men were ordered to Jaffna. MSP, Volume 24, pp. 3627-33
296   MSP, Volume 24, pp. 3627-33
297   PRO, CO, 54, 22, f. 211-12, Maitland to Windham, 24-11-1806
298   *Ibid.*, f. 223
299   William Bentinck, *op. cit.*, p. 39
300   MSP, Volume 23, pp. 3263-65, Buchan to Dyce, 25-11-1806
301   MSP, Volume 24, pp. 3555-57, Cradock's minute, 1-12-1806
302   *Ibid.*, pp. 3557-59. Lt. Col. Chamber was asked to succeed Grant.
303   *Ibid.*, pp. 3555-57
304   *Ibid.*, pp. 3560-62, Circular letter
305   MSP, Volume 24, pp. 3563-64, The Board's action. Petrie stated that Welsh's
        conclusion "contradicts every principle of human reasoning." UN, Pw Jb 38, pp. 191-
        201. Oakes added, ". . . all sober reflexion appears to have deserted him." Pw Jb 35,
        pp. 3557
306   MSP, Volume 24, pp. 3564-67
307   *Ibid.*, pp. 3647-49, Dyce to Campbell, 29-11-1806
308   *Ibid.*, pp. 3578-80, Dyce to Campbell, 27-11-1806
309   MSP, Volume 24, pp. 3646-49, 3652-54, 3690-94, 3833-34; Volume 27, pp. 244-
        45. The Ceylon detachment arrived at Tuticorin on November 29. It came to
        Palamcottah on December 3, at Dyce's order, as he put it, "to strengthen the public
        authority." Some Muslim sepoys had been fussy earlier. The detachment left
        Palamcottah for Ceylon on December 15. MSP, Volume 24, pp. 3690-3702; Volume
        25, p. 4007. The corps from Trichinopoly were halted at Madura except the first
        battalion of the fourth regiment which later released the first battalion of the third
        regiment. MSP, Volume 24, p. 3418
310   MSP, Volume 24, pp. 3679-80, Dyce to Grant, 24-11-1806; pp. 3650-51, Grant to
        Dyce, 26-11-1806
311   MSP, Volume 24, pp. 3650-51, 3676-81
312   *Ibid.*, pp. 3521-22; Volume 27, pp. 195-200
313   MSP, Volume 28, pp. 729-31

314   *Ibid.,* pp. 911-12

315   James Welsh did not die till 1861. *Gentleman's Magazine* (April, 1861), p. 351

316   MSP, Volume 28, pp. 731-81

317   MSP, Volume 28, pp. 936-970. To defend his position, Grant stated that the senior Subadar of the battalion, Huraman, when he heard about Grant's court-martial, went to Captain McDowall and "repeated his approbation of the measure, and expressed his sorrow at my having incurred on that account the displeasure of Government declaring that disgrace no doubt it was, but Gentlemen might think one way and Black people another." *Ibid.,* p. 963

Bentinck's observation in this connection is a truism: "I see in the court-martial a conversation with a Native officer alluded to, in which it is pretended that the troops were not sensible of any dishonour done to them in this act. We know that every Native will say what is pleasing without consideration of truth. The sentiment ascribed is repugnant to reason and to human nature; every soldier, in every service in the world, knows that he cannot be more dishonoured than by being deprived of his arms." MSP, Volume 28, pp. 1025-31

318   MSP, Volume 28, pp. 871, 1021-22

319   *Ibid.,* pp. 1025-31

320   *Ibid.,* pp. 1032-35

321   MSP, Volume 30, pp. 1786-89, Bentinck to Barlow, 28-4-1807

322   It had about 600 Hindus and 130 Christians. MSP, Volume 24, p. 3785

323   MSP, Volume 23, pp. 3373-75, Lang to Cradock, 27-11-1806

324   MSP, Volume 24, pp. 3463-69

325   *Ibid.,* pp. 3469-71

326   *Ibid.,* p. 3472

327   *Ibid.,* 3472-73, Bentinck's minute, 2-12-1806

328   *Ibid.,* pp. 3473-75, Cradock's minute, 2-12-1806

329   *Ibid.,* pp. 3475-82, Petrie's minute, 2-12-1806

330   *Ibid.,* pp. 3483-88, Oakes' minute, 2-12-1806

331   *Ibid.,* pp. 3488-92. Munro was asked to have a portion of Indian cavalry should he choose to call the cavalry.

332   *Ibid.,* pp. 3492-96; Secret Letters from Madras, Series I, Volume 3, 11-1-1807

333   This was done partly to prevent the corps from doing mischief, partly it was already under orders to go north.

334   These brothers were strangers in Wallajabhad; they had come from Burhanpore in the Deccan.

335   Another time Sheikh Nutter stated the number was less than 60. The largest meeting, he reported, was attended by only 30 sepoys.

336   MSP, Volume 24, pp. 3781-3805, Munro's report

337   *Ibid.,* pp. 3835-36, Buchan to Brown, 20-12-1806

338   *Ibid.,* pp. 3728-30

339   *Ibid.,* pp. 3737-43, Bose to Campbell, 7-12-1806

340   *Ibid.*

341   *Ibid.,* pp. 3733-36, Bose to Fuller, 8-12-1806

342   *Ibid.,* pp. 3725-30, Bose to Campbell, 6-12-1806

343   *Ibid.,* pp. 3737-43

344   *Ibid,* pp. 3731-32, Campbell to Bose, 9-12-1806

345   *Ibid.,* pp. 3743-44, The Board's action

346   Secret Letters from Madras, Series I, Volume 3, 11-1-1807

347   MSP, Volume 27, pp. 332-45, Hazlewood to Agnew, 3-1-1807

348   MSP, Volume 28, pp. 445-48

349   *Ibid.,* pp. 524-25

350 UN, Pw Jb 44, Tod to Bentinck, 12-2-1807

351 MSP, Volume 28, pp. 524-25, Hazlewood to Reynell, 7-2-1807

352 UN, Pw Jb, 44, Tod to Bentinck, 12-2-1807

353 MSP, Volume 28, pp. 522-23

354 *Ibid.*, pp. 528-29

355 *Ibid.*, pp. 618-39

356 *Ibid.*, pp. 644-45

357 MSP, Volume 29, pp. 1070-1217

358 However, there were some plans in Paris of seducing the country powers on invading India. In 1803, when Napoleon Bonaparte sent out Charles DeCaen as governor of L'Ile de France, he instructed him to intrigue with Indian princes in order to oust the English in the next opportunity. DeCaen was given a large number of young officers, about 1,250, with the intention of training a sepoy force. As late as 1805, Napoleon suggested that about 20,000 French troops and 3,000 Spanish troops should be sent to DeCaen in order to invade India. French agents had been active with the Rajah of Tanjore, the Marathas and several poligars. S. P. Sen, *The French in India, 1763-1816* (Calcutta, 1947), pp. 562-67, 573-80; Henri Prentout, *L'Ile de France sous DeCaen, 1803-1810, pp. 374-80*

359 MSP, Volume 29, pp. 1217-27

360 *Ibid.*, pp. 1226-30

361 UN, Pw Jb 687

362 MSP, Volume 28, pp. 471-504, 649-59; Volume 29, pp. 1258-64

363 MSP, Volume 27, pp. 207-209; Volume 29, pp. 1269-77

364 MJP, Range 322, Volume 19, pp. 768-89; Volume 24, pp. 3402-03; MSP, Volume 27, pp. 211-232, 234-42

365 MMP, Range 256, Volume 3, pp. 1201-07; Volume 4, pp. 1559-61

366 MJP, Range 322, Volume 20, pp. 1283-91, 1299-1334; MMP, Range 256, Volume 7, pp. 3644-67; Volume 8, pp. 4234-54

367 MJP, Range 322, Volume 25, pp. 4040-41

368 After the Nundydrug affair, the Supreme Government opted for *en masse* banishment. But against that, the Madras Government remonstrated. Consequently, the Supreme Government left the matter with the local government. MSP, Volume 29, pp. 1044-47, Barlow to Bentinck, 12-2-1807

369 MSP, Volume 30, pp. 1928-39. These were princes' adherents.

370 MMP, Range 256, Volume 12, pp. 6696-97

371 MSP, Volume 29, pp. 1059-63; MMP, Range 256, Volume 7, pp. 3672-74. Lt. Col. Lang, George Read, and William Wright in Vellore; Lt. Col. Copper, E. C. Greenway and David Cockburn in Madras. There were 391 military prisoners in Vellore and 180 in St. Thomas Mount. MSP, volume 30, pp. 1843-1980; MJP, Range 322, Volume 20, pp. 1357-61; MMP, Range 256, Volume 7, p. 3667

372 MSP, Volume 30, p. 1964

373 *Ibid.*, pp. 1967-71; W. Bentinck, *op. cit.*, p. 41

374 MSP, Volume 30, pp. 2122-24

375 MSP, Volume 31, pp. 344-52

376 MSP, Volume 30, pp. 1980-91

377 *Ibid.*; MMP, Range 256, Volume 26, pp. 2021-23

378 MMP, Range 256, Volume 12, pp. 6696-97

379 MSP, Volume 30, pp. 2027-29. Jemmal-ud-din's detention was much regretted because of the promised pardon.

380 MMP, Range 256, Volume 19, pp. 11065-93

381 *Ibid.*, pp. 11061-64, 11097-11101; Volume 23, pp. 581-82

CHAPTER VI: REACTION IN ENGLAND

1 The Times, December 23, 1806
2 The Morning Post, January 2, 9, 1807; The Times, January 5, 9, 12, 19, February 18, 1807; The Morning Chronicles, January 9, 1807
3 The Times, December 23, 1806
4 The Morning Post, January 2, 1807
5 The Times, The Morning Post, The Morning Chronicle
6 The Times, January 12, 1807
7 UN, Pw Jb 25, pp. 502-23
8 Quoted in J. W. Kaye, The Life and Correspondence of Major-General Sir John Malcolm (London: Smith, Elder, and Co., 1856), I, 374-76
9 BM, MSS, Add 29182, f. 50
10 UN, Pw Jb 25, pp. 502-23
11 HMS, Volume 510, p. 411
12 Secret Letters from Bengal and India, Volume 8, pp. 409-14, 30-7-1806
13 Secret Letters from Madras, Series 1, Volume 3, 8-8-1806
14 Ibid.
15 There was a report from Hyderabad of an invasion of the Marathas. Therefore, the Government detained the Sarah Christina till it was clarified.
16 About Leith, Bentinck wrote: "He is a silent, reserved, sensible and awkward man. His information is like the precious metals—difficult of extraction but valuable. He will execute the service upon which he is sent with safety and success. He will not speak without being questioned and his answers will be discrete." UN, Pw F 1203
17 Secret Letters from Madras, Series 1, Volume 3, 14-10-1806
18 Historical Manuscript Commission, Dropmore, Report on the Manuscripts of J. B. Fortescue, Esq (London: The Hereford Times, Ltd., 1915), IX, 50
19 Ibid., p. 52
20 The Court Book, Volume 115, pp. 1274-75
21 UN, Pw Jb 216a
22 The Court Book, Volume 115, pp. 1304-05
23 BM, MSS, Add 29182, f. 91
24 UN, Pw Jb 25, pp. 502-23
25 UN, Pw Jb 750
26 The Court Book, Volume 115, pp. 1466-67
27 HMS, Volume 510, pp. 765-850, paragraphs # 10, 14, 16, and 23
28 Ibid, paragraphs # 3, 10, and 22
29 UN, Pw Jb 25, pp. 502-23
30 Pw Jb 218a
31 Maya Gupta, Lord William Bentinck Madras, 1803-1807 (Ph. D. Dissertation, 1969, University of London), pp. 388-90; Peter Auber, Rise and Progress of the British Power in India (London: Wm. H. Allen and Co., 1837), II, 444-45
32 HMS, Volume 510, pp. 795-850, paragraphs # 11 and 12; Pw Jb 216a
33 BM, MSS, Add 29182, f. 142-43
34 Ibid., f. 171-72
35 The Court Book, Volume 115, p. 135
36 HMS, Volume 510, pp. 795-850, paragraph # 32. However, the Board of Control intervened on behalf of Darley stating that such a measure was tantamount to his recall, and in the light of his later success with his corps he should be given only a

severe censure. Letters from the Board to the Court, 1801-1808, Volume 30, pp. 485-94, 27-5-1807

37   UN, Pw Jb 25, pp. 502-23. The Duke of Portland became prime minister on March 24. Some of William Bentinck's friends asked him to intervene but he refused, as being a family matter.

38   UN, Pw Jb 216a

39   Board of Control, Draft, Volume 13 (F), pp. 533-34

40   Board of Control, Draft, Volume 13 (F), pp. 529-31

41   UN, Pw Jb 677/1, William Bentinck's journal

42   UN, Pw F 1203

43   MSP, Volume 28, pp. 608-18

44   UN, Pw Jb 677/1, William Bentinck's journal

45   William Bentinck, op. cit., p. 4

46   UN, Pw Jb 677/1. He also added, "I have no apprehension whatever for the result, but calculating upon. . . my hope of convincing the Court of Directors and my friends of the rectitude and I will think of the merit of my conduct; my conscience is perfectly at ease." Ibid.

47   John Cradock, Detailed Letter, p. 1

48   MPUP, Range 243, Volume 23, pp. 5067-72

49   Ibid.

50   Ibid., p. 5094

51   Ibid., pp. 5067-72

52   UN, Pw Jb 677/1

53   HMS, Volume 510, pp. 897-914. John F. Cradock, Sketch of the Situation of Sir John Cradock (London, 1808), pp. 1-15

54   UN, Pw Jb 260a

55   UN, Pw Jb 750

56   Pw Jb 261-63, 267-74

57   Pw Jb 677/1

58   Ibid.

59   Pw Jb 750

60   Pw Jb 667/1

61   Madras Courier, October 14, 1807

62   Madras Courier, September 30, 1807

63   John Cradock, Sketch, pp. 1-15

64   Ibid.

65   UN, Pw Jb 750

66   Pw Jb 317a

67   Ibid.

68   Ibid.

69   Ibid.

70   William Bentinck, op. cit., pp. 44-48

71   UN, Pw Jb 388

72   In the Detailed Letter, Cradock stated that in 1790 at Connatore, a regiment of cavalry, when a new turban was introduced, showed "the strongest symptoms of dislike." But Major Stevenson "quelled the mutiny by forcible measures" and that he "was honored with the approbation and received the thanks of Government." In 1806, the resistance would have petered out, he said, except for the work of the conspirators. I have not been however able to find any evidence of this in the documents.

73   Correspondence Reports, Volume 34, pp. 640-44, July 1810

74   The old 36th battalion

75   MMP, Range 256, Volume 24, pp. 808-30; Volume 25, pp. 1831-60

76   The Court Book, Volume 118, pp. 572-75

77   Ibid., pp. 575-76

78   Ibid., pp. 576-7, 583-5, 586-7

79   William Bentinck, op. cit., p. iii

80   HMS, Volume 510, pp. 915-28

81   The Court Book, Volume 118a, pp. 1065-66

82   UN, Pw Jb 337a

83   Pw Jb 340

84   Correspondence Reports, Volume 34, pp. 640-44; The Court Book, Volume 119, p.
     541

85   John Cradock still remained unsatisfied. As late as February 27, 1811, he sent a letter
     to the Court of Directors stating how much he had suffered in consequence "of his
     having accepted the command of the Company's forces at Madras." The Court Book,
     Volume 119a, p. 1478

86   Laurence Kitzan, The London Missionary Society in India and China, 1798-1834 (Ph.
     D. Dissertation, 1965, The University of Toronto), p. 32

87   Kenneth Ingham, Reformers in India, 1793-1833 (Cambridge: The University Press,
     1956), p. 1

88   Ibid., p. 2

89   E. M. Howse, Saints in Politics (Toronto: University Press, 1952), pp. 71-72; Henry
     Morris, The Life of Charles Grant (London: John Murray, 1904), pp. 174-93; G. R.
     Balleine, A History of Evangelical Party in the Church of England (London: Longmans,
     Green, and Co., 1908), pp. 147-48

90   John C. Marshman, The Life and Times of Carey, Marshman and Ward (London:
     Longman, Brown, Green and Roberts, 1859), I, 16-67

91   Richard Lovett, History of London Missionary Society (London: Oxford University
     Press,1899), I, 5-42

92   Charles Holes, The Early History of the Church Missionary Society (London: Church
     Missionary Society, 1896), p. 177

93   Robert Owen, The History of the Origin and First Ten Years of the British and Foreign
     Bible Society (London: tilling and Hughes,1816), I, 98-100, 275-77

94   H. Morris, loc. Cit.; G. R. Balleine, loc. cit.

95   J. C. Marshman, op. cit., pp. 25-28, 67-68; M. A. Sherring, The History of Protestant
     Missions in India (London: The Religious Tract Society, 1884), p. 25

96   In a minute, dated June 27, 1806, Bentinck recorded: "Our first wish must be to see
     the followers of Mahomet and of Bramah embrace Christianity. . ." He wanted to
     protect all Christian bodies including Catholics. HMS, Volume 59, pp. 335-37

97   John C. Marshman, op. cit., pp. 55-70. Until the Charter Act of 1793, the punishment
     for unlicensed person was deportation. The new act imposed fine and imprisonment,
     and it came into effect on February 1, 1794. C. Holle, op. cit., pp. 152-54

98   John C. Marshman, op. cit., pp. 75-77. 112-17

99   Quoted in Ibid., pp. 73-74

100 C. H. Philips, The East India Company, 1784-1834 (Manchester: The University Press,
     1961), p. 159

101 Quoted in J. W. Kaye, The Administration of the East India Company (London:
     Richard Bentley, 1853), pp. 635-36

102 J. C. Marshman, op. cit., pp. 155-57

103 Ibid., pp. 190-92; J. W. Kaye, The Life and Correspondence of Major-General Sir John
     Malcolm, II, 270-71

104 J. C. Marshman, op. cit., p. 247

105   A. T. Embree, Charles Grant and British Rule in India (London: George Allen and Unwin Ltd., 1962), p. 240

106   He offered three. The third one was, "A brief historic view of the progress of the gospel in different nations, since its promulgation, illustrated by maps, shewing its luminous tract throughout the world, with chronological notices of its duration in particular places." Hugh Pearson, op. cit., I, 350-51

107   Claudius Buchanan, The Works of Rev. Claudius Buchanan (New York: Whiting and Watson, 1812), pp. 208-214

108   Ibid., p. 208

109   Towards the close of 1805, Buchanan wrote to the Archbishop of Canterbury:
One observation I would make on the proposed Ecclesiastical establishment. A partial or half measure will have no useful effect. A few additional chaplains can do nothing towards the attainment of the great objects in view.

An Archbishop is wanted for India, a sacred and exalted character, surrounded by his bishops, of ample revenue and extensive sway, a venerable personage, whose name shall be greater than that of transitory governors of the land; and whose fame for piety, and for the will and power to do good, may pass throughout every region.
We want something royal in a spiritual or temporal sense, for the abject subjects of this great eastern empire to look up to . . . It is certain that men are ruled by the Church, though ostensibly by the state, in every country. The seeds of moral obedience and social order are all in the Church. . .
. . . It is certain that nothing would more alarm the portentous invader of nations, than our taking a 'religious possession' of Hindostan. Five hundred respectable clergy of the English Church, established in our Gentoo cities, would more perplex his views of conquest than an army of fifty thousand British soldiers. The army of fifty thousand would melt away in seven years; but the influence of an upright clergyman among the natives of his district would be permanent.. . .
If the Scriptures be from God, our nation does not deserve at his hand to retain the possession of this 'paradise of nation' a year longer; so greatly have we abused our sacred trust. We have, in one word, 'withheld the revelation of God, and permitted the libation to Moloch of human blood' . . But we do not fulfil the purpose for which the sceptre was given [christianizing India], why then should Providence withhold the country from a new invader? If we ultimately lose it, let us acknowledge the justice of God in the dispensation." H. Pearson, op. cit., I, 367-75

110   Quoted in J. W. Kaye, Christianity in India (London: Smith, Elder and co., 1859), p. 147

111   Quoted in J. W. Kaye, The Administration of the East India company, pp. 635-36

112   About the time of the mutiny, Buchanan was on a trip to South India to examine the conditions of Christians there. R. H. Kerr, who was in Malabar, was asked by Bentinck to report on the Syrian Christians. In his report, he stated, "We have, my Lord, been sadly defective in what we owed to God and man, since we have had a foot in this country, as well as by departing most shamefully from our Christian profession ourselves, as in withholding those resources of moral perfection from the natives." He recommended the establishment of English schools in order to educate the Indian children. Quoted in Claudius Buchanan, The Works of Rev. Claudius Buchanan, Report, 3-11-1806

113   Chater and Robinson came in August, 1806. As Chater's wife was "near her confinement" and as there was "no surgeon on board" the missionaries were allowed

to stay in Bengal. Meanwhile the Government cooled off; however the missionaries were sent to Burma and Penang. J. C. Marshman, op. cit.,I, 259-61

114 BM, MSS, Add 29182, f. 171-72
115 UN, Pw Jb 218a
116 BM, MSS, Add 29182, f. 171-72
117 Ibid.
118 Ibid., f. 177-86
119 UN, Pw Jb 218a
120 BMS, Andrew Fuller to William Ward, 9-7-1807
121 Ibid.
122 C. H. Philips, op. cit., p. 162
123 Ibid., p. 163
124 Quoted in Henry Morris, op. cit., pp. 300-02
125 Parry and Grant referred to the "drain theory." They said, "The public tribute which we derive as sovereigns, the private wealth individuals among us require, is transferred from India, whereby the growth which that country naturally productive, would have in prosperity, is prevented."
126 President's Secret Correspondence, Volume 1 (1807-10), pp. 1-36
127 HMS, Volume 816, pp. 138-42, Parry-Grant to Dundas, 21-9-1807
128 Ibid.
129 President's Secret Correspondence, Volume 1 (1807-10), pp. 27-30
130 HMS, Volume 816, pp. 138-42
131 C. H. Philips, op. cit., p. 162
132 A. T. Embree, op. cit., p. 246
133 Thomas Twining was in Bengal from 1792 to 1805. J. C. Marshman, op. cit., I, 333-34. He was a son of a tea merchant, aged about 40. BMS, Fuller to Marshman, 12-2-1808.
134 The British and Foreign Bible Society had formed a Correspondence Committee in Calcutta in 1806. To which, it had sent one thousand pounds in 1806 and another thousand in 1807, and also 500 copies of English Bible, 1,000 copies of English New Testament, 500 copies of German Bible, and another 500 copies of German New Testament. Robert Owen, op. cit., I, 98-100, 275-77
135 Thomas Twining particularly capitalized Buchanan's incautious remark: "A wise policy seems to demand that we should use every means of coercing this contemptuous spirit of our native subjects." Upon it, he exclaimed, "Gracious Heaven! What sentiment are here sent forth amidst the population of our provinces in India."
136 BFBS, Thomas Twining, A Letter to the Chairman of the East India Company

About Twining's pamphlet, William Wilberforce wrote to Rev. Francis Wrangham on November 23, 1807: "You may probably have heard, that the late melancholy tragedy at Vellore, has furnished to the adversaries of Christianity an occasion for endeavouring to obstruct the efforts which were made for its diffusion. How far this is gone you will judge, when I tell you that a quondam servant of the Company has been lately publishing a pamphlet in the shape of a letter to the chairman, of which it is the direct object to reprobate the translation or circulation of the Holy Scriptures in Indostan; and so confident was the author in the rectitude and wisdom of his own opinions, that he called on the chairman one morning to express his surprise that the Court of Directors had not publicly declared their determination to suppress so pernicious a practice.. .

". . .We are the more criminal, because there is not a pretence for connecting the Vellore transaction with the missionary labours. . ." Robert Isaac and

Samuel Wilberforce, *The Life of William Wilberforce* (London: John Murray, 1838), III, 350-53

137 John C. Marshman, op. cit., I, 353

138 Robert Owen, An Address to the Chairman of the East India Company Occasioned by Mr. Twining's Letter. BFBS's Collection

139 J. C. Marshman, op. cit., I, 376

140 Ibid.

141 He said that he had seen one of Thomas Marriott's letters exculpating the princes and their adherents, and therefore he changed his position.

142 Joseph Farington, Farington Diary (London: Hutchinson and Co., 1925), V, 16; BFBS, Lord Teignmouth, Considerations on the Practicability, Policy and Obligation of Communication to the Natives of India the Knowledge of Christianity, Preface

143 The Christian Observer, December, 1807; BMS, Andrew Fuller to Joshua Marshman, 12-2-1808

144 The Christian Observer, December, 1807

145 C. H. Philips, op. cit., p. 163

146 BM, MSS, ADD 29183, f. 158-59

147 BMS, Fuller to Marshman, 12-2-1808

148 BFBS, Andrew Fuller, An Apology for the Late Christian Missions to India

149 Ibid.

150 BFBS, A Letter to John Scott Waring Esq. in Refutation. The author said that he had been in India for about 20 years.

151 BFBS, John Scott Waring, A Letter to the Rev. John Owen A.M. in Reply; John Scott Waring, A Reply to a Letter Addressed to 'John Scott Waring'

The Christian Observer accused Waring as a disciple of Voltaire. To that accusation, he stated: ". . . The conductors of the Christian Observer and those who concur with them are in truth the disciples of Voltaire, because they wished to destroy institutions, which have been established in India for ages. I admit that their motive to be as good as Voltaire's were infamous and wicked. But men of reflection will consider that the very same effects may be produced by an imprudent attempt to change a system bad as it is, to which an immense population is invincibly attached. . ." Scott Waring contended that he was not "an enemy to the extension of Christianity in India," but "an enemy to the new and dangerous measures adopted for extending Christianity in India." Scott Waring at this time was an old man. He had been a Major in the Bengal Army. He had returned to England to defend Warren Hastings against his enemies. He was a member of the Parliament for several years.

152 The officer was Colonel Stewart, sometimes called "Hindu Stewart" inasmuch as he was a Hindu proselyte.

153 After pointing out that proselytism divided families and community, he admonished the missionaries: "Cease, then, worthy missionaries, to disturb that repose that forms the happiness of so many millions of the human race; a procedure that can only tend 'to set a man at variance against his father, and the daughter against mother, and the daughter-in-law against the mother-in-law' . . ." He also defended Hindu morality saying: "Wherever I look around me, in the vast region of the Hindoo mythology, I discover piety in the garb of allegory; and I see morality, at every turn, blended with every tale; and, as far as I can rely on my own judgement, it appears the most complete and ample system of moral allegory, that the world has ever produced." He admitted that sati and sacrifices in Jaganath temple were cruel, but stated that they were voluntary, and if one did not want to do, none would compel one.

154 BFBS A Bengal Officer, *Vindication of the Hindoo*

155 BFBS, A Late Resident at Bhagulpore, *The Danger to British India*

156   John Lord Teignmouth was of course incorrect. At that time there were fourteen missionaries in South India. Kenneth Ingham, op. cit., pp. 125-27

157   BFBS' Collection. Teignmouth's was published under the name "A late Resident in Bengal," but most people knew who the author was. Towards the end, Teignmouth became too evangelical in the presentation: "I think it my duty to make a solemn appeal, to all who still retain the fear of God, and who admit, that religion and the course of conduct which it prescribes, are not to be banished from the affairs of nations, now when the political sky, so long overcast, has become more lowering and black than ever, whether this is a period for augmenting the weight of our national sins and provocations, by an exclusive toleration of idolatry; a crime which . . . had actually drawn forth. . . the most fearful inflictions of the divine displeasure."

158   The Christian Observer, February, 1808, p. 124

159   The Christian Observer (September, October, November, 1808), pp. 569-73, 639-51, 702-04; (February, April, 1809), pp. 83-84, 220-25

160   As an example it was stated that Scott Waring supported slave trade strenuously in the Parliament and then congratulated William Wilberforce when it was abolished in 1807.

161   *The Eclectic Review* (January to June, 1808), Volume IV, Part I, pp. 70-77, 154-72, 253-72, 336-50, 440-51; (July to December, 1808), Volume IV, Part I, pp. 627-32, 1115-23; (January to June, 1809), Volume V, Part I, pp. 420-34

162   The Edinburgh reviewers were liberal churchmen. The author of this particular article was Rev. Sydney Smith. He was extremely vicious towards the Baptists. He got hold of some accounts of the Baptist missionaries, which had been inadvertently published, and culled out those which would be most fit for satire and ridicule and printed them with such quaint captions as: "Brother Carey's Piety at Sea," "Mr. Ward is Frightened by a Privateer," "Mr. Ward feels a Regard for the Sailors," "Mr. Ward sees an American Vessel and longs to preach to the Sailors," "Mr. Fountain's Gratitude to Harvey." (April, 1808), pp. 151-85

    John Styles, of the Congregation Church, gave a severe rebuke for its attack on the Baptist missionaries. See Strictures on Two Critiques on the Edinburgh Review on the Subject of Methodism and the Missions (London, 1808)

163   It also argued that proselytism was not a Christian "duty," and described the Hindus as "a civilized and moral people.

164   The Edinburgh Review (April, 1808), pp. 151-84

165   The author was Rev. Southey. The article appeared in the February issue, 1809

166   It added: "This is looking far before us!—but in an age when there are serious apprehensions entertained of overstocking the world, it is surely allowable to look on for some half a millennium." The Quarterly Review (February to May, 1809), pp. 193-226

167   J. C. Marshman, op. cit., I, 380-511

168   T. C. Hansard, The Parliamentary Papers, XXV, 425-499

CHAPTER VII: THE CONSPIRACY THEORY

1   A selective list of authors who held the Muslim conspiracy theory: R. R. Gillespie, *A Memoir of Major-General Sir Robert Rollo Gillespie*, pp. 92-106; John Blakistan, *Twelve Years' Military Adventure*, I, 282-312; Edward Thornton, *The History of the British India* (London: Wm. H. Allen and Co., 1843), II, 58-83; Harriet Martineau, *The History of the British Rule in India*, pp. 215-21; Henry Beveridge, *A Comprehensive History of India* (London: Blackie and Son, 1862), pp. 814-16; Charles F. Kirby, *The Adventures of an Arcot Rupee*, III, 246-59; John W. Kaye and G.

B. Malleson, *History of the Indian Mutiny of 1857-58,* I, 178-183; Arthur F. Cox, *Madras District Manual: North Arcot* (Madras: The Government Press, 1895), I, 106-07; A. Keene, "The Mutiny at Vellore, July 10th, 1806," *United Service Magazine* (London), XXXIV (October, 1906, to March, 1907), 95-104; Arthur Stanley, "Gillespie of Vellore," *The Army Quarterly,* (London), XXII (July, 1931, 337-44; Richard Hilton, *The Indian Mutiny* (London: Hollis and Carter, 1957), pp. 22-23. Among the Indians, Haripado Chaudhuri holds on to the conspiracy theory. "The Vellore Mutiny: A Reappraisal," *The Modern Review* (Calcutta), August, 1955, pp. 1125-28. C. S. Srinivasachari has no conclusive view. "The Vellore Mutiny of 1806," *Indian History Congress Proceedings,* Delhi, 1948, pp. 195-98

2   MSP, Volume 25, pp. 88-89

3   HMS, Volume 510, pp. 87-177

4   *Ibid.,* pp. 350-54

5   See pages 218-229

6   See pages 216-219

7   HMS, Volume 510, pp. 179-217, 375-97

8   See pages 39-40

9   See pages 56

10   UN, Pw Jb 687

11   HMS, Volume 507, pp. 207-14; Volume 508, pp. 122-290

12   HMS, Volume 508, pp. 103-120

13   See pages 38-39

14   HMS, Volume 507, pp. 137-39; MSP, Volume 28, pp. 1025-31

15   UN, Pw Jb 687

16   W. J. Wilson, *op. cit.,* III, 193-94

17   MMP, Range 256, Volume 24, pp. 815-17

18   HMS, Volume 508, p. 287

19   HMS, Volume 508, p. 166. On the morning after the suppression of the mutiny, when Marriott went to see if she and her son were safe, the first thing she did was to exclaim: "Marriott Sahib, did not I tell you what would be consequence of the making the sepoys disaffected."

20   Edward Locker, "Vellore," *Plain Englishman* (1821), pp. 487-90

21   See page 123

22   See page 125-126

23   HMS, Volume 509, pp. 62-68; MSP, Volume 21, pp. 2280-87

24   See pages 157-159

25   See pages 71-73

26   HMS, Volume 508, p. 181

27   *Ibid.,* pp. 210-12

28   *Ibid.,* p. 269

29   Mrs. Pritchard stated that after she returned home, "She had occasion to observe that both the men's and women's hats had been particularly abused and crushed." HMS, Volume 508, pp. 179-81. Forbes and Coombs stated that if the sepoys had been really upset with the turban, they would have crushed the hats "with every mark of indignity, revenge and detestation." They stated that the hats were left hanging "undestroyed and untouched." MSP, Volume 25, pp. 4185-4244, paragraph # 27. The only explanation for these contradictory statements is that in some homes the sepoys destroyed them, and in other homes they did not.

The fourth appendix of the Forbes-Coombs Report of October 15, 1806, states: "Extract from the evidence of Ramdoo sepoy 1st batt. 1st reg. During the mutiny in the fort as I was standing at the paymaster's house, with Mahommed Jaffer, he said to me, 'They will all think we are fighting for the turband. No, pointing to the Mysore flag, which was flying, it's that we are fighting for, that and our faith.' Signed J. M. C. MSP, Volume 25, p. 4253. I do not find this statement in Ramdu's deposition either before the Military Court, or the Mixed Commission, or anywhere. This singular deposition is isolated and without base. I strongly question both its authenticity and reliability.

30 HMS, Volume 508, p. 104
31 HMS, Volume 507, pp. 587-588
32 See pages 141-148
33 MSP, Volume 24, pp. 3843-3860
34 MSP, Volume 27, pp. 6-128, Bentinck's minute, 8-1-1807
35 See pages 161-163
36 UN, Pw Jb 726, pp. 55-63
37 See page 65
38 See pages 71-73
39 See page 148-153
40 See pages 179-181
41 MMP, Range 256, Volume 3, pp. 1053-55
42 See pages 75-76
43 See page 94; MMP, Range 256, Volume 9, pp. 4898-4900
44 UN, Pw Jb 49, pp. 337-48
45 Later in September, 1806, Subadars Kader Beg, Amar Ali and Sheikh Hussain were picked as inciters of disaffection. HMS, Volume 509, pp. 356-64. In his letter, Sydenham stated, "I have even heard that some Hindoos, who were supposed to have been very well affected towards the service performed after the publication of Colonel Montresor's order a solemn religious ceremony for having escaped the occurrence of the dreadful alternative between the sacrifice of their faith and an insurrection against the Company's government." HMS, Volume 509, pp. 259-280, paragraph # 10
46 See pages 78-80, 175-180
47 See pages 151-153
48 UN, Pw Jb 726, pp. 55-63, Bentinck to Thomas Grenville, 1-12-1806
49 MSP, Volume 23, pp. 3443-60; Volume 24, pp. 3501-05; Volume 27, pp. 96-128; UN, Pw Jb 49, pp. 442-61
50 See pages 148-150
51 UN, Pw Jb 726, pp. 55-63, Bentinck to Grenville, 1-12-1806
52 HMS, Volume 509, pp. 387-408, Sydenham to Barlow, 31-8-1806
53 MSP, Volume 27, pp. 9128, Bentinck's minute, 8-1-1807
54 See pages 165-166
55 See pages 126-128; 151-153
56 MSP, Volume 25, pp. 88-95. On the report John Cradock expressed his highest approbation and added, " . . . that had the Commission at Vellore exhibited equal ability and labour, misrepresentation and delusion would not have maintained so long in Empire, and that a great part of the mischief that has continued from that hour to the present would have been averted by promptitude and vigour." But Bentinck described the authors of the report as "principal actors in these proceedings, the most implicated in responsibility, the most biased that selection could have assembled from the whole army," and added that the report was "the statement of an advocate who defended an opinion already formed, rather than a judge who without any preconceived opinion searches for truth in the midst of contradictory assertions and documents." MSP, Volume 27, 82-88
57 MSP, Volume 20, pp. 1225-45
58 MSP, Volume 25, pp. 4185-4244, paragraph #39

59 Jemmal-ud-din had earlier refused to say anything despite the promise of full pardon. HMS, Volume 508, p. 290

60 See page 28-29

61 UN, Pw Jb 687, Hazlewood's narrative

62 The first of the first was almost annihilated in Colonel Baillie's defeat in 1780. Then it was reconstructed by the recruits from Tanjore. W. J. Wilson, *op. cit.*, III, 176

63 The second of the twenty-third arrived in Vellore on May 16, 1806.

64 See pages 72-73

65 MSP, Volume 20, pp. 1225-45

66 *Ibid,*

67 HMS, Volume 507, pp. 332-36; Volume 508, pp. 191-6, 220-22, 274-76

68 MSP, Volume 22, p. 2397

69 HMS, Volume 508, pp. 288-90

70 MSP, Volume 22, 2409-10

71 HMS, Volume 508, pp. 194-98

72 See pages 83-84

73 MSP, Volume 22, p. 2415

74 HMS, Volume 508, pp. 219-220

75 MSP, Volume 25, pp. 4295-96, Appendix # 26

76 MSP, Volume 24, p. 2420

77 HMS, Volume 509, pp. 259-280, Sydenham to Barlow, 22-8-1806, paragraph # 27

78 Maya Gupta, *op. cit.*, pp. 355-57

79 MSP, Volume 28, pp. 548-607

80 Maya Gupta, *op. cit.*, pp. 357-58

81 Schwartz asked the Rajah of Tanjore many times to protect the Christians from persecutions.

82 The following were the missionaries in South India at the time of the mutiny: J. P. Rottler, A. F. Caemerrer, C. S. John, Christian Pohle, John C. Kohlholl, C. H. Horst, William T. Ringeltaube, Holzberg, H. D. Schreyvogel, C. W. Paezold, George Cran, Augustus des Granges, William C. Loveless, and Johnm Taylore. Out of these 14, 7 had come after the beginning of the century. Kenneth Ingham, *op. cit.*, pp. 125-27

83 About this time, the British and Foreign Bible Society sent a great number of New Testament and Bible to Bengal. There is no account of anything being sent to the Coast.

CONCLUSION

1 The rumour of forced proselytism reached even Central India. Mountstuart Elphinstone, the Resident in Nagpore, reported to the Supreme Government on September 3, 1806, that Jeswant Rao "was particularly inquisitive about our ideas on the propriety of compelling men of other religions to embrace the Christian Faith." BSPP, Volume 196, Entry Correspondence, September 25, 1806

2 MSP, Volume 28, pp. 548-607, Bentinck's minute, 28-2-1807

3 Quoted in J. F. Cradock, *Detailed Letter,* p. 31 H. H. Wilson, *op. cit.*, p. 130

4 H. H. Wilson, *op. cit.*, p. 130

APPENDIX A: MAP OF SOUTH INDIA

APPENDIX B: AN OUTLINE OF THE VELLORE FORT

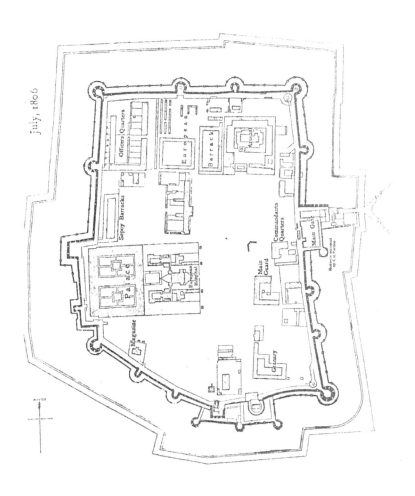

APPENDIX C

NOTES ON MOUSTACHES, BRARDS, EAR RINGS, SECT MARKS, AND UNIFORMS

The following testimonies were given after the Mutiny for the information of the Court of Directors, and they are recorded in MMP, Range 256, in Volume 25.

"It has been so universally and constantly the custom for the native soldier to appear clean shaved upon duty and the reverse would be noticed as an offence."   - Lt. Col. I. Durand, 17th Regiment

"Invalids sometimes wear their beards but they are in general privileged men."   - Major Paul Bose, 14th Regiment

"Most undoubtedly no beard was allowed, as much as it was for Europeans to do so."   - Lt. Col. E. Reilly, 8th Regiment

"I positively affirm that no corps I have ever served in or associated with admitted of the men appearing with their beards."
          - Lt. Col. Cuppage, 18th Regiment

"It was customary to allow whiskers to be worn but at all times to have their beard clean."   - Lt. Col. G. Wahab, 17th Regiment

"It was never permitted (in the 2nd of the 4th) that any man should wear a long beard when dressed for parades or other duty. I have the same to observe of the 1st of the 14th. In the   36th battalion

there was a particular standing order. . . The men of the 1st of 4th
have always shaved their beards and they continue to do so."

- Major R. Scott, 4th Regiment

"The standing orders [of the 2nd of the 13th] stated: 'The native
officers, non-commissioned, drummers, and sepoys to have their
beards clean shaved at least twice a week, vizt Wednesday and
Saturday. If the battalion furnished the guards on those days they
must shave the day before.'"   - Captain A. Frith, 13th Regiment

"It never has been usual . . . with the native troops . . . to wear
painted marks of cast or large ear rings under arms of duty."

- Lt. Col. I Durand, 17th Regiment

"It never . . . was the usage for the native troops to appear on
parade with or without arms with marks of cast on their faces,
very trifling ones excepted or with ear rings, I mean those large
ones worn by Hindoos."   - Major Paul Bose, 14th Regiment

"It was not customary for sepoys to appear on parade with marks
of cast painted on their faces, and should a recruit do so (which
was sometimes the case) he was cautioned against it, and never
came on parade with the mark again. It was in like manner with
the ear rings. They were never allowed on parade. Sometimes
perhaps you might see one man in a hundred with a small plain
ring at the lower part of the ear that was hardly visible but this
was uncommon and taken notice of when perceived."

- Lt. Col. E. Reilly, 8th Regiment

"I know the usage of the service and the positive regulations of
every corps I have served with to have been, 'That no man shall
appear on parade or any duty with ear rings or the large mark of
cast on his forehead.' To appear on parade with either would be
considered irregular and probably punishment would follow. A

small ring in the ear of the size of a common finger ring was not objected."   - Lt. Col. Cuppage, 18th Regiment
"I have never known it customary in any sepoy corps to wear any mark of cast or ear rings under arms or in anyway connected with their duty."   - Lt. Col. G. Wahab, 17th Regiment

"It never was customary in any corps I ever served in for the men to wear the large ear rings that are generally worn by the Natives of India . . In the 36th battalion no marks of cast of any kind or size whatever were permitted to be worn by any man in his regimental dress. In the 1st of the 14th to which I was Adjutant when it was raised we tacitly admitted of a mark, about the size of a large pearl to be painted on the lower part of the forehead, but we never allowed the large and various discriminating marks of cast to be worn by any man in his regimentals. In the different corps I have been in, excepting the 36th battalion I think small gold checks have not been forbidden, but the custom was rather discouraged than approved of."   - Major R. Scott, 4th Regiment

There are a few drawings and paintings of the sepoys and Indian officers in the Art and Picture Library (India Office, London), Army Museums Ogily Trust (Northumberland House, London) and National Army Museum (Sandhurst, Camberley). Besides the testimonies, my conclusion is based on these drawings and pictures.

GLOSSARY

Amildar	district governor, collector of revenue
Arrack	indigenous spirituous liquor
Bang	a type of narcotic
Bazaar	market place
Betel	a type of leaf, chewed with dauk and lime
Chucklers	buffoons
Coffers (kafir)	aliens or foreigners, referred particularly to British
Colleries	a caste, commonly infamous for its ingenuity
Diwan	chief officer of state
Dooly	covered carriage
Duragh	small place of Muslim worship
Fakir	a wandering Muslim mendicant
Feringhees	foreigners, referred primarily to Europeans
Gun lascars	Indian seamen who manned guns
Havildar	Indian sergeant
Havildar major	Indian regimental sergeant major, senior non-commissioned officer in the battalion
Havildar writer	Indian sergeant clerk, responsible for the paper work in the commanding officer's office
Hirkarh	personal guard
Hookahs	smoking pipes
Jagir	tenure granted for the collection of revenue
Jemadar	Indian lieutenant

Kachheri	a court or hall where public business is transacted
Kot havildar	Indian sergeant in charge of regimental stores
Lance naique	lance corporal, junior non-commissioned officer
Mahal	harem
Maravas	a middle-ranking caste in Tinnevelly and neighouuring districts
Mirasdarism	a system of landholding where the village was assessed as a whole for taxation
Munshi	writer or secretary
Murdandh	an occasion when women were excluded and male relations and adherents were allowed to spend the night
Muri-admians	gentleman companions
Naique	Indian corporal
Nautch	exhibition of dancing girls
Nullah	river
Palanquin	covered litter for one, carried usually by four or six men
Panchayat	village council
Pandarum	a wandering Hindu mendicant
Parcherry	low-caste or non-caste hamlet
Pariah	low-caste or non-caste man
Pauk	a type of nut, chewed with betel and lime
Peon	inferior police man or messenger
Pettah	extramural suburb of a fortress
Pioneers	non-combatants who worked on roads etc to facilitate troop movements
Pir	Muslim teacher
Poligar	semi-feudal chieftains in Southern India
Puckaulas	high-caste cooks

Ryotwarism	a system of landholding where the individual cultivator was assessed directly
Salaam	greeting, "peace"
Sect marks	usually painted on the forehead to distinguish one's sect
Sepoy	Indian infantry soldier
Sherbet	a kind of cool drink, popular in South India
Sirdars	high officials in Indian court
Sowaris	horsemen
Subadar	Indian captain
Syrang	commissioned officer in gun lascar corps—equivalent to jemadar
Tappal	mail
Tindel	non-commissioned officer in gun lascar corps
Topie	turban
Zamindar	landlord
Zamindarism	landlordism
Zillah	district

BIBLIOGRAPHY

PRIMARY SOURCES

Manuscripts:

A. Army Museums Ogilby Trust, Northumberland House, London, England
    1. Box "Madras Cavalry"
    2. Box "Madras Infantry"

B. Baptist Missionary Society, Gloucester Place, London, England
    1. Letters to Serampore, 1806-1810

C. Bodleian Library, University of Oxford, Oxford, England
    1. MSS. Eng. Misc. b. 30

D. British Museum, Great Russell Street, London, England
    1. MSS. ADD. 29182-29183, Warren Hastings' Correspondence

E. India Office Library, Blackfriars Road, London, England
    1. Bengal Proceedings
        a. Secret and Political Proceedings, Volumes 193-202
    2. Court of Directors etc.
        a. Court Minutes or Books, Volumes 115-119a (1806-1810)
        b. General Court Minutes: Proprietors
            (1) Volume B/264, April 11, 1804 to September 23, 1807
            (2) Volume B/265, December 23, 1807 to March 18, 1814
    3. General Committees and of Correspondence
        a. Minutes of the Committee of Correspondence, Vol. 2
        b. Correspondence Reports, Volumes 30-34 (1806-1810)

4. General Correspondence

    a. Home Correspondence: Miscellaneous Letters received from Madras, Volume 113-116

    b. Correspondence with the Board of Control

        1. Letters from the Court to the Board Volume 3

        2. Letters from the Board to the Court, Volumes 30-31

    c. Correspondence with India

        1. Letters from Madras, Volumes 334-336

        2. Despatches to Madras, Volumes 899-900

5. Home Miscellaneous Series, Volumes 59, 459-460, 464-465, 507-510, 816-817

6. Madras Proceedings

    a. Judicial Proceedings, Range 322, Volumes 19-20, 24-27

    b. Military Proceedings, Range 255, Volumes 43, 50, 69-80, Range 256, Volumes 1-11

    c. Military and Political Proceedings, Range 254, Volumes 39-41

    d. Political Proceedings, Range 316, volumes 113-122, Range 317, Volumes 1-18

    e. Public Proceedings, Range 243, Volumes 22-23

    f. Revenue Proceedings, Range 276, Volumes 6-7

    g. Secret Proceedings, Volumes 11, 17-31

7. Political and Secret Department

    a. Secret Committee Minutes, Volumes 1-2

    b. Home Correspondence

        1. Secret Committee's Home Correspondence

            a. Secret Miscellancy Book, Volume 1

        2. Board's Secret Home Correspondence

        a. President's Secret Correspondence, Vol.1

    c. Secret Correspondence with India

    1. Secret Letters from Madras

    2. Board's Drafts of Secret Letters and Despatches to India

3. Secret Correspondence with India

    a. Secret Letters from Bengal and India, Volumes 8-10

    b. Political Letters Received from Bengal, Volumes 1a-2

8. MSS, Eur. C. 133, Letters to Warren Hastings

F. National Army Museum, Sandhurst, England

There are some drawings of the uniforms of Indian troops of the East India Company. Some of the drawings go back as early as 1780.

G. Public Records Office, Chancery Lane, London, England

  1. War Office Records, 1, 3l57, 360

  2. Colonial Office Records, 54, 22

H. Salop County Council, Abbey Foregate, Shrewsburry, England SRO 761/12

I. University of Edinburgh, Edinburgh, Scotland

  1. MSS 913, Abbotsford Collection

J. University of Nottingham, Nottingham, England

  1. Pw F. Portland of Welbeck Manuscripts, Third Duke of Portland

  2. Pw Jb, Portland Collection, Lord William Bentinck, Madras Period, 1803-1807

MEMOIRS*

(Anonymous). *Fifteen Years in India*, 1805-1819.London: Longman, Horst, Rees, Orme and Brown, 1822

Arbuthnot, Alexander J. *Major-General Sir Thomas Munro, Governor of Madras, Selections from His Minutes and other Official Writings*, 2 Volumes. London: C. Kegan Paul and Co., 1881

Major-General Sir Thomas Munro, Governor of Madras: A Memoir. London: Kegan Paul, Trench and Co., 1889

Bentinck, William Cavendish. *Memorial Addressed to the Honourable Court of Directors . . . Containing an Account of the Mutiny at Vellore with the Causes and Consequences of that Event. London:* John Booth, 1810

Blakistan, John. *Twelve Years' Military Adventure in Three Quarters of the Globe . . . between the Years 1802 and 1814*, 2 Volumes. London: Henry Colburn, 1829

Buchanan, Claudius. *An Apology for Promoting Christianity in India.* London: T. Cadel and W. Davies, Strand, 1813

Christian Researches in Asia. London: T. Cadell and W. Davies, Strand, 1812

The Works of Rev. Claudius Buchanan. New York: Whiting and Watson,1812

Cradock, John F. *Detailed Letter Relative to the Insurrection at Vellore.* London: 1808

Sketches of the Situation of Sir John Cradock. London: 1808

Farington, Joseph, *The Farinton Diary*, Volume 5. London: Hutchinson and Co., 1925

Fay, Anthony, *Original Letters from India.* Calcutta: 1821

Gillespie, R. R. *A Memoir of Major-General Sir Robert Rollo Gillespie.* London: T. Egerton, 1816

Gold, Charles. *Oriental Drawings, Sketched between the Years 1791 and 1798.* London: Bunney and Co., 1806

Historical Manuscript Commission. *Report on the Manuscripts of J. B. Fortescue, Esq., Preserved at Dropmore.* Volume 9. London: The Hereford Times, Ltd., 1915

Martin, Mongtomery (Editor). *The Despatches, Minutes and Correspondence of the Marquess Wellesley, K. G. During his Administration in India, 5* Volumes. London: W. H. Alllen, 1837

Martyn, Henry. *Memoir of the Rev. Henry Martyn.* London: J. Hatchard, 1819

Minto, *the Countess of. Lord Minto in India, 1807-1813.* London: Longmans, Green, and Co., 1880

Munro, Thomas. *Disaffection in the Native Army. London:* n. p., n. d.

Pearson, Hugh. *Memoirs of the Life and Writings of the Rev. Claudius Buchanan,* 2 Volumes. Oxford: The University Press, 1817

Spencer, Alfred (Editor). *Memoirs of William Hickey, 1790-1809,* Volume 4. London: Hurst and Blackett, Ltd., 1925

Teignmouth, Lord. *Memoirs of the Life and Correspondence of John Lord Teignmouth,* Volume 2. London: Hatchard and Son, 1843

Valentia, George. *Voyages and Travels to India, Ceylon, the Red Sea, Abyssinia, and Egypt in the Years 1802 to 1806,* Volume 1. London: William Miller, 1809

Welsh, James. *Military Reminiscences,* 2 volumes. London: Smith, Elder and Co., 1830

Wilberforce, Robert Isaac and Samuel. *The Life of William Wilberforce,* Volume 3. London: John Murray, 1838

*PRINTED

PAMPHLETS

(Anonymous). *Candid Thoughts . . . Occasioned by 'Mr. Twining's Letter to the Chairman'.* London: Hatchard, 1807

An Essay to Shew That no Intention has Existed or Does Now Exist of Doing Violence to the Religious Prejudices of India. London: John Hatchard, 1808

A Letter to John Scott Waring, Esq. in Refutation of His 'Observation'. . . London: John Hatchard, 1808

A Letter to the President of the Board of Control on the Propagation of Christianity in India. London: John Hatchard, 1807

Two Letters to the Proprietors of East India Stock Occasioned by Mr. Twining's Late Letter. . . London: Williams and Smith, 1807

A Bengal Officer. *Vindication of the Hindoos.* London: R and J. Rodwell, 1808

Cunningham, J. W. *Christianity in India.* London: John Hatchard, 1808

Fuller, Andrew. *An apology for the Late Christian Missions to India.* London: J. W. Morris,1808

A Late Resident at Bhagulpore. The Dangers to British India from French Invasion and Missionary Establishments. London: Black, Parry and Kingsbury, 1808

Marshman, Joshua. *Advantages of Christianity in Promoting the Establishment and Prosperity of the British Government in India.* London: Smith's Printing Office, 1813

Owen, John. *An Address to the Chairman of the East India Company.* London: John Hatchard, 1807

Porteus, (Bishop of London). *A Few Cursory Remarks on Mr. Twining's Letter.* London: John Hatchard, 1807

Scott Waring, John. *A Letter to the Rev. John Owen*, A. M. London: James Ridgway, 1808

    Observations of the Present State of the East India Company. London: James Ridgway, 1808

    Remarks on the Rev. Doctor Buchanan's Christian Researches in Asia. London: James Ridgway, 1812

A Replay to a Letter Addressed to John Scott Waring, Esq.' London: James Ridgway, 1808

Styles, John. *Strictures on Two Critiques in the Edinburgh Review on the Subject of Methodism and Missions.* London: Williams and Smith, 1808

(Teignmouth, Lord John). *Considerations on the Practicability, Policy, and Obligation of Communicating to the Natives of India the Knowledge of Christianity.* London: John Hatchard, 1808

Twining, Thomas. *A Letter to the Chairman of the East India Company on the Danger of Interfering into the Religious Opinions of the Natives of India.* London: James Ridgway, 180

PERIODICALS AND NEWSPAPERS

The Asiatic Register, London, 1807-1810

The Christian Observer, London, 1807-1812

East India Register, London, 1805-1811

The Eclectic Review, London, 1807-1812

The Edinburgh Review, Edinburgh, 1807-1812

The Evangelical Magazine, London, 1807-1812

Gentleman's Magazine, London, 1861

Madras Courier, Madras, 1806-1807

The Morning Chronicle, London, 1806-1807

The Morning Post, London, 1806-1807

Plain Englishman, London, 1821

The Quarterly Journal of the Mythic Society, Mysore, 1915

The Quarterly Review, London: 1807-1810

The Times, London, 1806-1807

REGULATIONS AND REPORTS

An Abstract of the Annual Reports and Correspondence of the society for Promoting Christian Knowledge from the Commencement of its connection with East India Missions, A. D. 1709, to the Present Day. London: F. C. and J. Rivington, 1814

A Code of Regulations for Various Department of the Military Establishment of Fort St. George, 1806. Madras: Government of Fort St. George, 1806

SECONDARY SOURCES

MANUSCRIPTS: DISSERTATIONS

Gupta, May. *Lord William Bentinck in Madras, 1803-1806*, Ph.D., University of London, 1969

Kitzan, Laurence. *The London Missionary Society in India and China, 1798-1834*. Ph. D., The University of Toronto, 1965

Ramanujam, Chidambaram Srinivaschari. *British Relations with Tanjore, 1748-1799*. Ph.D., University of London, 1968

BOOKS

Aiyar, S. Ramanath. *A History of Travancore.* Madras: Srinivasa Varadachari and Co., 1938

Allen, W. O. B. and Edmund McClure. *Two Hundred Years: The History of the Society for Promoting Christian Knowledge,* 1698-1898. London: SPCK, 1898

Auber, Peter. *Rise and Progress of the British Power in India,* 2 Volumes. London: Wm. H. Allen and Co., 1837

Balleine, G. R. *A History of the Evangelical Party in the Church of England.* London: Longmans, Green, and Col, 1908

Ballhatchet, Kenneth. *Social Policy and Social Change in Western India,* 1817-1830. London: Oxford University Press, 1957

Barnes, R. Money. *Military Uniforms of Britain and the Empire, 1742 to the Present Time.* London: Seeley Service and Co. Ltd., 1960

Bearce, George D. *British Attitude Towards India, 1784-1858.* London: Oxford University Press, 1961

Begbie, P. J. *History of the Services of Madras Artillery,* 2 Volumes. Madras: Christian Knowledge Society's Press, 1852

Beveridge, Henry. *A Comprehensive History of India.* London: Blackie and Son, 1862

Biddulph, John. *The Nineteenth and Their Times.* London: John Murray, 1899

Bjornstjerna, Count. *The British Empire in the East.* London: John Murray, 1840

Boase, Frederick. *Modern English Biography, of Persons Died between 1851 and 1900.* London: Frank Cass and Co. Ltd., 1965

Bose, Pramatha Nath. *A History of Hindu Civilization during British Rule,* Volume 1. Calcutta: W. Newman and Co., 1894

Boulger, Demetrus. *India in the Nineteenth Century.* London: Horace Marshall and Son, 1901

Lord William Bentinck (Rulers of India Series). Oxford: The Clarendon Press, 1892

Bradshaw, John. *Sir Thomas Munro and the British Settlement of the Madras Presidency (Rulers of India Series).* Oxford: The Clarendon Press, 1894

Briggs, Henry George. *The Nizam: His History and Relations with the British Government,* Volume 2. London: Bernard Quaritch, 1861

Cadell, Sir Patrick. *The History of Bombay Army.* London: Longmans, Green and Co., 1938

Cardew, Alexander. *The White Mutiny.* London: Constable and Co. Ltd., 1925

Carman, W. Y. *Indian Army Uniforms Under the British from the Eighteenth Century to 1947 Artillery, Engineers and Infantry.* London: Morgan-Grampian, 1969

> *Indian Army Uniforms under the British from the Eighteenth Century to 1947—Cavalry.* London: Leonard Hill (Books) Ltd., 1961

Chase, Margaret H. *South Asian History, 1750-1950. A Guide to Periodicals, Dissertations, and Newspapers.* New Jersey: Princeton University Press, 1968

Choksey, R. D. *A History of British Diplomacy at the Court of the Peshwas, 1786-1818.* Poona: Israelite Press, 1951

Cnattingius, Hans. *Bishops and Societies: A Study of Anglican colonial and Missionary Expansion, 1698-1850.* London: SPCK, 1959

Collen, Edwin. *The Indian Army: A Sketch of Its History and Organization.* Oxford: The Clarendon Press, 1907

Compton, Herbert. *A Particular Account of European Adventurers of Hindustan, 1784-1803.* London: T. Fisher Unwin, 1892

Cotton, Julian James. *List of Inscriptions on Tombs or Monument in Madras Possessing Historical or Archeological Interest.* Madras: The Government Press 1905

Cox, Arthur F. *Madras District Manuel: North Arcot,* 2 Volumes. Madras: The Government Press, 1895

Cox, F. A. *History of the Baptist Missionary Society,* 1792-1842, 2 Volumes. London: T. Ward and Co., 1842

Crawshay, George. *The Immediate Cause of the Indian Mutiny as Set Forth in the Official Correspondence. A Lecture Delivered. . . on November 4, 1857.* London: Effingham Wilson, 1857

Dodwell, Henry H. (Editor). *The Cambridge History of the British Empire, British India,* 1497-1885, Volume 4. Cambridge: The University Press, 1929

The Cambridge History of India, Volume 5, British India, 1497-1858. Delhi: S. Chand and Co., 1963

Dodwell, Henry H. *Dupleix and Clive: The Beginning of Empire*. London: Methuen and Co. Ltd., 1920

Sepoy Recruitment in the Old Madras Army. Calcutta: Government of India, 1922

Embree, Ainslie Thomas. *Charles Grant and British Rule in India*. London: George Allen and Unwin Ltd., 1962

Fraser, Hastings. *Our Faithful Ally: The Nizam*. London: Smith, Elder and Co., 1865

Garratt, Geoffrey T. and Edward J. Thomas. *Rise and Fulfilment of British Rule in India*. London: Macmillan and Co., Ltd., 1934

Ghose, Sailen. *Archives in India. Calcutta: Firma K. L. Mukhopadhyay*, 1963

Gleig, G. R. *The Life of Major-General Sir Thomas Munro, Bart and K. C. B. London:* Henry Colburn and Richard Bentley, 1830

Grant, James. *Cassell's Illustrated History of India*, 2 Volumes. London: Cassell and Company, Ltd., 1891

Haswell, Miller A. E. and N. P. Dawnay. *Military Drawings and Paintings in the Collection of Her Majesty the Queen*. London: Phaudon, 1969

Hill, S. Charles. *The Army in India and Its Evolution*. Calcutta: Government of India, 1924

Yusuf Khan. London: Longmans, Green d Co., 1914

Hilton, Richard. *The Indian Mutiny*. London: Hollis and Carter, 1957

Hole, Charles. *The Early History of the Church Missionary Society for Africa and the East to the End of A. D. 1844*. London: CMS, 1896

Hough, James. *History of Christianity in India*, Volumes 3 and 4. London: 1839-45

Howse, Ernest Marshall. *Saints in Politics. The "Clapham Sect" and the Growth of Freedom*. Toronto: University of Toronto Press, 1952

Ingham, Kenneth. *Reformers in India, 1793-1833*. Cambridge: The University Press, 1956

Kaye, John William. *The Administration of the East India Company: A History of Indian Progress*. London: Richard Bentlley, 1853

318

Christianty in India: A Historical Narrative. London: Smith, Elder and Co., 1859

The Life and Correspondence of Major-General Sir John Malcolm, G. G. B., 2 Volumes. London: Smith, Elder, and Co., 1856

Kirby, Charles F. *The Adventures of an Arcot Rupee,* 3 Volumes. London: Saunders, Otley, and Co., 1867

Lord, Walter Frewen. *Sir Thomas Maitland.* London: T. Fisher Unwin, 1897

Love, H. D. *Vestiges of Old Madras,* 3 Volumes. London: 1913

Lovett, Richard. *History of London Missionary Society,* 2 Volumes. London: Oxford University Press, 1899

MacFarlane, Charles. *History of British India.* London: George Routledge and Sons, 1881

Majumdar, B. N. *A Study of Indian Military History.* New Delhi: Army Educational Stores, 1963

Majumdar, Romesh Chandur. *The Sepoy Mutiny and the Revolt of 1857.* Calcutta: Firma K. L. Mukhopadhyay, 1957

Malcolm, John. *The Political History of India from 1784 to 1823,* 2 Volumes. London: John Murray, 1826

Malleson, G. B. (Editor). *Kaye's and Malleson's History of the Indian Mutiny of 1857-58,* Volume 1. London: W. H. Allen and Co. Ltd., 1891

Malleson, G. B. *History of the French in India, 1674-1761.* London: Longmans, Green, and Co., 1868

Marshman, John Clark. *The Life and Times of Carey, Marshman, and Ward,* Volume 1. London: Longman, Brown, Green, Longmans and Roberts, 1859

Martineau, Harriet. *The History of the British Rule in India.* London: Smith, Elder, 1857

Mayhew, Arthur. *Christianity and the Government of India,* 1600-1920. London: Faber and Gwyer, Ltd., 1878

Menon, P. Shungoonny. *A History of Travancore from the Earliest Time.* Madras: Higginbotham and Co., 1878

Misra, Bankey Bihari. *The Central Administration of the East India Company, 1773-1834.* Manchester: The University Press, 1959

Morris, Henry. *The Life of Charles Grant.* London: John Murray, 1904

Myers, John Brown. *The Centenary Volume of the Baptist Missionary Society, 1792-1892*. London: The Baptist Missionary Society, 1892

Northcott, Cecil. Glorious Company. *One Hundred and Fifty Years, Life and Work of the London Missionary Society, 1795-1945*. London: The Lingstone Press, 1945

O'Mallley, L. S. S. *The Indian Civil Service, 1601-1930*. London: 1931

Orme, Robert. *A History of the Military Transactions of the British Nation in Hindustan from 1745*, 3 Volumes. London: F. Wingrave, 1861

Owen, John. *The History of the Origin and First Ten Years of the British and Foreign Bible Society*, 2 Volumes. London: Tilling and Hughes, 1816

Pascoe, C. F. *Two Hundred Years of the SPG, 1701-1900*. London: SPG Office, 1901

Philips, C. H. *The East India Company, 1784-1834*. Manchester: The University Press, 1961

Phythian-Adams, E. G. *Madras Infantry, 1748-1943*. Madras: 1943

Potts, E. Daniel. *British Baptist Missionaries in India, 1793-1837*. Cambridge: The University Press, 1967

Prentout, Henri. *L'ilse de France sous Decaen, 1803-1810*. Paris : Librairie Hatchette et Clle, 1901

Prinsep, Henry T. *History of the Political and Military Transactions in India, 1813-1823*. 2 Volumes. London: Kingsbury, Parbury and Allen, 1825

Richter, Julius. *A History of Missions in India. Translated by Sydney H. Moore*. Edinburgh: Oliphant Anderson and Ferrier, 1908

Rivett-Carnac, S. *The Presidential Armies of India*. London: W. H. Allen and Co., 1890

Roberts, P. E. *History of British India under the Company and the Crown*. London: Geoffrey Cumberlege, 1952

    India under Wellesley. London: G. Bell and Sons Ltd., 1929

Sen, S. P. *The French in India, 1763-1816*. Calcutta: 1947

Sen, Surendra Nath. *Eighteen Fifty-Seven*. New Delhi: Government of India, 1957

    The Military System of the Marathas. Bombay: Orient Longmans, 1958

Sherring, M. A. *The History of Protestant Missions in India*. London: The Reliigious Tract Society, 1884

Singh, Rajendra. *History of the Indian Army. New Delhi: Army Educational Stores,* 1963

Smith, George. *The Life of William Carey.* London: John Murray, 1885

Smith, Lewis Ferdinard. *A Sketch of the Rise, Progress, and Termination of the Regular Corps Formed and Commanded by Europeans in the Service of the Native Princes of India.* Calcutta: J. Greenway, 1805

Smith, Vincent. *The Oxford History of India.* Oxford: The Clarendon Press, 1919

Spear, Percival. India: *A Modern History. Ann Arbor.* The University of Michigan Press, 1961

Thornton, Edward. *The History of the British India,* 6 Volumes. London: Wm. H. Allen and Co., 1843

Thornton, L. H. *Campaigners Grave and Gay. Studies of Four Soldiers of the Eighteenth and Nineteenth Centuries.* Cambridge: The University Press, 1925

Trotter, L. J. *History of India.* London: SPCK, 1889

Vibart, Henry Meredith. *The Military History of the Madras Engineers and Pioneers from 1743 up to the Present Time.* London: W. H. Allen and Co., 1881

Wainright, M. D. and Noel Matthews. *A Guide to Western Manuscripts and Documents in the British Isles Relating to South and South East Asia.* London: Oxford University Press, 1965

Wakeham, Eric. *The Bravest Soldier: Sir R. R. Gillespie, 1766-1814.* Edinburgh: William Blackwood and Sons Ltd., 1937

Wilks, Mark. *Historical Sketches of the South of India,* 2 Volumes. Madras: Higginbotham and Co., 1869

Wilson, Horace Hayman. *The History of British India from 1805 to 1835,* Volume 1. London: James Madden, 1848

Wilson, W. J. *History of the Madras Army,* Volumes 1-3 Madras: Government Press, 1883

ARTICLES

Adye, John. "Native Armies of India." *The Nineteenth Century (April, 1880), VII*, 685-709

(Anonymous). "Lord William Bentinck's Administration." *The Calcutta Review (August, 1844) I*, 337-371

Cadell, Patrick. "The Uniforms of the Madras Army." *Journal of Society for Army Historical Research, XXVII*, 171-173

Chauduri, Haripado. "The Vellore Mutiny: A Reappraisal." *The Modern Review, Calcutta (August, 1955)*, pp. 125-128

Cotton, H. E. A. "Thomas Hickey: Portrait Painter. . . Hickey's Portraits of the Mysore Family." *Bengal: Past and Present (1924)*, pp. 158-163

Grier, Sydney C. "The Mutiny at Vellore in 1806." *Bengal: Past and Present (1924)*, pp, 166-180

Hill, S. Charles. "The Old Sepoy Officer." *The English Historical Review (1913), XXVIII*, 260-272

Keene, A. "The Mutiny at Vellore, July 10th, 1806." *United Service Magazine (October, 1906, to March, 1907), XXXIV*, 95-104

Malcolm, John. "Origin and State of the Indian Army." *The Quarterly Review (October, 1817, to May, 1818), XVIII*, 387-403

Shearer, E. J. "The Madras Cavalry." *The Cavalry Journal (July, 1928)*, pp. 347-356

Srinivasachari, C. S. "The Vellore Mutiny of 1806: A New Study of Its Origin." *Indian History Congress Proceedings (1948, Delhi)*, pp. 195-198

Stanley, Arthur. "Gillespie of Vellore." *The Army Quarterly (July, 1931)*, XXII, 337-344

INDEX *

*As many South Indians did not have last names, we decided to arrange all the names as those people were called, addressed or titled.

Another view of the Vellore Fort

ACKNOWLEDGEMENTS

A NUMBER OF INDIVIDUALS AND INSTITUTIONS have extended their co-operations and assistance in the preparation of this manuscript [The Mutiny at Vellore and Related Agitations, 1806-1807]. It is not feasible to enumerate all of them. However I would like to express my sincere appreciation to the staff of the Library of the School of Oriental and African Studies, the University of London Library, the British Museum, the India Office Library, the Public Records Office, the University of Cambridge Library, the Departments of Manuscripts of the Bodleian Library, the University of Nottingham Library, and the University of Edinburgh Library, for their help. The same degree of appreciation must also be extended to Brigadier R. G. Thurburn, CB, CBE, Army Museums Ogilby Trust, Northumberland House, and the archivists of the National Army Museum, Sandhurst, the Baptist Missionary Society, the British and Foreign Bible Society, the Congregational Council of World Churches, and the Society for Propagating Christian Knowledge.

I should also record my sense of gratitude to Professor Kenneth A. Ballhatchet of the School of Oriental and African Studies, University of London, for his most valuable guidance and encouragement during my stay in England, and to Professor Llaurence Kitzan, my faculty advisor, for his sound advice and willing help. [Ballhatchet was the one who told me about the Vellore mutiny and suggested that it would make an excellent topic for a doctoral dissertation.] I may add that without the financial assistance of the University of Saskatchewan, the benefit of the Canada Student Loan Plan, and the encouragement of my friend, Professor D. C. Doss, this dissertation would not have been possible.

In converting the doctoral dissertation into a book, I had help from the following caring people: My friend Frank Burke edited the entire manuscript; my wife Suzanne went over it and did her best to pick up typo errors; my son Mischaël provided the necessary computer assistance, and finally my nephew Joseph Pakkianathan shepherded it for publication.

I am alone responsible for any error in this book.

BIOGRAPHY

SAMUEL RAJ, THEN KNOWN AS PAKKIANATHAN SAMUELRAJ, graduated from Spicer Memorial College, Poona in 1962, with three majors: Religion, History and Education. Since the degrees from Spicer were not recognized by the educational insitututions in India, he came to do graduate work in Canada.

Samuel's primary interest was in Religion. However, at the University of Saskatchewan, he chose to do his graduate studies in History. He obtained his M. A. in 1968 and Ph. D. in 1972. He returned to his first love and studied Religion at McMaster University, Hamilton (1973-74) and Carleton University, Ottawa (1978-79). A few years later, he obtained a Masters in Counselling from Saint Paul University (1982).

Samuel founded the Orleans Centre for Marriage and Family in 1986, and started writing *Catalyst* and *Table Talk and Pillow Talk,* quarterly bulletins. Later on, many of those articles were put together in three different books: *Table Talk and Pillow Talk—A Guide to a Happier and Richer Life and Relationship* (2014); *Catalyst—A Journey in Reflective Faith* (2016) and *Catalyst Plus—Reflections on History and Politics, Relationship, Religion and Theology* (2017). He authored *A Secret— Reflection on a Theological Innovation* (written in 1978 but published in 2016) and co-authored *Sustained by God's Grace—A Brief History of the SDA Church in Prakasapuram, South India* with Margaret Selvi Solomon. In theOttawa area, Samuel is known primarily for his counselling ministry.

Samuel Raj has been married to Suzanne Brisson since 1976, and they have two wonderful adult children: Althia, a journalist, and Mischaël, a civil engineer.

OTHER BOOKS

Samuel Raj's books have been reviewed in Canada and the US . . . Acclaimed by reviewers and the reading public alike, his writings reflect his experience and journey through life as a historian, counselor and seeker of Truth.

Here is a list of books published and are available on www.amazon.com

TABLE TALK AND PILLOW TALK
A Guide to a Happier and Richer Life and Relationship

CATALYST
A Journey in Reflective Faith

CATALYST PLUS
Reflections on History and Politics, Relationship, Religion and Theology

A SECRET
Reflections on a Theological Innovation

SUSTAINED BY GOD'S GRACE
A Brief History of the Seventh-Day Adventist Church in Prakasapuram, Tamil Nadu, India (co-authored by Margaret Selvi Solomon)

GOD'S COMRADE
A Reflective Meditation on Jesus of Nazereth

Made in the USA
Middletown, DE
27 October 2020